FALCONBRIDGE

FALCONBRIDGE

Portrait of a Canadian mining multinational

John Deverell and the Latin American Working Group

BRESCIA COLLEGE
LIBRARY
55878

James Lorimer & Company, Publishers
Toronto 1975

Copyright © 1975 by the Latin American Working Group. All rights reserved. No part of this book may be reproduced or transmitted in any form or by any means, electronic or mechanical, including photocopying, or by any information storage or retrieval system, without permission in writing from the publishers.

ISBN 0-88862-077-2 paper   0-88862-078-0 cloth

Cover photo: Michael Kazim Emre
Design: Lynn Campbell

Printed and bound in Canada

James Lorimer & Company, Publishers
35 Britain Street
Toronto

Canadian Shared Cataloguing in Publication Data

Deverell, John.
   Falconbridge: portrait of a Canadian mining
multinational/John Deverell and the Latin American Working
Group. —

1. Falconbridge Nickel Mines Ltd. 2. International business
enterprises. 3 Nickel industry — Canada. I. Latin American
Working Group. II. Title.

HD9539.N52C24   338.4'7'669733
ISBN: 0-88862-078-0; 0-88862-077-2 (pbk.)

Dedication

To the political prisoners of the Dominican Republic and Namibia, and to the mine workers of the world in their struggle to forge bonds of solidarity.

Table of Contents

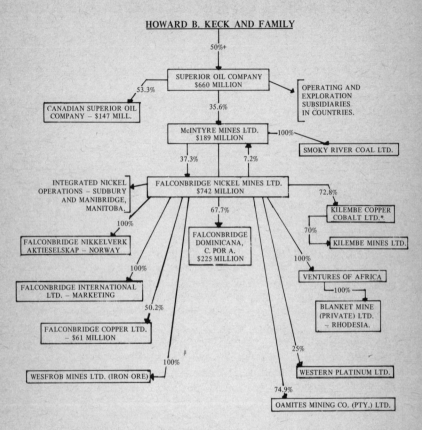

HOWARD B. KECK AND FAMILY

50%+

SUPERIOR OIL COMPANY
$660 MILLION

53.3%

CANADIAN SUPERIOR OIL
COMPANY — $147 MILL.

OPERATING AND
EXPLORATION
SUBSIDIARIES
IN COUNTRIES.

35.6%

McINTYRE MINES LTD.
$189 MILLION

100%

SMOKY RIVER COAL LTD.

37.3%   7.2%

FALCONBRIDGE NICKEL MINES LTD.
$742 MILLION

72.8%

INTEGRATED NICKEL
OPERATIONS – SUDBURY
AND MANIBRIDGE,
MANITOBA.

KILEMBE COPPER
COBALT LTD.*

70%

KILEMBE MINES LTD.

100%

FALCONBRIDGE NIKKELVERK
AKTIESELSKAP – NORWAY

67.7%

FALCONBRIDGE
DOMINICANA,
C. POR A.
$225 MILLION

100%

VENTURES OF AFRICA

100%

FALCONBRIDGE INTERNATIONAL
LTD. – MARKETING

100%

BLANKET MINE
(PRIVATE) LTD.
– RHODESIA.

50.2%

FALCONBRIDGE COPPER LTD.
– $61 MILLION

25%

WESTERN PLATINUM LTD.

100%

WESFROB MINES LTD. (IRON ORE)

74.9%

OAMITES MINING CO. (PTY.) LTD.

NOTES:–Kilembe Copper Cobalt was recently nationalized by the Ugandan
government.
  –dollar amounts express assets in millions as of 1974.

SOURCES: *"FALCONBRIDGE – MADE IN U.S.A.", BY FRED GOFF, IN*
DOMINICAN REPUBLIC, MILITARY "DEMOCRACY", *NACLA'S*
LATIN AMERICA AND EMPIRE REPORT, VOL. VIII, #4, APRIL
1974.

FINANCIAL POST SURVEY OF MINES, 1975, *FINANCIAL POST,*
TORONTO, 1975.

Introduction

Canadians, like the citizens of other relatively prosperous industrial countries, are now living in the eye of a growing international storm. Its buffetings have begun to disturb some of the comfortable complacency we have been permitted over the past three decades of prosperity, but the warning signs have not yet begun to produce any substantial or widespread re-evaluation of our society's place in the world, how it is likely to change, or how we want it to change. In this sense we continue to live day to day with remarkable delusions, realizing only vaguely that somehow they are unsustainable and will be, in some yet unimagined way, rudely shattered.

The broad outlines of the dilemma are familiar. The world of the 1970s is characterized by an incredible inequality in the distribution of resources both within "rich" countries like our own, and between countries. More precisely the widening gulf between rich and poor is a gulf between social classes, since even the wealthiest of countries host substantial poverty, while the poorest countries are burdened with small elites of extremely wealthy people.

What is less well understood is the intimate relationship between wealth and poverty, both within individual countries and on the international scale. Population explosion, food shortages, and famine and disease are not the problems of societies that yet remain to be integrated into the world economy. They are striking hardest in precisely those countries which have been harnessed to world markets and a world production system in ways which produce exploitation and hardship rather than authentic development and rising living standards for the vast majority of their people.

At centre stage in the unfolding world drama of the 1970s is a phenomenon which represents the pinnacle of capitalist economic development, the multi-national corporation. A logical extension of the growth of monopolies within national capitalist economies, the multinationals have burst the confines of national markets and are rapidly organizing labour, resources and technology for the production and movement of goods and services on a world scale.

Within the last ten years these large corporations have grown so fast that their combined total sales exceed the gross national product of every country except the United States and the Soviet Union. Their combined assets now exceed $200 billion, and projections of current trends indicate that within another decade or two between 50 and 80 percent of everything worth owning in the way of productive assets in the non-communist world will be controlled by about 300 corporations.[1]

> In the process of developing a new world, the managers of firms like GM, IBM, Pepsico, GE, Pfizer, Shell, Volkswagen, Exxon and a few hundred others are making daily business decisions which have more impact than those of most sovereign governments on where people live; what work, if any, they will do; what they will eat, drink and wear; what sorts of knowledge schools and universities will encourage; and what kind of society their children will inherit.[2]

The significance of this phenomenon is a matter of vigorous dispute. Some analysts, like Barnet and Muller in their comprehensive survey *Global Reach,* suggest that the multinationals have risen above nationalism and transcend the outmoded nation state. On the other hand it is obvious that all the so-called multinationals operate from a definite national base, until now primarily the United States of America. Although production may ignore national boundaries, the top management of American-based multinationals is overwhelmingly American, as is stock ownership. Furthermore, the ultimate defense of property requires armed force, and in the absence of world government the "multi-nationals" continue to depend for this service on the strongest "outmoded" nation states. In this respect the U.S. government and military occupy a pre-eminent role which they show little sign of abandoning.

The multi-national outlook of these giant corporations, and their inherent tendency to pursue global profit-maximization independently

1.   R. Barnet and R. Muller, *Global Reach: The Power of the Multinational Corporations,* Simon and Schuster, New York, 1974, p.26.
2.   *Ibid,* p. 15.

of national political policies are circumscribed by this compelling tie to the strongest national governments. For this reason the established term, "multi-national corporation", cannot be accepted at face value, and in this book we follow the usage of those United Nations agencies which speak of "transnational corporations".

Beyond any doubt, the transnational corporations are engaged in a fantastic centralization of control over world resources and production. This process cannot be smooth or unopposed because it operates to the detriment of a huge portion of the world's population. Studies documenting the monopolization of world resources by the industrial countries which spawn transnationals are numerous, as are those which describe the deteriorating terms of trade between raw materials and manufactured goods. New studies following the U.N.'s Decade of Development of the 1960s show the economic position of millions of people in the Third World actually declining rather than improving, even as the transnational companies extend their world power and influence.

The world productive system they are organizing and managing is increasingly divorced from the basic needs for food, clothing and shelter of the vast proportion of humanity. This widening chasm, in our opinion, is the most fundamental political problem facing the modern world, the grand contradiction from which most others spring.

This case study of the Falconbridge Group, an important transnational complex of resource companies, is intended to illuminate a number of the mechanisms of normal business and political practice which feed on and regenerate the human catastrophe. Concentrating on the nickel industry, in which Falconbridge is the world's second largest producer, we examine the principal aspects of corporate behavior.

The first chapter outlines the strategic importance of nickel as an industrial base metal, the relationship between nickel industry development and 20th century militarism, and the corporate drive into the Third World in pursuit of higher profits and a scarce raw material. Chapters two and three outline the historical development of monopoly in the nickel industry and the vital role of government contracts for the monopoly corporations. The fourth and fifth chapters describe the increasing coordination of monopoly power across industry lines by financial groups, and the intimate relationship between such groups and government, in this case principally the government of the United States.

The following three chapters deal with Falconbridge's impact in three quite different political, economic and social settings: Canada, the Dominican Republic and southern Africa. Our conclusion is that the objectives of this transnational corporation are substantially at odds with the aspirations and needs of the working people in all three areas, and we examine the corporation's response to various manifestations of this political problem.

By this study of a single corporate group we have tried to indicate how such seemingly disparate issues as pollution, occupational health and safety, town planning, resource taxation, foreign investment, militarism, imperialist intervention, and the corruption of representative government all find a common nexus in the ownership, control and behavior of the world's most influential institutions, the transnational corporations.

In advancing this argument we are aware of the limitations of a single case study, and make no pretense of putting forward a definitive work. The Latin American Working Group remains engaged in monitoring the behavior of many transnationals, and other groups are also involved in this kind of corporate research that seeks to uncover the relationships of power in Canada and internationally.

However, we are satisfied that Falconbridge is no "black sheep", but rather a typical representative of the globe-trotting resource corporation flock. One of our chief difficulties in circumscribing the scope of this book was determining where to stop in tracing the intricate web of financial, personal and political links between the Falconbridge Group and the larger system of which it is a part. While the case study approach has some limitations, we are convinced that it can also lead to new insights overlooked by a "macro-investigation" of transnationals. Finally, we hope that the specific focus on Falconbridge, while uncovering part of the larger system, will also assist the local and national struggles by those in Canada, the Dominican Republic and southern Africa most directly affected by the global operations of this set of companies.

The selection of the Falconbridge Group from a list of other worthy transnational candidates was made because its operations raise so many of the questions Canadians must face and deal with in the near future. The Falconbridge Group claims to be Canadian, and uses the Canadian image to some advantage in its overseas operations, but the appearance is an illusion. Much of the duality and ambiguity of Canada's position as both a resource colony and a junior partner in imperialism is expressed in the business and political affairs of the Falconbridge Group.

*   *   *

Preparation of this book has at different stages involved the efforts of a large number of people. Much of the preliminary research was supported financially by the Task force on the Churches and Corporate Responsibility; the writing in part by a grant from the Ontario Arts Council; and the space and facilities by the generous and supportive staff of the Catholic Information Centre in Toronto.

Many members of the Latin American Working Group shaped both the research and the discussion which preceeded the actual writing. Among those others who gave freely of their time and research information were: Jonathan Forbes and Jamie Swift of the Development Education Centre (DEC); Mike Locker and Fred Goff of the North American Congress on Latin America (NACLA); Elie Martel and Bud Germa, both Sudbury area MPPs; the Ontario NDP research office; Jim Tester and other members of the Mine, Mill and Smelter Workers Union, Local 598 in Sudbury; John Lang of the C.C.U.; the Union of Workers of Falconbridge Dominicana in Bonao; the Central General de los Trabajadores of the Dominican Republic; representatives of the South West Africa Peoples Organization (SWAPO) who have travelled from Namibia to help North Americans better understand the struggles of their peoples; and the numerous others who assisted us, including those whose names must remain confidential.

Bob Carty, Louise Casselman and Tim Draimin, members of the Latin American Working Group conceived the project and provided much of the impetus for it. They gathered and coordinated the research materials and provided supplementary research, constructive criticism and numerous improvements chapter by chapter as the manuscript took shape. The resulting book is very much a collective effort. While many other people have offered indispensable cooperation, the responsibility for interpretation and for the accuracy of what follows lies with the four of us.

John Deverell and
Bob Carty
Louise Casselman
Tim Draimin of the
Latin American Working
Group

Toronto, February, 1975

CHAPTER ONE

Nickel: Vital Raw Material

The Third World directly threatens the interests of the United States in obtaining assured supplies of primary products at reasonable prices and avoiding the loss of jobs and exports. It threatens relations among the United States, Western Europe and Japan, triggering scrambles among them for specific deals with commodity suppliers. . . . And it could threaten world peace as well, both indirectly through economic conflicts and directly through nuclear proliferation and regional hostilities.

> —C. Fred Bergsten, Fellow of the Brookings Institute and former economic advisor to U.S. Secretary of State Henry Kissinger, November 17, 1974.

As a developer of natural resources outside Canada for some 30 years, the Falconbridge Group of companies has learned to live, work and think internationally. The first-hand experience gained over this period of time, in a variety of climates and cultures and under varying political regimes has shaped our operating philosophy along very practical lines. . . . As a member of the international mining community, we compete worldwide with other companies exploring for mineral deposits that can be developed on an economic basis to help meet market demands and at the same time to produce an adequate return for Falconbridge shareholders. Our field of search, therefore, has no geographical boundaries; we must go wherever ore deposits can be found. Consequently we may find ourselves in countries where the economic and/or the political environments differ greatly from Canada's.

> —Marsh Cooper, president of Falconbridge Nickel Mines and chairman of McIntyre Mines, April, 25, 1974.

A WAR METAL

Nickel is prominent on the United States Department of the Interior list of 13 basic raw materials required by an industrial society, a list which is receiving closer attention in 1975 than ever before. The oil crisis of 1973-74 has made obvious to all a truth which American policy makers have long understood; secure supplies of raw materials at reasonable prices are the lifeblood of any industrial nation, and especially of a military, economic and diplomatic superpower like the United States.

The Interior Department reported in 1973 that the United States was already importing 85 percent of its nickel and more than half its supply of five other basic materials: aluminum, chromium, manganese, tin and zinc. By 1985 it will also depend on foreign sources for more than half its iron, lead and tungsten. By the year 2000 this will also be true of copper, potassium and sulphur. Only in phosphorus does the United States have any reasonable prospect of self-sufficiency. The same report claims that Europe and Japan are even more dependent on raw materials imports than the United States.[1]

Such extensive dependency causes policy problems at all times but particularly in the event of war. As a superpower the United States has more than its share of interest and involvement in military conflicts around the globe. Security of basic materials, when both the outcome of wars and the ability to maintain the uneasy balance of terror between wars are closely related to economic strength and performance, is a paramount objective.

Within the general scheme of raw material supplies, nickel has a special place. The U.S. Defence Department warned in 1954 that nickel "comes closest to being a true 'war metal'. It deserves the first priority among materials receiving conservation attention. Since the start of the Korean War, nickel has remained the world's most critical material; this condition is likely to continue for some time."[2]

In the past twenty-five years that prediction has proved quite accurate. Throughout the 1950s and 1960s the world demand for nickel has outstripped increases in productive capacity. In 1975 the nickel industry is embarked on the largest but also the most difficult expansion program in its entire history.

The properties which make nickel such a useful and strategic

1. *Wall Street Journal,* December 26, 1973, p.1, also see: *U.S. Natural Resource Requirements and Foreign Economic Policy,* Interim Report by the International Economic Policy Association, Washington, July 18, 1974.
2. *Annual Materials Conservation Report,* U.S. Department of Defense, Office of Assistant Secretary of Defense, Washington, 1954, p.4, cited in Percy Bidwell, *Raw Materials,* Council on Foreign Relations, New York, Harper Bros., 1958, p. 132.

metal are its strength, hardness, ductility, and resistance to corrosion, plus the ability to retain these features at extremely high and low temperatures. It imparts these same benefits to other metals like iron, steel, copper, tin, zinc, magnesium and aluminum when combined with them in alloys.

Although there are substitutes for nickel in certain of its uses, these possibilities are in no way sufficient to alter its classification as an essential industrial commodity. Faced with chronic nickel shortages and extensive informal rationing for most of the last 25 years, American industry has long experience in attempting to find substitutes, but nickel consumption continues to grow rapidly. The growth in demand continues despite rising prices for the metal.

The reason for this strong demand, not only in the United States but also in Western Europe and Japan, is the key role nickel plays in many high-technology products and processes. This also helps to explain its classification as a war metal. One of the chief activities of the massive military establishments in industrialized countries has been the pioneering of advanced technology and its application to enormous, expensive, ever-growing and ever-changing stocks of military hardware. The expansion of the nickel industry from its earliest beginnings during the 1890s and throughout the twentieth century has been intimately linked to the rise of military expenditure in times of peace and war.

Commercial production of nickel in Canada, the world's leading producer for nearly 70 years, was begun for military purposes. In 1889 Samuel Ritchie, president of the Canadian Copper Company (later part of the International Nickel Company), persuaded U.S. Secretary of the Navy B.F. Tracy to test the potential of nickel-alloyed steel as armour plate material for the American fleet. Ship armour of the day had reached a thickness of two feet of iron backed by 17 inches of teak and was still inadequate to resist improvements in artillery; the U.S. navy moved quickly to pursue the technological advantage nickel seemed to offer. Nickel steel passed the artillery punishment tests with flying colours and was judged "the most wonderful armour plate ever made."[3] Another commentator on the widely publicized tests lamented "when the irresistible nickel plated breech-loader confronts the impenetrable nickel plated ironclad then indeed. . . . war as a fine art will come to an end."[4]

Whatever the consequences for war as an art, the Canadian

3. *New York Times,* July 30, 1892; cited in J.F. Thompson and N. Beasley, *For the Years to Come,* Toronto, Longmans, Green and Co., 1960, p.66.
4. *Glasgow Herald,* October 27, 1890; cited in Thompson and Beasley, *op. cit.,* p.61.

Copper Company made its first big sale of nickel in 1891 to the United
States Navy, and the new industry was on its way.

For the period until 1918, expansion of nickel production was
based primarily on meeting the demand of the various national military
establishments. Recession and naval disarmament following World
War I presented the nickel industry with the unfamiliar problem of large
excess capacity but the major producer, INCO, met this crisis with an
aggressive scientific research program to develop new civilian industrial uses for its product and an equally vigorous sales program to
broaden its markets. It has maintained both to the present day. These
policies met with considerable success; the civilian uses of nickel alloys
multiplied, but military demand remained the fundamental strength of
the nickel industry throughout the 1930s.

World War II inspired a further large expansion in production.
The mild lag in demand of the post-war years was quickly superceded
by the stimulus of the Korean War and then the combination of United
States government strategic stockpiling and the arms race of the Cold
War years. During the 1960s the increasing civilian uses of more than
3000 nickel alloys competed with the military requirements of the Vietnam war to encourage a further strong growth in productive capacity.

WHY NICKEL IS ESSENTIAL

The major nickel companies, INCO, Falconbridge and Le Nickel, call
their product the wonder metal, the friendly metal, "the metal that
makes other metals better metals," and the claim is not exaggerated.
Nickel has found its way into thousands of products in both heavy
industry and the consumer sector. There is nickel in all stainless steel
houseware from cutlery to cookware to the kitchen sink; in the heating
elements of home ranges, washers, dryers, space heaters and kettles;
and beneath the chrome electroplating on kettles, toasters and so on. In
the field of basic production, nickel alloys are important in bridges,
structural steel for heavy construction, railroad rolling stock, gears,
bearings, transmissions and all manner of machine parts. The hull of
Humble Oil's tanker Manhattan which penetrated the crushing ice floes
of the Canadian northwest passage was reinforced by nickel alloys.

In the early 1970s the largest intermediate product was stainless
steel, using 40 percent of all nickel, and its share of nickel use was still
rising. Electroplating accounted for 16 percent of nickel use, high
nickel alloys for 14 percent, construction alloys 11 percent, and iron
and steel castings nine percent of the total.[5]

5. "The Wonderful World of Nickel", mimeo reprinted from *Falcon,* Falconbridge
    Nickel Mines Ltd., undated.

The long term demand for the metal until recently seemed very strong, on the assumption of a continuation of the past growth patterns of the major industrial countries. Every car sold in North America contains about four pounds of nickel, which on 10 million vehicles accounts for about 40 million pounds annually. "Add to this the millions of cars also being turned out in England, Japan, Germany, France and other countries and you begin to see how much nickel already rides the highways, and how much more will be needed," enthuses a Falconbridge brochure. The company also looks forward to the advent of stainless steel backyard swimming pools "instead of the traditional concrete, fibreglass and other plastic types now generally in use."[6]

In recession-ridden 1975 all this seems a little ridiculous, but even if some of the frivolous uses which in the past have kept the order books full are severely pruned, the basic strength of nickel demand remains. Many of the latest space age technological advances have a "nickel intensive" aspect which is opening up big new markets for the metal. Ordinary stainless steel contains an average of 10 percent nickel, but some of the new super alloys essential to high technology have a nickel content as high as 80 percent. The hardware in the American Apollo program which landed man on the moon in 1969 indicates the trend:

> In the spacecraft itself and in the Saturn V launch vehicle, nickel alloys were used in a large number of critical components including pressure vessels and fuel tanks, and in the spacecraft's nose cone and heat shield. Additionally there were millions of pounds of nickel stainless steels in the mobile launcher and in storage and transfer equipment in the two Apollo launch pads at Cape Kennedy. A nickel stainless steel plaque still sits on the moon, placed there by the Apollo II astronauts to mark man's first visit to a body in outer space.[7]

Leaving the plaque aside, the point made is fundamental. Space and military technology and all related civilian production dealing with intense stress and heat require extremely high-performance materials in large quantities, as for example in the large and powerful jet engines of the aircraft industry.

The change in the scale of demand is indicated by the changing nickel requirements of that industry: a four engine piston driven plane required only about 125 pounds of nickel; a commercial four engine jet requires 4,000 pounds; the Boeing 747 jumbo uses 11,000 pounds; and

6. *Ibid.*
7. *Ibid.*

the supersonic transports, if their day ever comes, will each need about 18,000 pounds of nickel.[8] The same trend appears in any productive activity where the power, size and speed of machinery is increasing.

Another special feature of nickel, its non-corroding quality, spreads the demand for nickel to other high-technology growth industries. The petroleum industry in the capitalist world now uses 64 million pounds of nickel annually, mainly in refinery process equipment. The new nuclear power plants require large amounts of nickel alloy tubing in their heat exchanger systems, and a similar need for miles of nickel-alloy tubing arises from the desalinization plants which will be needed to increase fresh water supplies. The same is true of pollution control systems for the treatment and disposal of industrial wastes.

These trends in technology mean that the future demand for nickel, even if its price rises significantly, will be very strong. On this basis the major nickel corporations and independent analysts of the industry foresee a need to increase the industry's productive capacity by six to seven percent annually over the next ten years.[9] While the setbacks of 1975 may lower this estimate slightly, only an economic collapse would render it false. The present annual capacity of 1.2 billion pounds of nickel must rise to about 2.2 billion pounds by 1985 if the industry's forecasts of the shape of things to come are to be realized.

THE SOURCES OF NICKEL

There are two basic types of nickel ores available to meet the growing needs of industrial countries: lateritic and sulphide. [10] They are located in distinct areas of the world, and each requires a different technology of extraction. It is these differences in geography and technology which set the stage for dramatic changes in the politics of nickel.

The countries responsible for consuming most of the capitalist world's nickel — the United States, Great Britain, Germany, Japan, France, Italy and Sweden—have almost no nickel reserves within their borders. Their needs have until recently been met from the extensive

---

8. ''Who controls the 'War Metal'?'', *Pacific Imperialism Notebook*, Volume V., #7, July 1974, P.140.

9. ''Long-term nickel growth rate still intact'', *The Northern Miner*, November 28, 1974, p. 83-4.

10. In addition to the laterite and sulphide varieties of nickel, the big mineral companies are also beginning to look at sources under the sea. In many areas of the ocean floor are billions of nodules, spherical masses about the size of golf balls, that contain manganese, copper, iron, nickel, and cobalt. By the late 1970s several companies may be recovering and processing these nodules but one of the impeding factors at this time is the lack of jurisdictional clarity. Conflicting claims to the seabeds are presently being aired in the United Nations. See: ''The scramble for resources'', *Business Week,* June 30, 1973, p.56.

sulphide nickel ore deposits of Canada, and to a much smaller extent, New Caledonia. The Sudbury Basin has yielded about 20 billion pounds of nickel during the 20th century, and potential for further expansion seems limited. The major companies regularly bemoan their rising costs as they push deeper underground and move into lower grades of the sulphide ores.

The rapid rise of nickel demand is forcing a major change in traditional supply patterns toward the lateritic ores, a globe-girdling band of large, low grade nickel deposits in the tropical zone. These lateritic ores are the geological result of a long weathering process. Their most attractive feature is surface location, which will allow their exploitation by cheap and capital intensive strip mining techniques in contrast to the more expensive underground pursuit of Canada's sulphide nickel ore.

The countries with large and promising reserves of laterites include Guatemala, the Dominican Republic, Venezuela, Colombia, Brazil, the Solomon Islands, New Caledonia, the Philippines and Indonesia. There have also been finds in Southern Africa, Australia and Greece. Some of the world's best reserves of lateritic nickel are located in Cuba, but in general the prospect of extensive trade between capitalist and communist countries in a strategic commodity like nickel is highly unlikely.

The major nickel corporations have long realized the inevitability of the current nickel supply problem, and have made extensive preparations to meet it. INCO, Falconbridge and Le Nickel are all moving into major new projects to exploit the tropical lateritic ores. A worrisome feature of the new separation processes for the laterites is a very high energy requirement; the ores cannot be concentrated before smelting, meaning the production of ferro-nickel from laterites involves melting down the entire low grade ore body. For this reason the oil price revolution of 1973-74 has slowed the rush of major nickel producers to the sunnier climes, but only temporarily.

With nickel prices rising, the urgency of demand growing, and 80 percent of all known nickel reserves outside communist countries tied up in the lateritic formations, a strong shift in the traditional pattern of supply toward the tropical countries is inevitable.[11] The cost of production will be higher than in the past, but that cost will have to be paid.

THE MONOPOLY ORGANIZATION OF NICKEL
The drive of nickel producers into the tropics will be remarkably

11. "Good-bye to Motherhood", *Forbes,* June 15, 1974, p. 30-1; also see: "Laterites: future source for world nickel", *Engineering and Mining Journal,* October 1968, p. 73.

orderly, because nickel is perhaps the most highly monopolized industry in the capitalist world economy. For seventy years nickel and the International Nickel Company have been synonymous, and in the mid-1970s INCO is still by far the dominant producer.

In the 1940s and early 1950s the giant company, with its strangle-hold over the rich sulphide ores of Canada's Sudbury basin, supplied the vast majority of Canada's nickel production which in turn accounted for close to 90 percent of all nickel production in the non-communist world. As late as 1956 INCO provided 80 percent of Canadian production and 62 percent of all nickel consumed outside communist countries.

In 1946 the U.S. Department of Justice filed a complaint against INCO alleging it had established a monopoly and that it had entered into agreements with foreign producers "to impose limits on world production, to fix world-wide prices, and to allocate and restrict sales in world markets."[12] The case never came to trial, and a U.S. Senate subcommittee noted that the out-of-court agreement with the company "did almost nothing to affect the basic monopoly INCO enjoys over the sale of nickel and nickel products in the United States."[13]

INCO's current share of total supply has declined to about 40 percent with the rapid growth in capacity of the industry, but it still retains its role of industry price leader. INCO's extended reign is due in large part to its long-range view of the industry. It has used its monopoly pricing powers and potential to discriminate among customers in a relatively cautious manner. "We could be in worse hands," was the resigned attitude of a major buyer during the short supply period in 1970.[14]

The long, stable and profitable history of the INCO monopoly has inspired other companies to try the nickel business, and several have gained a foothold. Société Le Nickel, the Rothschild company which has dominated the New Caledonia fields since the nineteenth century, embarked on renewed expansion in 1968.[15] The French company has been negotiating with American Metal Climax (AMAX) for a joint venture in New Caledonia. AMAX is already taking part in a nickel project in Botswana with Anglo-American, South Africa's largest corporation.

12. Percy Bidwell, *op. cit.*, p. 142.
13. *Ibid.*, p. 142.
14. "The Beguiling New Economics of Nickel", *Fortune*, March 1970, p. 100.
15. For an examination of the Rothschild's Le Nickel in New Caledonia see: "The Rothschild's Nasty Little New Caledonia Nickel Monopoly", *Pacific Imperialism Notebook, op. cit.*, p. 147. Through various banks and holding companies the Rothschilds control 78.7 per cent interest in Le Nickel S A.

The Western Mining Company of Australia has become a significant producer, with about 90 million pounds annual capacity. Sherritt Gordon, a Canadian company linked to the American Newmont Mining group, has a modest capacity in Canada of about 35 million pounds, but has interests in the Marinduque Mining project in the Philippines and another prospect in Indonesia.[16] Sherritt has done much of the pioneering research in the processing of lateritic ores.

The biggest moves in the tropical adventure will not be made by these companies, however, but by INCO itself and its fastest growing rival, Falconbridge Nickel. Falconbridge has moved into the number two position in the industry by virtue of its 100 million pound capacity in the Sudbury area, and its $195 million plunge into the Caribbean with a 65 million pound facility in the Domincan Republic.

INCO, which seems to have lagged a step behind in its battle with Falconbridge over shares of the nickel market, in fact has a major and geographically diversified expansion program on the drawing boards, based on its long term policy of exploration and tying up promising reserves. The industry leader is poised for moves into New Caledonia to create 50 to 100 million pounds capacity; into Guatemala in alliance with the Hanna mining and steel group to create 28 million pounds capacity; and into Indonesia in alliance with Japanese interests where the 100 million pound Soroaka mining project and related smelter and hydro-electric facilities will bring its investment to $600 million by 1979, the target full-production date. INCO is also actively exploring in Mexico, Brazil, Papua-New Guinea and Africa.

The financial impact of this expansion program, through which the industry plans by 1985 to add an estimated one billion pounds to the 1973 capacity of 1.1 billion pounds, is staggering. Falconbridge capital costs for the Dominican Republic venture were about $3 per pound of installed capacity, but more recent cost estimates have been running at $7 per pound, which places the entire investment program in the $7 billion-plus range.[17]

None of the companies, not even mighty INCO, can begin to finance activity on this scale out of retained earnings. Decisions of this magnitude require the extensive collaboration of whole financial groups, which explains the growing tendency toward joint ventures between the nickel corporations and oil and steel companies in close alliance with major financial institutions.

16. "Who controls the 'War Metal'?", *op. cit.*, p. 141. The Newmont Mining Corporation of New York holds a 37.6 percent controlling interest in Sherritt Gordon Mines Ltd. (*Inter-corporate Ownership, 1969*, Statistics Canada, Ottawa, 1971).

17. "Optimism indicated for nickel demand", Toronto *Globe and Mail,* November 19, 1974.

INCO, which is the only one of the trusts formed by J.P. Morgan at the turn of the century to survive unscathed, retains working relations with the powerful Morgan Guaranty Trust of New York and an impressive array of associated companies. Falconbridge has become part of a coalition of Texas oil and First National City Bank of New York interests, while Le Nickel has its Rothschild connection. During the next decade, the financial and political clout of these powerful groups will be essential to the further development of the nickel industry.

THE POLITICS OF EXPANSION

The imperatives of producing ever larger quantities of nickel each year, and of acquiring the vast sums of capital needed to pursue the investment program, are counterbalanced by major components of risk. These exclude the risk of failures in exploration, or fluctuations in markets; the nickel monopolies are large enough to withstand any temporary inconveniences which arise from these quarters. The risk which they now find most difficult to control is political, and the ever-keen interest of these corporations in politics has become, if possible, even more acute.

Perhaps the best illustration of the importance of the interplay between politics and corporate interests in nickel is the Cuban experience. With 40 percent of the known nickel reserves outside communist countries in the late 1950s, Cuba had long been an important part of American strategic planning. Reporting to the United States Council on Foreign Relations in 1958, P.W. Bidwell wrote of Canada and Cuba:

> It is clearly a matter of national interest that production should be maintained at a high level in both countries, and that they should not in any way impede our access to their output. This amounts to saying that the provision of adequate wartime supplies of nickel hinges upon the ability of the United States to retain Cuba and Canada as partners in a system of collective defense.[18]

Cuba initially proved its value in this respect during World War II, when a mine owned by the United States government and operated by Freeport Sulphur contributed 60 million pounds of nickel to American needs between 1943 and 1947. The facility was closed, then reopened in 1952 by the National Lead Company, and expanded to 49 million pounds capacity in 1953 as part of the United States government stockpiling program. The U.S. government investment was valued at about $100 million.

In 1957 Cuba's importance was further increased when the United States government signed a contract with the Cuban American

18. Percy Bidwell, *op. cit.*, p. 172.

Nickel Company, a Freeport Sulphur subsidiary, for delivery of an eventual 271 million pounds of nickel. Initial production was scheduled for 1959, and American officials were pleased that the United States' severe dependence on Canada and INCO for nickel was being reduced.

The triumph of Fidel Castro's revolutionary nationalist government in Cuba upset all these calculations. Strict new Cuban government mining laws in late 1959 led the American companies to slow their activities, and the Castro government responded by nationalizing the American properties in late 1960. With the subsequent American embargo on trade with Cuba, Cuban nickel has not been available for United States needs ever since.

The "Cuban problem" is what haunts the United States government and major resource corporations like INCO and Falconbridge as they try to harness the world's resources for consumption in the industrial nations. W.G. Dahl, the president of Falconbridge International, observed in 1968 that the lateritic óres his company wants are in countries "which are not renowned for the stability of their governments . . . or their fervor to deal fairly with free-enterprise business. Cuba provides an example of what can happen to perfectly good nickel capacity."[19] His associate G.T.N. Woodrooffe, a Falconbridge vice-president, added precision to the company's concept of fairness: "A mine must earn back its investment in five years if it wants investors to entrust their savings to it."[20]

The corporations' concern for favourable tax treatment and respect for property rights translates at another level into a major objective of American foreign policy: maintaining wherever possible a climate conducive to the free movement of goods and capital. This task has become more difficult as the enormous appetite of the advanced countries for raw materials runs afoul of the rising, often revolutionary nationalism of Third World countries desperate for economic development more suited to the needs of their own populations.

The "Cuban problem" has in the last 30 years popped up prominently in China, Korea, and Vietnam, as well as Cuba, in all cases with concerted opposition from the United States. However, this does not begin to indicate the extent to which the United States has been obliged to intervene militarily, diplomatically and economically in the affairs of other countries to pursue its overall objectives.

This imperialist dimension of United States foreign policy toward non-industrial countries is closely tied up with the activities of transnational companies, many of them American-based. In the Third World a

19. *Barrons,* March 4, 1968, p. 3.
20. *Ibid.*

primary concern of the transnationals is resource extraction, which simultaneously provides large profits and essential raw materials for the leading industrial countries. The important link between power politics and raw materials extraction is universal, but the point can be illustrated by examining briefly the political situation in just those countries which are of future importance to the transnational nickel corporations.

Guatemala: Jacobo Arbenz, elected in 1950 with 63 percent of the popular vote, pledged to transform Guatemala from a state of underdevelopment and dependency into "a modern capitalist country." His agrarian reform, aimed at redistributing uncultivated land, affronted the United Fruit Company. The CIA, State Department and United Fruit engineered a coup in 1954 which toppled Arbenz and brought in a government led by Castillo Armas. The Armas government and its successors have been extremely well disposed to foreign investment, and today many transnational corporations, including INCO, are active in the country.

The American intervention was particularly crude in Guatemala; during the Armas invasion CIA planes flown by American pilots bombed Guatemala City until Arbenz gave up. At the time Allan Dulles was director of the CIA. His brother John Foster Dulles was Secretary of State, a former legal counsellor to the United Fruit Company, and for 27 years until 1948 a director of INCO.

INCO has a $180 million nickel project scheduled to begin production in Guatemala in 1977. [21]

The Philippines: A Spanish colony for 300 years, the Philippines became part of the American empire after the Spanish-American war in 1898. The country achieved formal independence in 1946. The economy is dominated by American capital, and the government headed by president Ferdinand Marcos rules under martial law.

Brazil: In the early 1960s the government of Joao Goulart attempted to introduce land reforms, nationalize the electrical power utility owned by Brazilian Traction, Light and Power, and impose control on capital

21. "Exmibal: Take another nickel out", *Guatemala,* North American Congress on Latin American (NACLA), Berkely, 1974. This NACLA publication contains excellent material on the history, political economy and state of repression in Gautemala. The INCO Exmibal project in Guatemala has recently come under attack by NDP MP John Rodriguez who charged that Canadian taxpayers are paying millions of dollars to help the company exploit Guatemala resources. Rodriguez was attacking a $17.25 million loan by the Canadian Export Development Corporation (EDC) To Exmibal. (see: "Ottawa helping U.S. firm exploit Central America mineral resources", *Windsor Star,* November 22, 1974). Also see: "INCO Plans 1975 capital outlay of more than $400 million", Toronto *Globe and Mail,* February 25, 1975, p. B10.

exports. Goulart was overthrown by an army coup in 1964, with much evidence that the coup was encouraged by the United States government. Brazil is now a paradise for transnational corporations, and the military government is notorious for its contempt for civil liberties and extensive use of torture and death squads to suppress political dissent.

New Caledonia: New Caledonia became a French possession in 1853. Long a penal colony, the island is dominated by Le Nickel and Rothschild banking interests. The convict and indentured labour system used in the mines was not abandoned until after World War II. About 40 percent of all known nickel reserves in the capitalist world are on the Pacific island.

Dominican Republic: An American protectorate from 1916 to 1930, the Dominican Republic suffered under American-trained and sponsored dictator Rafael Trujillo from 1930 to 1961. Following the CIA-engineered assassination of Trujillo in 1961, the country's politics were tumultuous. Nationalist reform leader Juan Bosch was elected president with 60 percent of the popular vote in 1962, but deposed by a right wing coup in 1963. Constitutionalist forces attempted to reinstate Bosch in 1965, at which point U.S. president Johnson sent in 20,000 marines "to protect American lives."

With the United States preserving order, onetime Trujillo ally Joaquin Balaguer assumed the presidency. His regime has been characterized by political assassination, rigged elections, and suppression of opposition parties. Balaguer has also provided a warm welcome for major foreign interests: ALCOA, Gulf and Western, and Falconbridge Nickel.

Indonesia: Indonesia achieved national independence from the Dutch after World War II under President Achmed Sukarno, who became by the middle 1950s the self-styled leader of the neutralist or non-aligned block of Third World countries. Sukarno ruled increasingly in alliance with the Indonesian Communist Party (PKI). The Indonesian army stripped Sukarno of power in 1965, and consolidated its position during an extended reign of terror in which over one million people were massacred. The military regime of President Suharto has reversed Sukarno's policies of independent development and avidly pursues investment from transnational corporations, INCO among them. In the foreign policy field, Indonesia is now closely aligned with the United States.

In nearly every area where the nickel corporations must seek new supplies, the governments are essentially unpopular and military regimes. They rule with various degrees of terror, sustained by raw police and military force. Operating in such a climate of instability, the corporations and their major shareholders have every reason to be concerned with the risks of sinking billions of dollars into fixed capital investments.

There are only two major forms of insurance against the risk of losing control over capital and important sources of raw material. Transnational resource corporations like INCO, Falconbridge and the others have taken out both kinds by: supporting any national government which favours foreign investment on generous terms, regardless of its political character; and maintaining close connections with strong governments, particularly the United States government, so that if things go wrong at the local level, strong outside pressures up to and including armed intervention can be brought to bear.

As the nickel industry increases its overseas activities, in the years ahead, these patterns of behavior can only intensify. The consequences for the politics of the industrial countries, and for both the politics and economic evolution of the less developed countries, are truly disturbing.

CHAPTER TWO

Forging the Nickel Monopoly: INCO

Thayer Lindsley, a geologist, engineer and entrepreneur from the United States, pushed Falconbridge into the world nickel business in 1928. To the rest of the business community it must have seemed more an act of faith than a rational initiative. Many other companies had preceeded Lindsley's and none had survived the attempt to compete with one of the world's most formidable monopolies, the International Nickel Company. Despite the record of competitive disasters in the nickel industry and apparently against long odds, Falconbridge has survived and prospered. To understand the unlikely and startling achievements of Number Two, we must start with an examination of the history and strategy of Number One: INCO.

U.S. CAPITAL MEETS CANADIAN RESOURCES[1]

International Nickel was incorporated as an American company in 1902, but the roots of the giant monopoly reach back more than a decade further to the pioneering activities of two forerunners, the Canadian Copper Company and the Orford Copper Company. At a time when the potential importance of nickel was appreciated by very few, these companies operating in combination gained control over two key seg-

1. O. W. Main's excellent book, *The Canadian Nickel Industry: A study in market control and public policy,* (University of Toronto Press, Toronto, 1955), is used as a major source for the historical data and interpretation in this chapter. Other historical materials include two "company" histories: D.M. LeBourdais' *Sudbury Basin: The Story of Nickel,* (Ryerson Press, Toronto, 1953) which was underwritten by the Falconbridge company; and *For The Years to Come,* (Longmans, Green & Co., Toronto, 1960), by former INCO Chairman and Chief Officer John F. Thompson with Norman Beasley.

ments of the nickel industry—the ore supply and the military market.

The Canadian Copper Company, organized by the American promoter Samuel Ritchie and a group of Ohio backers, laid early claim to vast areas of nickel-copper deposits in the Sudbury Basin in the mid-1880's. Canadian Copper's interest in acquiring mining properties was encouraged by the open-handed policies of the Ontario and Canadian governments, which aimed to attract development capital to mining by removing all restrictions in its path.

This was part of a more general pattern in Canadian mining history, in which American capitalists, promoters and speculators found few obstacles in buying up Canadian non-renewable resources. Mineral patents were sold for one dollar an acre, with no limit on the size of a claim, no taxes on undeveloped land, and no requirements for improvement. These conditions were a speculator's dream, and an invitation to monopoly.[2]

By 1886, before the rules governing mining claims were tightened up, Ritchie and friends controlled most of the accessible ores. These holdings, as Ritchie realized, would be tricky to develop. There was no large-scale market for nickel and the Sudbury ores presented unfamiliar refining problems. To create a profitable outlet for large quantities of nickel, Ritchie approached the United States Navy with his proposals for nickel-steel armour plate, and met with great success. In 1890, the Navy committed $1 million (out of an annual U.S. Goverment budget of only $75 million) to purchases of nickel and experiments with it.

Canadian Copper had no proper method to separate and refine its complex Sudbury ores. Navy Secretary Tracy assigned that promising contract to his friend R. M. Thompson, president of the Orford Copper Company of New Jersey. Colonel Thompson—"a man who thought in capital letters" — was no ordinary industrialist. His diverse activities were to earn him the sobriquets "King Cotton" and "King Copper" — grudging tribute to his skillful speculation in commodity markets.

Orford knew little more than Canadian Copper about handling the nickel-copper matte derived from the smelting of the complex Sudbury

2. In 1890, the Ontario Mineral Resources Commission noted that one-half of the mines in the province were owned by Americans. Promoters and speculators from the U.S. were not discouraged by the report's attitude to foreign capital: "As long as the mineral development in Ontario continues to depend largely upon investments of foreign capital, and especially American capital, a liberal policy must be followed; mining lands must be not less free here than in the United States, where with the single exception of New York there is neither reservation nor royalty." *Report of the Royal Commission on Mineral Resources of Ontario,* Toronto, 1890, p. xv cited in H. V. Nelles, *The Politics of Development,* Macmillan Co., Toronto, 1974.

ores, but the opportunity opened up by the Navy contract was not lost upon Thompson. By 1892, Orford had developed a satisfactory method of separating nickel and copper. In 1890, Canadian Copper and Orford entered into an exclusive five-year supply contract to cement a combination giving both companies substantial advantages over their competitors: for Orford, guaranteed supplies of ore at known prices; for Canadian Copper, a guaranteed market.

Colonel Thompson held the upper hand in this combination through his special relationship with the largest buyer of nickel, the U.S. Navy. The official INCO history, *For the Years to Come* obliquely provides some clues on the strength of this relationship and how it was maintained:

> Thompson never missed an Army-Navy football game. Engaging a special train, he filled it with guests including—more often than not—the Commandant of the Military Academy of West Point, decorated the train with Navy colors, and jewelled it with hundreds of chrysanthemums. Going to the game, luncheon was served; returning to New York after the game, dinner was served; at the game, Thompson, with top hat and cane, always led the Navy Team onto the field.[3]

The whole arrangement appears to have been vintage military-industrial complex.

From this secure starting point Orford and Canadian Copper grew rapidly, and soon possessed greater capacity than the Navy alone required. With the American civilian market still very narrow, Orford began selling to the European nickel market in 1893. This invasion immediately led to a price war with the established firm, Rothschild's Le Nickel. Safe behind the Navy contract and the U.S. tariff, Orford quickly took over about one-third of Le Nickel's sales. During this trial of strength between the American and French rivals, the price of nickel in Europe fell from 60 cents a pound to 25 cents. Peace broke out in 1895 when Thompson and Rothschild reached an understanding over prices and division of the market. The official INCO history describes the result:

> Société Le Nickel had finally arrived at the opinion that there was something in Canadian nickel . . . Singularly, in the rough and tumble struggle, Thompson and Baron Adolphe de Rothschild became friends . . . This was the sort of competition the Rothschilds appreciated — and understood. It brought casualties.[4]

3. J.F. Thompson and N. Beasley, *op. cit.*, p. 139, 140.
4. *Ibid.*, p. 93.

Not only had Orford captured a major share of Le Nickel's markets, but several competitors of Canadian Copper crumbled under the onslaught of the drastic temporary price-cutting and Orford's market control. The Drury Nickel Company, the Dominion Mineral Company, and H. H. Vivian & Sons all discontinued their Canadian mining operations, leaving Canadian Copper in sole control of the Sudbury district.

A WEAK NATIONALIST RESPONSE

The rapid growth of this American-controlled nickel combination from the outset created political tensions in Canada. As early as 1890, Samuel Ritchie had been caught making contradictory appeals to both Canadian and American nationalism to further the affairs of Canadian Copper. In Canada he defended Canadian Copper's American ownership by emphasizing the employment it created and the company's plans to build a Canadian refinery. In Washington, with a view to building a refinery in Ohio and monopolizing a protected American market, he lobbied Congress to remove the tariff on Canadian ores and matte, but not the tariff on refined nickel. Canadian Copper's struggling rivals were quick to point out these inconsistencies to the governments of Ontario and Canada. However, in 1891, Ritchie and Canadian Copper parted ways. Ritchie's personal financial interests in other Canadian projects placed him in conflict with his major shareholders, who removed him from office. While Canadian Copper went on to develop its connections with Orford, the embittered Ritchie overnight became one of the most ardent advocates of a Canadian nickel refinery and nickel-steel industry. Although this change of heart was blatantly self-serving, Ritchie's thinking was in tune with that of Canadian capitalists and speculators led by the Hamilton-based MacLaren syndicate. They resented the power of the Canadian Copper Company, and harboured visions of a major steel industry under their own control. The Canadian-Ritchie interests focussed their attack on the question of a nickel refinery, and demanded suspension of the Canadian Copper charter to force the Ohio group out of Canada. They also advocated an export tax on ore and matte to undercut the dominant position of Orford in the protected United States market and bring refining to Canada.

Canadian Copper fought vigorously against all these proposals. They claimed that a Canadian export duty on ore and matte would result in the decline of Canadian production. The American market would turn away from Sudbury ores to use the New Caledonian supplies. The debate reached a climax in 1897 when the Laurier Liberal government enacted export tax legislation, but failed to put it into effect after the Canadian Copper Company threatened to close its Sudbury mines.

The arguments and behavior of the Canadian Copper-Orford combination deserve close attention because, with slight modifications, they have since been used repeatedly to beat back recurring outbursts of Canadian nationalism on the nickel question. Similarly, the behavior of the Laurier government in 1897 established an example which was taken up at later points in history by other Ottawa regimes: first strike a nationalist pose to placate public opinion, then quietly back away to avoid a confrontation with American corporate power.

There is considerable evidence to suggest the Canadian Copper shutdown threat was pure bluff. The cost advantages of Sudbury over New Caledonia were large, and the technology of the day made expansion of production in New Caledonia improbable. Nor was nickel refining tied to Orford's New Jersey location by any insurmountable economic or technological factors. In 1897, Orford's Colonel Thompson argued in Washington against an American tariff on nickel ore and matte on the grounds that it would shift refining out of the United States. Thompson did point out, however, that refining involved four times as much operating expenditure as mining, but that "as Americans, naturally we wish to see the refining done in the United States and the work provided for American citizens."[5]

In retrospect it appears that the economic arguments used by Canadian Copper and Orford to back up their blackmail tactics were a combination of exaggeration and fabrication. The Laurier government's capitulation in failing to proclaim the export tax on unrefined nickel was based on either ignorance of the facts, or collusion with the American interests involved.

There was suspicion of the latter possibility. A member of the Hamilton group allied with Ritchie against Canadian Copper, John Gibson, wrote accusingly to Laurier "that before your general election (1896) took place, the Canadian Copper Company had an understanding with your government that this act would be disallowed."[6]

Evidence of such machinations appears in correspondence between Colonel Thompson and Prime Minister Laurier in 1906 describing a cheque for an undisclosed amount — including a profit of $5,000 on stock which Thompson claimed to have purchased for the Prime Minister.[7] Other correspondence from that period indicates a close personal relationship between Thompson and Laurier. Another hint of Thompson's influence with the Liberal Cabinet appeared in the Finan-

---

5. Ontario Bureau of Mines, *Report*, 1897, p. 44 cited in O.W. Main, *op. cit.*, p. 41.
6. Cited in H.V. Nelles, *op. cit.*, p. 99.
7. *Laurier to Thompson*, October 20, 1906 cited in H.V. Nelles, *op. cit.*, p. 329.

cial Post in 1916, when it claimed that two Liberal cabinet ministers received large gifts of shares during the formation of INCO in 1902.[8]

When the federal government failed to challenge the Canadian Copper-Orford combine in 1897, its opponents turned to the Ontario government to impose license fees on exports of unrefined ore and matte. Ontario passed such legislation, with rebates for refining in Canada, but it too was never proclaimed. Again the fear of retaliation by the companies and loss of employment in Sudbury were given as the reason for inaction.

A fascinating situation arose when Orford allowed its refining patents to lapse in Canada in 1900. The Ontario legislature passed a motion advising Ottawa that the Canadian national interest would best be served by refusing to renew the patents, a move which would create an opening for a Canadian nickel refinery using the Orford process. Apparently, Laurier found Colonel Thompson's views more persuasive. Ottawa ignored Ontario's advice and renewed the Orford patents, thus perpetuating conditions favourable to the monopoly.[9]

The Canadian Copper-Orford combine survived the criticism of the late 1890's with its image in Canada severely tarnished but its power untrammeled. The two companies were in an excellent position to enjoy the benefits of the naval boom generated by the Spanish-American War of 1898, a conflict which exercised a strong influence on the naval strategists of the world's major powers. The superiority of the United States Navy had been total.

> In . . : two battles (Manila Bay and Santiago de Cuba) the American warships clad in nickel steel armour destroyed almost the entire Spanish fleet without the loss of a single vessel. The American casualties were one dead and seven wounded. Immediately there was a quickened economic and political interest in nickel. [10]

That quickened interest soon translated into orders for nickel; but while Orford and Canadian Copper reaped substantial profits, their very prosperity invited renewed competition. New York nickel prices soared from 35 cents a pound in 1899 to 57 cents two years later, and the combine did not expand production rapidly enough to satisfy demand.

8.   *Financial Post,* Toronto, July 15, 1916.
9.   Of this period in Ontario mining history H.V. Nelles concludes: "In mining it would seem that the regulated group experienced greater success in bringing the regulator under control than the other way around." (Nelles, *op. cit.,* p. 491).
10. Thompson and Beasley, *op. cit.,* p. 121.

The Hamilton-based MacLaren group finally moved to join the fray against Canadian Copper by forming the Nickel Steel Company and the Nickel Copper Company of Canada. Encouraged by an arrangement with British steelmakers, these companies began to bid for nickel properties in the Sudbury area. Another entrant with close connections to British steelmakers was Mond Nickel, owned and managed by the Mond family. High nickel prices also attracted Boston capital in F. H. Clergue's Consolidated Lake Superior Corporation, a well-financed venture which intended to supply ferro-nickel to the Krupps in Germany.

J.P. MORGAN SHAPES THE FUTURE

The ascendancy of Canadian Copper and Orford was threatened by the plans of these rival mining and refining companies, but also from a more dangerous quarter. Large steel companies with strong financial connections were taking interest in both the profitability of nickel and the potential for control of the even more profitable steel markets through regulating nickel distribution.

In Europe, a number of armaments manufacturers and steelmakers formed the Steel Manufacturers Syndicate. It beat back high prices by threatening to enter the nickel business, and persuaded Le Nickel to enter into long-term contracts with its members at 25 cents a pound.

In the United States a parallel process was underway. The continuation of tremendous profits from armour plate, until then the private preserve of Carnegie and Bethlehem Steel Companies, depended ultimately on control of nickel. J. Pierpont Morgan and Company, the powerful New York investment bankers who had just organized the United States Steel trust, formed a nickel syndicate and began assembling nickel properties.

Colonel R.M. Thompson of Orford and the Ohio owners of Canadian Copper were not slow to understand the hazard facing them. Although it would be expensive, Morgan and the U.S. Steel corporation had the resources to circumvent their combine and develop an independent nickel supply. Rather than suffer through a long, costly and ultimately losing struggle with big steel, the nickel men sensibly decided to bow to superior strength and maximize their personal gains. Thompson negotiated a reorganization of the nickel industry with J. P. Morgan.

In 1902, the Morgan syndicate formed the International Nickel Company, incorporated in New Jersey, by purchasing the Orford Copper Company and the smaller Wharton refinery, the mining operations and holdings of Canadian Copper, the other minor nickel holdings in Canada and New Caledonia. Colonel Thompson became INCO's first

Chairman, but the board of directors was controlled by U.S. Steel appointees.[11]

The creation of INCO gave Morgan several advantages: assured nickel supplies, domination of the armour plate business in the United States, and a strategic position in foreign markets. Morgan financial power would protect this empire by denying capital to potential competitors in nickel or steel. In addition, the direct profits on promotion of the new trust were tremendous. Purchase of the assets of companies absorbed into INCO cost about $10 million, but Morgan promoted the new company with a capitalization of $27.7 million, thus giving himself the potential for effective control without tying up a cent.[12] The floating of the new INCO shares demonstrated the proven Morgan formula for creating a trust: initially the stock was watery, but the increased monopoly power of the company soon gave substance to its inflated share values.

The reaction in Canada to Morgan's coup was nervous, with renewed speculation that Sudbury mines would be closed down in favour of New Caledonia. Since this same fear had supposedly been guiding Canadian policy on export taxation, the statements of the director of the Ontario Bureau of Mines in 1902 are highly interesting:

> I have no fear that (the Sudbury mines) will be closed down, as the product is needed . . . The only other sources of supply for the world's wants are the mines of New Caledonia, which cannot successfully compete with ours, on account of their great distance, the fact that they are worked by convict labour, and other disadvantageous conditions . . . The deposits are too valuable, and the metal in too active demand, to warrant anything like a stoppage in production. It is a mere change between American companies.[13]

The formation of INCO was not a "mere change between American companies." It dashed the dreams of Canadian capitalists and the Ontario government for a powerful North American nickel-steel industry based in Canada. While the New Caledonian ores alone could not

11. A majority of the 1902 directors of INCO were closely associated with J.P. Morgan and U.S. Steel. A. Monell, formerly with Carnegie Steel; Max Pam, counsel for U.S. Steel; E.C. Converse of U.S. Steel; M. Hunsiker of Nickel Corporation: J. Wharton of Bethlehem Steel; Robert Thompson, Orford Copper Co.; Leslie Ward, A.W. Maconochie and Charles Schwab of U.S. Steel; and also S.H.P. Pell, A.H. Wiggin and E.F. Wood. (Main, *op. cit.*, and Thompson, *op. cit.*)

12. O.W. Main, *op. cit.*, p. 45. "Morgan and Company was thus able to retain control without being required to invest anything in the new company."

13. Toronto *Globe*, March 21, 1902, cited in Thompson and Beasley, *op. cit.*, p. 147. 148.

defeat the Canadians, the alliance through INCO of Orford refining facilities and stockpiles, U.S. steelmakers and Morgan control of capital markets made their vision impossible. INCO's existence rendered ineffective the notion of export taxation on unprocessed nickel as a tool to force industrial development in Canada. "The new company, with its vast financial resources, could hold the United States market and forestall the establishment of a nickel-steel industry in Canada without relying on Canadian ores."[14] Canadian nationalist agitation around the nickel question petered out, not to reappear until World War I.

CONSOLIDATING THE INCO MONOPOLY

Between 1902 and 1913, INCO rode the European armaments race, increasing its production more than fourfold. By keeping the price in the 35 to 40 cent range throughout the period, the company captured all the new demand for its Sudbury mines under long-term contracts. INCO's dominance over Le Nickel and the New Caledonia mines was undisputed. Although INCO frequently denied the existence of a cartel, it quite clearly negotiated changes in the division of the world market with Le Nickel to avoid unnecessary disruption and loss of revenue through price competition. The Rothschilds had learned their lesson once, and didn't need to learn it again. "We have made important changes in our foreign relations ensuring for us for some years to come a larger participation in the foreign demand," noted INCO president Ambrose Monell in his 1904 annual report.[15]

INCO was faced with several competitive threats during the pre-war years, but the long shadow J.P. Morgan cast in capital markets was sufficient to prevent creation of a serious rival. Competitors found great difficulty raising equity or loan capital from American financial institutions. Clergue's Consolidated Lake Superior Corporation became overextended in diverse and ambitious projects in Sudbury and Sault Ste. Marie, and found itself unable to raise money in the United States to develop its promising holdings. The company went bankrupt in 1904.

Morgan's heavy hand was also in evidence in the failure of four separate attempts by the Nickel Copper Company to secure American markets and financial backing. The company's plans to build a Canadian refinery made it an intolerable threat to INCO, which was not interested in seeing any revival of that type of proposal for its own operations in Canada.

The Nickel Copper Company properties by 1912 passed into the

14. Main, *op. cit.*, p. 59.
15. *Ibid.*, p. 64.

hands of the Canadian Northern railroad interests of Mackenzie and Mann in alliance with New York promoter H.F. Pearson.[16] Together they formed the British America Nickel Corporation (BANCO) and planned to build a mining-refining capacity sufficient to supply one-third of the existing American nickel market. BANCO also ran into insurmountable obstacles in raising funds to finance its development and the expected cost of breaking into INCO's market. The Company was further set back when Pearson went down with the *Lusitania* in 1915 while on a money-raising voyage to London.

The only new nickel company to do well before the war was Mond Nickel, which succeeded because it had INCO's blessing. The Mond family operated from a relatively strong position with adequate sources of capital and a guaranteed market in Great Britain. From INCO's point of view, there were points in Mond's favour. Its very existence would give the industry an appearance of competition where none existed. The British ties of Mond would serve a valuable public relations function in Canada where empire loyalism still meant British Empire, not American. Finally, Mond was interested in selling only to Great Britain, not to INCO's primary market in the United States. Mond Nickel was admitted to the cartel in 1904 and dealt exclusively through Henry Merton and Sons, the same sales brokers used by INCO and Le Nickel to supervise prices and market division.

EARLY POLITICAL MISHAPS
INCO's decision to tolerate Mond Nickel was rewarded in 1910 when the American company came under the scrutiny of a federal Parliamentary committee and the charges of "foreign monopolist" were raised once again. Ignoring its American control, INCO made much of its Canadian and British shareholders. Mond intervened in the debate to

16. William Mackenzie, Donald Mann and H.F. Pearson were members of an elite of "super-promoters" in turn-of-the-century Canada. Mackenzie and Mann parlayed some disconnected railway holdings into a new trans-continental, the Canadian Northern Railway, which as it approached bankruptcy, was nationalized by Robert Borden's Conservative government to become the foundation of the Canadian National Railway. Pearson emerged as a prominent promoter and financier of Mexican Light, Heat and Power Companies, the Dominion Coal Company, and several Canadian hydro-electric projects. The threesome, along with William Van Horne of CPR fame, worked together in 1912 to incorporate the Brazilian Traction, Light and Power Company. Mackenzie became the first Chairman of Brazilian Traction and the company prospered in Brazil. Today BRASCAN is that country's largest privately-held company with almost two billion dollars in assets. For further information see: "How much is that in cruzeiros?", *Let Us Prey*, James Lorimer and Co., Toronto, 1974; Main, *op. cit.*, p. 70; John Porter, *The Vertical Mosaic*, University of Toronto Press, Toronto, 1965, p. 542-3; and Frank and Libby Park, *Anatomy of Big Business*, James Lorimer and Co., Toronto.

deny that INCO monopolized ore reserves and hauled out the old
chestnuts about the inferiority of Sudbury ores to those of New
Caledonia.[17] Once more INCO, this time with the aid of its "competitor", escaped the scrutiny of Canadian politicians, all the while
stepping up its activity in Sudbury and shunning the siren call of the
Pacific island.

A more serious embarrassment overtook INCO in 1914. At the
outbreak of World War I, the company shut down its Sudbury mines
and smelters. This caused widespread indignation in Canada, with
public opinion favouring full production of nickel as a vital war material
for Great Britain. The problem for INCO was that by 1913 it had been
sending 40 percent of its entire output to the German armament program. When this became generally known, the public reaction was
fierce. The *Toronto Telegram* blasted INCO editorially: "The present
situation," shrilled the Tely, "is that Britishers and other enemies of
the Teutonic armies are being shot down by machine guns hardened
with Ontario nickel and not an Ontario boy goes into action except at the
risk of having to face bullets barbed with the nickel of which his own
native province has a monopoly."[18] The press clamoured for an export
ban on nickel, public ownership of the industry, and the construction of
a refinery in Canada to permit firmer control over the destination of
Canadian nickel.

INCO had just completed another refinery at Bayonne, New
Jersey in 1913 and was not inclined to yield to such demands. The
Borden government in Ottawa tried to justify the company position, but
found public sympathy non-existent.[19] In 1915 the Ontario government
created a commission to study the possibility of refining nickel in
Canada. The studies of the Ontario Commission and the Munitions
Resources Commission finally prompted Ottawa to inform INCO
"there should be established in this Dominion a nickel refinery sufficient at least to supply all the requirements of the British Empire, under
any conditions and in any emergency."[20] The company promised to do
this, but its troubles weren't over.

17. Mond told the parliamentary committee which was proposing an export duty on
     nickel that such a duty would "favour the products of convict labour in the penal
     colony of New Caledonia." (Nelles, *op. cit.*, p. 332) Such statements of social
     concern from the corporate elite usually recur when they are supportive of underlying
     financial concerns.
18. Toronto *Telegram*, December 27, 1914, cited in Main, *op. cit.*, p. 153.
19. In 1916, the Toronto *Telegram* reflected part of the public resentment against
     INCO's avoidance of a Canadian refinery site: "A few boarding houses around two
     or three holes in the ground, plus Sudbury, represents all that Ontario has to show for
     a monopoly of 90 percent of the world's nickel supply." (Nelles, *op. cit.*, p. 307).
20. Toronto *World*, February 8, 1916 cited in Main, *op. cit.*, p. 84.

Canadian industrialists belatedly realized they were missing out
on large profits from war production, which were instead piling up in
the United States. The Liberal Party took up the cry for a Canadian
nickel steel industry, with some members even calling for public
ownership.[21] Public sentiment was further aroused when the German
submarine *Deutschland* made two Atlantic crossings from the United
States (still a neutral nation) in 1916 carrying, among other things,
nickel presumed to be from INCO. The company pleaded inability to
control the final destination of all its sales, but as atonement announced
Port Colbourne as the site of its promised Canadian refinery and began
construction immediately.

The Ontario nickel commission, reporting in 1917, seemed satisfied with INCO's gesture. It had been unable to find any evidence of the
existence of a cartel, because INCO and Mond claimed that none
existed! It ruled out expropriation of the company on the grounds that
compensation of $100 million would have to be paid. The commission
did recommend government encouragement for the British America
Nickel Corporation, and a five percent profits tax aimed at INCO which
the government enacted.[22] INCO thus survived the most serious threat
to its existence, a political threat, almost untouched. It was poised to
consolidate the monopoly position the Royal Commission said it didn't
have.

CRUSHING A CHALLENGER
In the years following the 1918 Armistice, INCO faced two problems: a
slump in sales during the post-war recession aggravated by naval
disarmament; and competition from the British America Nickel Corporation. The war and government intervention in nickel procurement had
enabled BANCO to outflank the Morgan control over investment in
nickel production. Sir Robert Borden, the war-time Prime Minister of
Canada, became a director of the company. The urgency of wartime
demand and the need for secure nickel supplies had drawn the British
government into financial and contractual arrangements with Norwegian nickel producers who had an interest in BANCO. With these
government assurances in hand, the company seemed to have solved its
financial problem. In 1918 it commenced mining and construction of a
smelter near Sudbury. A refinery at Deschenes, Quebec was completed
in 1920.

BANCO suffered serious reverses almost immediately. The
British government backed out of its purchase contracts and the demand

21. "Whip hand held by Nickel Trust", *Toronto World,* Nov. 18, 1916, p. 1.
22. *Report of the Royal Ontario Nickel Commission,* Toronto, 1917.

for nickel collapsed in the sharp post-war recession of 1921. Still, by 1923, the company had gained important contracts in the United States and posed a serious threat to INCO. International Nickel responded with a monopolist's weapon of last resort: price warfare. Nickel prices fell from 37 cents a pound in 1920, to 34 cents a pound in 1922, and 25 cents by 1924. At the same time BANCO lost a law suit, and its precarious, debt-ridden financial structure was shattered. The company was forced into liquidation having spent an estimated $15 million in equity and issued another $20 million from securities for properties and processes. There were, despite approaches to a number of major corporations, no buyers for the company although its organization, personnel and production techniques were sound.

Finally, the unknown Anglo Canadian Mining Company picked up the assets at the sacrifice price of $5 million. Only when the transaction was completed was it learned that Anglo Canadian was a dummy corporation set up by INCO. The reluctance of any other company to buy BANCO was attributed to pressure from J. P. Morgan and Company and its allies. INCO dismantled the facilities of its vanquished rival and brought the last threat of real competition under control, acquiring superior refining techniques as an added bonus.

During the 1920's under a new president, R.C. Stanley, INCO concentrated on developing its American markets, leaving Europe largely to Mond and Le Nickel. Stanley realized that, although INCO had always protested the "merchant of death" and "warmonger" labels, it had been excessively dependent on the armaments industry. The company history inadvertently acknowledged the accuracy of its critics' charges:

> When the United States entered the war, the demand for nickel was such that practically all orders were listed as priority items for nickel to be used in the manufacture of ammunition, ordnance, armour plate, guns, gun mounts, etc. — and a study of the order books disclosed that for twenty years the steady increase in nickel sales had been due, almost entirely, to the competition between nations in the building of armaments.[23]

To wean INCO from war, Stanley organized a program of research and market development designed to diversify sales. This strategy met with considerable success, as the growing automobile and radio industries provided substantial new outlets for the various nickel alloys the company's expanding staff of scientists and engineers was discovering. It was a period of rapid technological advance in both the production and use of nickel.

23. Thompson and Beasley, *op. cit.*, p. 172-173.

Competition between Mond Nickel and INCO was carefully confined to the winning of new customers for new uses of the product. Each company stuck to the agreed base price of 35 cents and avoided tampering with the other's established customers. The INCO-supervised strategy of maintaining a moderate and steady price encouraged buyers to adopt nickel for new uses, and at the same time reduced customer speculation on price increases with the attendant inconvenient fluctuations in orders and production. Gradually through the 1920's production recovered to the levels reached during the all-out effort of World War I.

INCO BECOMES "CANADIAN"

Among nagging problems of the day was a growing anti-monopoly sentiment in the United States. Private ownership was not under attack, but the U.S. government was forcing the reorganization of some of the more formidable trusts like Standard Oil, the Aluminum Company of America, U.S. Steel and others. Some of J.P. Morgan's proudest handiwork was threatened, and INCO presented an obvious target for the trustbusters.

The company escaped this potential inconvenience by moving to Canada. INCO's Canadian subsidiary, which had been incorporated as part of the effort to placate Canadian opinion in 1916, became the parent company during a purely technical reorganization in October, 1928. The move was accompanied by considerable fanfare about serving Canadian interests, but the facts remained otherwise. Although 90 percent of the company's assets were located in Canada and share ownership had been somewhat dispersed over the years, control of INCO remained firmly in American hands. In the succeeding half-century the apparent dispersal of ownership has continued, and the company seems to have evolved as a private utility, with its control divided among several important financial groups including the original Morgan network.[24]

The "Canadianization" of INCO was part and parcel of another major consolidation of its monopoly position, this time involving Mond Nickel. The period of peaceful coexistence between the two companies had created a technical problem for both as they contemplated the

24. Wallace Clement in his recent book *The Canadian Corporate Elite,* McClelland & Stewart, Toronto 1975, states INCO "is 70 percent controlled outside Canada with over 50 percent of the total ownership located in the U.S." (p.107). The *Financial Post* of August 3, 1974 shows an American ownership of only 31 percent and 17 percent in other countries, with the balance at least registered in Canada. Clement points out that at the time of his study 12 of INCO's 24 directors lived in the United States and four more elsewhere outside of Canada, a strong indication of the general locus of control.

expansion of mining in the Sudbury district. Mond owned the centre portion of the extensive Frood deposit, an ore body estimated at 150 million tons, while INCO owned both extremities. Separate development of Frood, in the view of both companies, would require costly duplication of investment and result in a highly inefficient waste of ore. They reached the same conclusion: technical considerations demanded a single operation.

The Boards of Directors concluded that a merger was more suitable than a joint venture approach. As Sir Alfred Mond, president of Mond Nickel, observed, "there must be more than a temporary armistice; there must be a permanent peace. The cartel . . . is really nothing more than an armistice in industrial warfare; and people are not going to hand over arms and methods of warfare to those who might fight them again."[25] The Mond family's willingness to merge with INCO was also increased by its growing interest in managing its British chemical industry holdings. Stronger than technical mining considerations, however, was the realization by both companies that circumstances were ideal for a killing on the stock market. They made the most of the opportunity.[26]

INCO prepared for the merger of December 1928 in several ways. It moved to Canada to avoid the expected anti-trust action in the United States, talked down the value of its shares to permit insiders to increase their holdings at minimum expense, and stoutly denied rumours of the planned merger in the spring of 1928. In August, INCO issued 167,338 shares to common shareholders and 35,653 shares to its preferred shareholders at a price of $60 when the current market price was about $150. The debasing of the stock was probably designed to take advantage of the feverish and often uninformed stock market speculation prevalent at the time.

Mond's shares, which rocketed from $35 to $100 with the first merger rumours and then slid back in response to the denials, were split two for one in June, 1928. At the same time the management issued 600,000 new shares for cash, optioning 100,000 to itself at low prices.

The pre-merger manipulations and stock-watering were only a prelude to the depredations during the actual merger. The mechanics of the merger involved INCO taking over all Mond Nickel assets, and dividing its own original shares in seven. Former INCO shareholders exchanged their stock for the new shares on a one-for-six basis, while Mond shareholders traded one-for-one, giving them roughly one-seventh of the enlarged INCO. Beyond this share swapping, the man-

25. Alfred Mond, *Industry and Politics*, London, 1937, p. 236 cited in Main, *op. cit.*, p. 104.
26. The facts on the Mond-INCO merger are drawn from Main, *op. cit.*, p. 105-106.

agement of Mond, still dominated by members of the Mond family, was offered an additional 100,000 new INCO shares, while the preferred shareholders in INCO secured a large portion of the issue of additional common stock. These new shares rose to $75 by the middle of 1929. On an undivided basis this was the equivalent of $450 compared to the $150 price of August, 1928, for the original INCO shares, a threefold increase in less than one year.

No doubt the general market speculation of 1929 was partly responsible for the rise of the stock prices, but a good portion of it can be attributed to the effect of the merger. The principal owners and managers had contrived, by a combination of market manipulation and gifts to themselves of undervalued shares, to create an opportunity for tremendous personal gain. How much of this potential they actually reaped before the 1929 crash is an open question. In any case, the whole episode obviously had much more to do with making money than it did with making nickel.

It is illuminating to contrast the reality of this performance with the language used to describe it. Surveying the history of INCO, a past president, J. F. Thompson, later wrote:

> It is my confident belief that the real protection for a country is not found in laws, but in the integrity of its people; likewise, it is my confident belief that the real protection for a company's shareholders is not found in the size of the company's bank accounts but in the integrity of its directors. In fact, that is the shareholder's greatest protection. The Nickel Company has always been fortunate in its directors.[27]

The extravagant elimination of Mond, its main "competitor", made absolutely clear what INCO had long been at pains to deny: it was a monopoly enjoying world wide control over 90 percent of the nickel market, with the power to raise that share to 100 percent at will.

The decade of the great depression did little to shake INCO's dominion over nickel. The total nickel production of the capitalist world doubled between 1929 and 1939, with INCO accounting for about 80 percent of the total on the eve of World War II. The market diversification program of the 1920's did not cushion the shock of 1931-33 as much as company management had hoped; the United States' basic steel industry experienced a horrendous slump, and INCO's sales plummeted in direct sympathy with steel. The remedy, an all too familiar one, was at hand. The escalating arms race in Europe and Japan from 1933 quickly put INCO's financial statements solidly back in order.

Once again during the 1930's INCO found itself under public

27. Thompson and Beasley, *op. cit.*, p. 353.

attack in Canada as its pursuit of profit joined with the needs of foreign militarism. The Canadian Legion called for embargos on nickel exports to armament makers, and the Trades and Labour Congress advocated the nationalization of INCO to control the traffic in nickel. The company blandly claimed it had "no reason to think that the increased consumption in Europe is due, in any substantial extent, to its use for armament purposes." [28]

Public criticism of INCO in Canada this time around lacked the intensity of the World War I era, partly because INCO was a major employer in a depression-ridden country, and partly because its extended advertising campaign linking the fortunes of the company to the well-being of Canada seemed to have altered public attitudes. First the Conservatives and then the Liberal government in Ottawa adopted the view that nickel was not really being sold for armaments, and if it was there was nothing they could do about it.

Too Small to Squash: Falconbridge

Some competitive weeds grew in INCO's garden during the 1930's. In Europe this was related to the attempts by the Axis countries to develop nickel supplies for strategic reasons without regard to international prices. In Canada, the Falconbridge Nickel Mines Ltd. made its modest debut.

Falconbridge was incorporated in 1928, the year the INCO-Mond merger provided most of the news about nickel. Falconbridge was an outgrowth of Ventures Ltd., a mineral exploration company directed by Thayer Lindsley which specialized in locating and acquiring promising mines properties not only in Canada but around the world. Lindsley's guiding philosophy sometimes frustrated his production men and shareholders: "Paper currencies will continue to depreciate everywhere," he was fond of saying. "One form of protection is to have good ore in the ground." [29]

Still, some part of the Ventures properties had to generate capital to support the rest, and the choice fell on the Sudbury nickel-copper deposits. With the backing of a New York group, Lindsley outfitted a small mine and smelter to produce matte for shipment to Falconbridge's newly acquired refinery in Norway. Lindsley was in effect putting together some of the pieces of the old British America Nickel Corporation, including a number of the experienced staff from that unhappy venture. Falconbridge's entire complex when it started production in 1930 was on a much smaller scale, its total value estimated at about $5 million.

28. *Financial Post*, May 20, 1933 cited in Main, *op. cit.*, p. 118.
29. *Current Biography 1957*, Toronto, p. 326.

The new company ran straight into the worst of the depression, and nearly went bankrupt as nickel markets dried up. Only a price cutting venture into the U.S. market in 1932 saved it from the fate of so many of its forerunners. INCO seems to have tolerated the upstart because of its small size, and its orientation to European rather than American markets. The "deviation" of 1932, again on a relatively small scale, was no doubt unwelcome but the cost of eliminating tiny Falconbridge through price warfare would have been excessive. Once again, the existence of Falconbridge gave the appearance of competition in the industry.

Falconbridge grew quickly under the price umbrella of INCO, its production rising from 5 million pounds of nickel in 1931 to 20 million pounds by 1939, with marketing concentrated in Europe. This was still only six percent of non-communist world consumption and no serious threat to INCO. World War II sparked a surge of nickel consumption and production to the highest levels in history, more than twice the 1935 output. Most of this was produced by the Allied countries, and most of Allied production came from Canada with an assist from Cuba. The New Caledonia shipping routes were unsafe for most of the war.

With the French refineries of Le Nickel and Falconbridge's Norwegian refinery under German control, INCO's facilities in Canada and Great Britain processed nearly all refined nickel for the Allied war effort. This served to emphasize once again the overwhelmingly dominant position of Canada and INCO in the entire world nickel market. This dependency made the United States government and military strategists profoundly uneasy, and would lead in the post-war period to strong measures to develop alternative suppliers, among them Falconbridge Nickel.

Despite its attempts at diversification, INCO throughout its history found itself repeatedly in the same position. It was an outgrowth of the boundless military demands of the twentieth century. Its markets sometimes were private corporations operating on their own account, but frequently and increasingly INCO had to deal directly with governments and their military resource allocation agencies. The affairs of big business like INCO were becoming inseparable from the affairs of big governments at war or preparing for war.

The Allied victory over Germany and Japan brought no change in this trend. Ahead, in close succession awaited the Cold War, Korea, the missile race, the space race and Vietnam. There would always be a place for nickel and a place for INCO. Yet the two could no longer amount to the same thing. There were too many risks, particularly for the United States, in having such a vital commodity come from one location, Sudbury, and one organization, the International Nickel Company.

CHAPTER THREE
The Rise of Falconbridge

SECRET EMPIRE

For its first 34 years Falconbridge Nickel was the heart of Thayer Lindsley's shadowy mining empire. With considerable success Lindsley shielded both himself and Falconbridge's parent company, Ventures Limited, from general publicity and scrutiny. When the enormity of his Canadian holdings began to penetrate the public consciousness in the early 1950s, Lindsley found himself being written up as a mystery man, a Canadian Howard Hughes minus the affinity for beautiful women and worldly pleasures. Even in 1962 Falconbridge's historian D.M. LeBourdais could write: "Hundreds of thousands of investors have held shares in his various companies, yet (Lindsley) could walk down Bay Street without being recognized."[1]

The self-effacing Lindsley was a case study in work addiction, a man without any apparent interests outside his business. "His work is studying his own mines," an acquaintance once said. "His recreation is studying someone else's."[2] He remained dominant in Ventures until he was well over 70 years of age, and continued to maintain a pace that exhausted younger associates.

Lindsley was not only energetic and single-minded beyond normal bounds, but combined these traits with an extremely keen knowledge of both geology and finance, making him according to *Macleans* the "undisputed No. 1 figure in Canadian mining."[3] The accolades were based on Lindsley's personal role in creating eleven major operating mines, and the high esteem accorded him by other figures in the

---

1. "Thayer Lindsley and his Ventures", *Saturday Night,* February, 17, 1962, p. 18.
2. "The Unkown Giant of Canadian Mining", *Macleans,* August 15, 1951, p. 7.
3. *Ibid.*

mining industry. His ability to solve the jigsaw puzzles of geological structures seems to have been exceptional. Said a mining engineer describing the analytic process,

> You've fitted together a few pieces and you have a man's head at one spot and his foot somewhere else. On the strength of those two clues you figure out where his left hand should be. That's how mining exploration works. Some men have to waste a couple of million dollars putting drill holes in the wrong spots before they see the picture. Lindsley can usually figure a thing out at the beginning. His judgement is not limited to just what he can see. He can visualize the underground structure with uncanny accuracy.[4]

During this active 30 year career in Canada, Thayer Lindsley parlayed $30,000 into control of a world mining empire with assets estimated variously from $150 - 250 million. His mines produced nickel, copper, cobalt, gold, silver, platinum, palladium, lead, cadmium, selenium, magnesium, and zinc; there were oil and gas wells for good measure.

These multiple enterprises, including Falconbridge Nickel, were interrelated in a byzantine structure of companies, all under the umbrella of the ultimate holding company, Ventures Limited. "Mr. Lindsley holds the strings for all of them," said one Ventures executive, "and he pulls like the dickens." [5]

Lindsley was sometimes criticized for being a "modern Midas", a man more interested in discovering ore bodies than in bringing them into production. This is far from accurate. For example, Lindsley made a success of the Beattie low-grade gold ores in Quebec during the 1930s by applying a new technology which surprised the rest of the mining industry.

What some observers mistook for a hoarding instinct was a combination of Lindsley's shortage of development capital and his desire to maintain control of his discoveries, if necessary at the expense of immediate profit. The most notable aberration in his behavior was not so much his reluctance to tie up limited capital in operating investments, but his failure to provide an heir for the domain he was so busily creating. He married in 1929 at the age of 48, but the union produced no children and ended in divorce five years later.

During three decades of expansion the Ventures empire repeatedly threatened to outstrip Lindsley's financial ability to maintain

4. *Ibid.*
5. *Ibid.*

it, but his feel for geology was matched by tremendous imagination in the games of corporate structure. Lindsley's record of juggling, pyramiding and share-swapping among an eventual 15 operating companies, 20 development companies and 145 other mining, research and metallurgical companies has few parallels in Canadian history. As late as 1951 he controlled the entire Ventures complex with a personal fortune estimated at only $7 million.

Falconbridge was the key to the whole intricate endeavour. Lindsley sometimes sold its shares to raise cash for weak subsidiaries or traded its shares for those of other subsidiaries which then posted the Falconbridge stock as security for loans otherwise unobtainable. Falconbridge stock was the "supermoney" which held everything together, and by 1951 Ventures still held the absolute majority of it, 51 percent.

Lindsley's success as a lone-wolf entrepreneur in a world increasingly dominated by big finance capital was certainly remarkable. By the middle 1950s, his undercapitalized, resource-rich, undervalued Ventures was a jewel, a potential bonanza of profit. Inevitably it fired the imagination of several important financial groups and became the object of titanic takeover battles.

THE LINDSLEY METHOD

A son of the CPR's manager in Japan, Lindsley was born there in 1882, but lived in a Boston suburb from the age of 15 and graduated from Harvard University as a civil engineer. His developing interest in mining finally brought him to Canada in the early 1920s as an employee of McIntyre Porcupine Mines. He soon struck out on his own into prospecting and staking activities in the Sudbury Basin.

Ventures Limited and Falconbridge Nickel were both incorporated by Lindsley and a small group of associates in 1928, with Falconbridge as the producing company. They paid $2.5 million for the Falconbridge mining properties, then the highest price on record for mineral rights in the area, and quickly added a refinery at Kristiansaand, Norway for another $323,000.

Lindsley's lifelong strategy toward the mining business found immediate expression after the creation of his two main companies. "Because of his belief in the riches contained in the rocks of the Sudbury Basin, Lindsley adopted a policy of acquiring by purchase or by staking every available piece of ground, especially along the north rim, and this in after years was to pay off handsomely in Falconbridge's remarkable expansion."[6]

6.   "Thayer Lindsley and his Ventures", *op. cit.*

While Falconbridge struggled for survival during the early depression years and then began to profit supplying a reviving and rearming Europe from the Norwegian refinery, Lindsley busily accumulated new properties not only near Sudbury, but all around the world. Among the companies associated with Ventures over the next three decades were Sherritt Gordon, Frobisher Limited, Giant Yellowknife Gold Mines, United Keno Hill Mines, Hoyle Company Limited, Consolidated Sudbury Basin Mines, Kiena Gold Mines, Alminex, Metal Hydrides (later Ventron), and Canadian Malarctic Gold Mines. Among the overseas operations were Kilembe Copper (Uganda), La Luz Mines (Nicaragua), and International Titanium (Australia).

Lindsley united all these holdings in a web of associated companies, holding companies, subsidiaries, and subsidiaries of subsidiaries. The Ventures conglomeration was a lawyer's delight and an accountant's nightmare. Expansion was always the aim, and Ventures' corresponding reluctance to release capital in the form of dividends became the hallmark of Lindsley business methods. Sometimes other shareholders in Ventures' partially-owned subsidiaries protested this policy strenuously. After one such episode in the early days of Sherritt Gordon, Lindsley unloaded Ventures' piece of the company with the observation: ''What's the sense in owning a horse if you can't ride him?'' [7]

Ventures' wide-ranging interests carried Thayer Lindsley into unusual arenas. Shortly after the start of World War II he took a full-page ad in the New York Times to urge his old Harvard classmate and friend President Franklin Delano Roosevelt to lend 100 overaged U.S. Navy destroyers to Great Britain, a suggestion which closely resembles the lend-lease agreement later concluded between the two countries. One of the considerations behind this unorthodox foray into public affairs may have been nervousness over the destination of Falconbridge Nickel sales in the previous decade, including a record year in 1939. A large part of this production almost certainly found its way into German stockpiles, and Lindsley was old enough to remember INCO's embarrassment in Canada over the question of sales to Germany prior to the first Great War. Cancelling out some of his boss's public relations effort Gordon Hardy, president of Falconbridge, stumbled badly in his 1943 report to shareholders. ''Incidentally,'' he wrote, ''you will be glad to hear—as I was—that through indirect channels it is reported that your Norway refinery is safe so far and is being maintained. It is in operation by your Norwegian staff under German

7. *Ibid.*

control on the same Norwegian nickel-copper ore production that we formerly handled on a toll basis.''[8]

Hardy's pleasure at the preservation of company capital was not shared by CCF leader M.J. Coldwell who pointed out to the House of Commons that people had been imprisoned for less. ''If some individual should come to Canada and say 'You will be happy to know that our brother is safe and fighting on the side of the Germans' he would be treated immediately as a dangerous and subversive individual,'' claimed Coldwell.[9] Prime Minister Mackenzie King agreed the statement by the Falconbridge official was ''shortsighted, unwise . . . and unpatriotic''[10] but the matter went no further. After losing the Norwegian refinery, Falconbridge redirected its efforts to supplying the Allied war effort, pushing nickel production to record levels at frozen wartime prices and sending the ore to INCO for refining.

Another Ventures' company played an important role in the United States' military program during World War II, testifying to Lindsley's interest in research and advanced technology. The Metal Hydrides Company of Massachusetts was the only plant in the United States capable of producing uranium of the quality and quantity required for atomic research. It supplied the Fermi reactor in Chicago which pioneered development of the atomic bomb.

PEACE AS WAR: A PROFITABLE REDEFINITION
Despite the diversity of Ventures' interests, Lindsley understood quite clearly that Falconbridge was the cornerstone of his operations. At the conclusion of World War II, the nickel company, still tiny in comparison to INCO, faced the predictable problems of converting to civilian markets and an expected reduction in demand. These short term hazards were offset, however, by a distinct opportunity: the United States government was clearly interested in reducing its almost complete dependence on INCO as the sole source of nickel for industry and the American military. This new policy direction was evident in the threat of anti-trust action against the nickel giant in 1946.

The United States' attempts to diversify its sources of nickel supply coincided with a more general development of American raw materials policy after World War II and all through the 1950s. Stockpiling of many strategic materials became the order of the day during that

8. *Debates of the House of Commons* (Hansard), Queen's Printer, Ottawa, May 11, 1943, p. 2593
9. *Ibid.*
10. *Ibid,* July 13, 1943, p. 4690

period of Cold War scares. From a military point of view the objective
was to have on hand sufficient supplies to sustain three years of
conventional warfare. The stockpiling program was also designed to
encourage new long-term sources of raw materials for American
civilian industry, and to serve as a bargaining weapon to discourage the
formation of cartels and monopoly pricing by resource-producing countries. As so often happens, national defense became the justification for
vast corporate welfare subsidies.[11] Between 1950 and 1957, the United
States government spent $789 million on its nickel expansion program
alone, including $655 million in direct purchase contracts. By 1962
some doubts over the worth of the stockpiling program had set in, and
there were complaints that the nickel inventory was 115 million pounds
in excess of planned maximum level, a thirty percent overrun.

   In the post-war period several small nickel producers, the Hanna
Mining Company, Freeport Sulphur, and Sherritt Gordon all cashed in
on the shift in American materials policy, but none so skillfully as
Lindsley and Falconbridge. Later investigations of the enormous profits
on stockpiling contracts were initiated under Democratic President John
F. Kennedy after his election in 1960 and concentrated on the Hanna
Mining Company contract. Its president, George Humphrey, had become Secretary of the Treasury during the early Republican years under
Eisenhower while Hanna benefitted mightily from supplying the
strategic stockpile. Attacking Falconbridge did not provide the Democrats with the same political mileage against Republicans, so Lindsley's
company received less attention.[12] In fact it had fared much better than
Hanna in the stockpiling sport, which took on the air of a corporate
turkeyshoot at the expense of the American taxpayer.

   In laying the groundwork for this escapade, Lindsley brought
expatriate Horace J. Fraser back to Canada as Falconbridge's mine

11. *Time* magazine explained in 1954 that the strategic stockpile program "assumed that
   in wartime all sources of supply except Canada and Mexico would be cut off from the
   U.S. . . ." Confident about Canadian responsiveness to U.S. demands *Time* added
   " . . . the U.S. should be spending its money only for those highly critical metals that
   cannot be found at home instead of buying aluminum, nickel, molybdenum, etc.,
   which are available in the U.S., Canada and Mexico." Finally, the article concludes:
   "Though operating under a heading of military necessity, such a program amounts to
   price supports for part of the U.S. mining industry."
   See: "Strategic Stockpile: Is it for security or subsidy?", *Time,* October 4, 1954, p.
   72. A more recent comment on another use of the stockpile program was reported in
   the *Wall Street Journal* (December 26, 1973): " 'What the stockpile has provided',
   an Interior Department planner says, 'is tremendous bargaining power for this
   country in the international sphere. With it, you don't let these bandits hold you
   up.' "
12. "Why Nickel Men on U.S. Hot Spot", *Financial Post,* November 17, 1962.

manager. Fraser, educated in Manitoba (chemistry) and Harvard (Ph.D. economic geology), already had three years' experience with the geological staff of INCO, as well as extensive teaching experience in American universities. His most recent tour of duty had been with the U.S. Office of Economic Warfare where he was in charge of foreign purchases of manganese, chromium, iron and *nickel*. LeBourdais' description of this appointment is tantalizing; during his years with the OEW Fraser "had become acquainted with Thayer Lindsley who in 1945 invited him to come to Falconbridge. . . . His advance was rapid, and much of the credit for Falconbridge's spectacular progress in recent years is due to him."[13]

The spectacular progress in question was due almost entirely to juicy stockpiling contracts with the U.S. government. Initial negotiations were inconclusive as Falconbridge offered in 1947 to supply 150 million pounds of nickel over ten years. The Bureau of Federal Supply recommended acceptance of the proposal, but the U.S. Munitions Board rejected it as providing too little nickel for the near future. Also the Board was not prepared to guarantee financing. The next year, however, Falconbridge landed its first major contract providing for the delivery of 40 million pounds over five years.

Two more attempts by Falconbridge to sew up guarantees failed in 1950 for reasons similar to those given in 1947. Then came Korea which changed the whole bargaining climate; Falconbridge's proposals suddenly found favour. In January 1951, the Defense Material Procurement Agency agreed to buy 50 million pounds of nickel over ten years at market prices, and sweetened the incentive for early delivery with a $6 million advance.

This was only a prelude to the big breakthrough in 1953. In that year, under contract DMP-60, the U.S. government agreed to buy 100 million pounds over nine years at market prices with options on a further 50 million during the same period and another 50 million in the following five years subject to certain conditions. What made this deal fabulous was an agreement to pay, in addition to market price, a premium of 40 cents a pound on the first 100 million pounds.[14]

This huge bonus provision, when the going price of nickel was 60

13. "Thayer Lindsley and his Ventures", *op. cit.*
14. According to then Falconbridge president, Horace Fraser, "The objective of DMP-60 as outlined by the U.S. Government negotiators was twofold. Furnish critically needed metals for the U.S. Strategic Stockpile as quickly as possible. Expand Falconbridge's productive capacity . . . thus making available to the United States in time of war or emergency a greatly expanded productive capacity in nearby Canada." See: "Those DMP-60 Details of Falconbridge Deals", *Financial Post*, May 5, 1962.

cents, was the making of Falconbridge. It was a gift of $40 million, enough to cover the entire estimated cost of the expansion program required to fulfill the contract. This promised handout allowed Lindsley to float a $30 million bond issue, a lifesaver when as Horace Fraser later remarked, the Ventures group had "reached the stage where its credit wasn't triple A."[15] Other insiders are more candid, admitting that Ventures was on the road to bankruptcy.

The U.S. government's largesse was soon reflected in the value of Falconbridge's shares, which were in the $11-$22 range in 1952. The company stock rose steadily to a high of $73 by 1961.[16] In anticipation of this great good fortune the company in 1952 made an optional offering to its shareholders of one share at $14 for each ten shares held. With 5 million shares outstanding the possible option sale could have reached 500,000 shares, but only 266,000 were taken up before the offer expired. [17] We may assume that insiders who knew of the DMP-60 contract negotiations and acted accordingly fared considerably better than outsiders who remembered only Lindsley's gambling tendencies and his constant need for other people's cash.

In addition Ventures Limited itself was somehow entitled to a further 75,000 shares on the 1952 offering at the same $14 price. It exercised this long-term option to the fullest, taking up 40,000 shares in May 1953, two months after DMP-60 was signed, and the remaining 35,000 in 1953 and 1954.[18] All in all these manipulations were likely the most lucrative of Lindsley's long career. Each $10 rise in Falconbridge stock was worth $750,000 to Ventures on the bonus stock alone. Lindsley personally owned about 35 per cent of Ventures, the rest of his control deriving from the proxies of relatives and friends.

During the fairytale decade of DMP-60, Falconbridge enjoyed its most rapid progress ever: production rose from 32 million to 65 million pounds of nickel annually; total revenue tripled; and profits, even after all the usual padding of costs, jumped from $2.5 million in 1952 to $16.9 million in 1961.[19]

LONE WOLF FALLS PREY TO THE PACK
While Falconbridge was booming, the aging Lindsley was getting

15. "Mining new markets for nickel", *Business Week,* September 5, 1964, p. 62.
16. The Financial Post Corporation Service, *Falconbridge Nickel Mines Ltd.,* Toronto, June 12, 1974, p. 9.
17. The Financial Post Corporation Service, *Falconbridge Nickel Mines Ltd.,* June 21, 1973, p. 8.
18. *Ibid.*
19. The Financial Post Service, *op. cit.,* June 12, 1974, p. 6, 7, 19.

Ventures into hot water on other fronts. Ventures' array of holdings had become too intricate and extended for one-man coordination, although Lindsley remained vigorous well beyond his 70th birthday in 1952.

> There never was a vice-president, managing director or general manager whose authority extended over the whole organization. Consequently, Thayer Lindsley was the only one who could speak for Ventures. There were times when despite the long hours he put in, an interview with Lindsley was almost as hard to secure as with the President of the United States; and, of course, he was away a good deal of the time. As younger and newer men came in, suggestions were made concerning the need to streamline the organization, but to this Thayer Lindsley could not agree; he had grown up with it and it was an intimate part of his life. [20]

Besides organizational problems, Ventures suffered from a severe shortage of capital. "The development of (its) varied interests called for ever increasing capital investment, which if not forthcoming resulted in a dilution of the company's equity and impairment of control."[21] Lindsley reached the end of the financial tether in the early 1950s by involving himself simultaneously in a flyer on the Eureka silver mine project in Nevada and a particularly grandiose $800 million hydroelectric-smelting scheme called Quebec Metallurgical Industries in the Yukon and British Columbia. Over the protests and then the resignation of his chief financial officer, W.B. Malone, Lindsley in 1954 issued $7.5 million in debentures, partly to post an advance on the Yukon projects. According to *Business Week,*

> Even Lindsley's best friends called this deal 'stupid'. Lindsley not only put up one million shares of Falconbridge—about half of Ventures' holding in this one big moneymaker — then selling at above $20 a share—but he also issued transferable stock purchase warrants to debenture holders entitling them to buy 50,000 shares of Ventures and 50,000 shares of Falconbridge at $20 a share.[22]

Lindsley was staking his control of Falconbridge on the highly speculative new projects.

These plunges brought Ventures to the brink of disaster. Notwithstanding all its mineral assets, Ventures in that year received dividend income from only six of its subsidiaries amounting to a paltry $1.3 million, with most of that from Falconbridge. Lindsley was forced into a major shakeup, dropping 11 of his own directors from the 16-man

20. "Thayer Lindsley and his Ventures," *op. cit.*
21. *Ibid.*
22. "Ventures, Ltd.: New Goal—Profits", *Business Week,* October 8, 1955, p. 68.

Ventures board and adding four outsiders: H.J. Carmichael of General
Motors; E.E. Lincoln, former adviser to the DuPonts; New York
underwriter H.B. Lake of Ladenburg Thalmann and Co., and metallur-
gist L.J. Buck.[23] These appointments seemed to portend a reorganization of Ventures and a major infusion of U.S. capital.

This possibility was reinforced dramatically in 1955 when Robert
B. Anderson, previously U.S. Deputy Secretary of Defense, became
the $100,000-a-year president of Ventures Limited, with Lindsley
leaving the post to become chairman of the board. Anderson was a man
on the move, boasting excellent connections with big oil money in
Texas, and in Washington where he was an Eisenhower favourite. It
was rumoured that Anderson's hiring had been recommended by the
new minority directors with prodding from General Motors.

It soon became clear, however, that Anderson was not the advance man for U.S. money because Lindsley was not interested in being
taken over by anyone. Anderson's political connections were useful,
according to one insider, "to babysit the stockpile contracts" on which
everything depended.[24]

Anderson began a reorganization of the company and secret
negotiations for new capital, but not in American financial circles
where he knew his way around. After an unsuccessful approach to Rio
Algom he struck a deal with a Canadian company, McIntyre Porcupine
Mines. Once the gold and coal corporation of Canadian mining magnate
J.P. Bickell, McIntyre by 1957 was not active in production but maintained an extensive investment portfolio as a holding company for
Canadian, British and South African interests. In that year McIntyre
suddenly invested $14 million in 400,000 shares of Ventures, with
options on another 250,000 at the $35 price and 250,000 at $40. This
purchase and option on 900,000 treasury shares when Ventures had
about 1.8 million common shares outstanding placed McIntyre in a
position of effective control and seemed to freeze out American capital.[25]

Regretfully noting this development, *Business Week* reported that
relations between Lindsley and Anderson had deteriorated badly.[26]
This was not surprising. According to one long-time director the deal

23. *Ibid.*
24. A company insider at the time claims that Anderson was sought out specifically
    because of his very high-level political connections in Washington. His presence in
    the Ventures-Falconbridge group helped safeguard the stockpile contracts that were
    coming under question in the United States.
25. "Shutting Door on U.S. Money", *Business Week*, May 25, 1957, p. 131.
26. *Ibid.*

between Ventures and McIntyre had been made behind Lindsley's back by Anderson and Horace Fraser, and sprung on the unsuspecting old commander-in-chief by a board of directors which was supposed to be under his control. In effect the hired help, realizing that Lindsley was losing his grip, had taken it on themselves to choose their next masters. Having helped steer an important U.S. defense supplier into safer hands, Robert Anderson immediately quit Ventures to become Eisenhower's Secretary of the Treasury.

TIDYING UP: MERGERS CENTRALIZE POWER

Horace Fraser was elevated to the presidency of Ventures in 1958, at the same time retaining the presidency of Falconbridge he had assumed the previous year. Under Fraser the consolidation of Ventures into a manageable structure forged ahead through a series of hard-fought mergers of the company's controlled subsidiaries. Ventures absorption of Frobisher Ltd. was particularly contentious and left the financial community in awe of Fraser's nerve and financial acumen. Insiders claim that Fraser never really understood what was happening, that he was in some respects a "financial child" and the prime mover of the consolidations was Toronto lawyer David Menzel, a director of several companies in the Falconbridge Group.

Considerable mystery still surrounds these events, one of the many untold stories in Canada's financial history. The importance of the mergers extended beyond tax advantages, presumably because they transferred wealth legally from the outside shareholders to those controlling the Ventures group, without corresponding compensation.

The consolidation of Ventures' subsidiaries set the stage for an even grander merger: the absorption of Ventures itself by Falconbridge in 1962. The publicly-stated purpose was "to inject some of Ventures' risk-taking spirit into Falconbridge and to temper some of Ventures' recklessness with Falconbridge's restraint."[27] Ventures Limited, Lindsley's personal vehicle for control of an empire, was thus eliminated entirely. Lindsley, then in his 80th year, remained a director of Falconbridge but was excluded from the executive committee.

The breakdown of Ventures' shareholders released during the transaction provides a telling commentary on "people's capitalism", a popular propaganda concept which persists to the present day. Of a total of 5,791 shareholders, three-quarters owned less than 100 shares each, accounting for only four percent of the stock. The preponderance of

27. "Mining New Markets for Nickel", *op. cit.*
28. See: *Falconbridge Nickel Mines Ltd.* application to list with the Montreal Stock Exchange, mimeo, May 15, 1962.

ownership, 88 percent, was held by only 175 people or institutions including the large blocks kept by Lindsley and McIntyre.[28]

The merger was a matter of some urgency for Falconbridge. The DMP-60 contract expired in 1961 and it had accounted for all but two percent of the company's business in the United States. Nickel sales in 1962 were down to 53 million pounds from 65 million the previous year, making it a time of difficult adjustments. The increased flow of dividends from old Ventures properties and an infusion of cash from McIntyre provided essential working capital while Falconbridge reoriented itself to civilian markets.

The Ventures-Falconbridge "upstream" merger, pre-negotiated with McIntyre-Porcupine, was a complicated family affair surrounded by secrecy and so much misinformation that trading in Ventures was suspended on the Toronto Stock Exchange in August 1961. The joining of the two Lindsley companies might have diluted McIntyre's control, since its 30 percent interest in Ventures translated into only 15 percent of Falconbridge. McIntyre offset this danger by plowing another $27 million or so into Falconbridge, picking up an estimated 180,000 shares of Ventures in pre-merger trading and 280,000 Falconbridge treasury shares at $62 as a part of the merger agreement.[29] This brought McIntyre's controlling interest in Falconbridge to about 25 percent, leaving it with effective control over the post-merger conglomerate.

The *Financial Post,* speculating on the future of this "evolving industrial-mining colossus. . . . top dog in what is now one of the biggest business empires in the world," asked if McIntyre would now move on to swallow Falconbridge, bringing the merger activity to an ultimate conclusion.[30] This proved to be the wrong question. No sooner had McIntyre established a streamlined authority over the newly organized Falconbridge group than it in turn faced takeover. The Falconbridge-McIntyre empire was large in Canadian terms, but only a midget in the transnational league.

29. "Will McIntyre Procupine Now Absorb Falconbridge?", *Financial Post,* February
    10, 1962.
30. *Ibid.*

CHAPTER FOUR

High Finance and Rivalry for Power

It has been said—only half-facetiously—that the less you know about the Superior Oil Company, the more you like it.
— New York Times, Feb. 7, 1974

THE "CANADIAN" INTERLUDE

Mergers and takeover battles afford rare but fascinating glimpses into the private world of high finance where most of the economic planning that there is in the capitalist world economy takes place. The struggle of four financial giants (McIntyre Porcupine, Power Corporation, Anglo American and Superior Oil) for control of Falconbridge Nickel and the rest of the new Falconbridge group is an excellent case in point.

When McIntyre Porcupine seized control of Ventures Limited in 1957 over the futile objections of Thayer Lindsley, the event was interpreted in some quarters as a victory for aggressive Canadian capitalists. Under the headline "Shutting Door on U.S. Money", *Business Week* said the takeover was swung with all-Canadian capital and added: "It looks like a sign of Canada's determination to keep control of its own industries. The country now has the resources and leadership to do it."[1]

McIntyre did appear to be a significant aggregation of Canadian talent and money. The chairman of the board, J.S.D. Tory, was an influential figure on Bay Street, with directorships at A.V. Roe, Algoma Steel, the Royal Bank and more than two dozen others. He was credited not only with the Ventures acquisition, but also with reorganizing the ownership of Algoma Steel following the death of Sir James

1. "Shutting Door on U.S. Money", *Business Week,* May 25, 1957, pp. 131-132.

Dunn, shepherding Massey-Ferguson into the fold of E.P. Taylor's Argus Corporation, and matching Sears, Roebuck & Co. with Robert Simpson Co. to form Simpson-Sears.[2]

McIntyre Porcupine, once an active and important gold mining company, had become a rather stuffy (some say moribund) investment holding company with an extensive portfolio including large blocks of INCO, Algoma Steel, Amerada Petroleum and Bell Telephone. The Canadian capital in McIntyre came from a number of estates managed in trust by the Canadian Imperial Bank of Commerce and National Trust, including that of McIntyre founder J.P. Bickell and the holdings of R.S. McLaughlin, the Canadian auto magnate who sold out to General Motors of Canada.

In a move to reactivate McIntyre as a producing company the board brought in J.D. Barrington as president and managing director. Barrington was a C.D. Howe protege and onetime president of Polymer, a federal Crown corporation.[3] It was the Barrington-Horace Fraser liason, some observers claim, which was central to plotting McIntyre's successful takeover against Thayer Lindsley at Ventures in 1957. However, behind this Canadian management and the Canadian trusts invested in McIntyre lurked a substantial (if loose) coalition of British and South African capital represented on the McIntyre board by Norman D'Arcy and later Jocelyn Hambro.

The Ventures coup was not so much a triumph of Canadian capitalists, as of a Canadian management supported by D'Arcy's Locana group. His company, Locana Securities, fronted in Canada for such prominent corporations as Cie. Financiere de Suez (successor to the Suez Canal Co.), Banque de L'Indo-Chine, Hambros Bank and, most important, the Anglo-American Corporation. Anglo-American despite its name is the principal holding company in the $5 billion gold and diamond-based mining empire of Harry Oppenheimer, South Africa's modern successor to Cecil Rhodes. These various companies represented by Locana together held about 25 percent of McIntyre in 1962 when Falconbridge swallowed Ventures and McIntyre simultaneously consolidated its control over Falconbridge. Thus what appeared superficially to be Canadian mining companies were already deeply enmeshed in the web of transnational empire.

A Canadian upstart, Power Corporation, tried to challenge this control mechanism in 1963 by making a public offering for one million

2.   *Ibid.*
3.   John Porter, *The Vertical Mosaic,* Toronto, University of Toronto Press, 1965, p. 430; see also Libbie and Frank Park, *Anatomy of Big Business,* Toronto, James Lewis & Samuel, 1973, pp. 59-60.

of McIntyre's 2.3 million outstanding shares. The prize Power Corporation sought was the Falconbridge group, but the cheap way to acquire control was to use the leverage made possible by McIntyre's controlling interest in Falconbridge. Power Corporation itself was floating in a sea of cash produced by the recent nationalization of two of its major assets, B.C. Hydro and Shawinigan Power.[4] Its vice-president, Maurice Strong, with a background in oil (and a future with the Canadian International Development Agency and the United Nations Environment Agency), was anxious to involve Power Corp. in the resources field, and from that perspective the diverse and untapped potential of the Falconbridge group was extremely attractive.

The Barrington management of McIntyre, however, had absolutely no interest in falling under the sway of Power Corporation, and resisted the takeover by every possible means. In this they were supported by both the Canadian Imperial Bank of Commerce and the Locana group. As bidding intensified, the market price of McIntyre shares leapt from $44 to more than $57 per share, which was the price of the Power Corporation offer. Locana increased its position, and in a neat bit of jiggery-pokery McIntyre had Falconbridge, which it controlled, buy about 7 percent of McIntyre's stock.

In a cable from London, Locana's Norman D'Arcy advised other shareholders to reject the Power bid: "We can read reports as well as anyone else," he said, "and we can work out the asset value for both McIntyre and Falconbridge. I certainly would not consider exchanging these assets for $57 Canadian."[5] With the controlling interests maintaining solidarity, and other shareholders heeding D'Arcy's counsel, Power's bid for control fell far short of the objective. Power Corporation ended up with only 200,000 shares and was denied even a representative on the board of directors.

PROSPECTIVE MASTERS

Two large transnational companies were as keenly attuned to the attractiveness of Falconbridge via the McIntyre route as Power Corporation had been. One was Anglo-American, which already had a piece of McIntyre but wanted to increase its position. Anglo-American is the pinnacle of a huge empire including De Beers Consolidated, and a myriad of controlled companies such as Engelhard Minerals & Chemi-

4. Frank Kaplan, "What may happen next in $$ drama as Power Corp. bidding for McIntyre", *Financial Post,* December 28, 1963.

5. *Ibid.* McIntyre management and its backers had once before frozen out an ambitious and powerful interloper — Cyrus Eaton. See Frank Kaplan, "'Moment of Truth' almost here for McIntyre-Power Corp. fans", *Financial Post,* January 18, 1964.

cals, Gold Fields of South Africa, Hudson Bay Mining and Smelting, Roan Consolidated Mines, Zambia Copper Investments and many smaller ones. It also has major investments in such well-known outfits as American Metal Climax, Rio-Tinto Zinc and Rio Algom Mines, all of which make Anglo Chairman Harry Oppenheimer one of the world's wealthier men.[6]

Tightening the grip on McIntyre should have been a fairly straightforward matter for Oppenheimer, but he was handicapped. Most of his wealth was concentrated in South Africa and Great Britain, and both countries had imposed controls on capital exports which seriously hampered his freedom to wheel and deal in the large sums needed to nail down the Canadian company.

While the South African wrestled with the problems of raising capital for his Canadian operations, another big customer was wandering the aisles of Canada's resources supermarket; the American Howard B. Keck of Superior Oil. Superior Oil was and is the largest of the independent oil producers in the United States. During an attempted merger with Texaco in 1959 which was blocked by the anti-trust branch of the U.S. Department of Justice, the company was valued at $810 million, and 51 per cent of that was owned outright by the Keck family. Although the Texaco deal was not consummated, Superior exchanged its Venezuelan oil properties for about 3 million shares of Texaco. Superior Oil has not been getting smaller in the intervening 15 years.[7]

By the early 1960s Superior, like other oil companies, was spinning off more cash than the owners knew what to do with. The general trend was diversification, often into competing energy industries like coal and uranium, and Howard Keck had similar ideas about the mining industry. In 1964 he formed Canadian Superior Explorations with former Rio Algom man James Booth as president, and told Booth to locate a suitable acquisition. After sorting through a number of possibilities, Keck chose Falconbridge as his target. A battle of titans was in the making between Keck and Oppenheimer.

POTENTIAL FOR EXPANSION

Meanwhile, the prize of the impending struggle, Falconbridge, was forging ahead both in development of the old Ventures properties and

6.   According to *Forbes* (June 15, 1973, p. 38) Oppenheimer controls assets estimated at $6 billion. *Forbes* described Oppenheimer's motivation in acquiring companies as "The group system: minimum investment, maximum control". McIntyre-Falconbridge fit the bill exactly; see also *Forbes,* December 15, 1972.
7.   Robert Metz, "Market Place: A Volatile Path in Superior Oil", *New York Times,* Feb. 7, 1974. *Forbes* (May 15, 1974) calculated the market value of Superior Oil at $1,189,735, 000.

competition with INCO in its basic activity, nickel. Expansion in Europe, where Falconbridge supplied more than half the nickel needs of the Scandinavian countries and was dominant in other markets, was not a practical option. "We felt frankly it was not in our interest or theirs to push those figures higher," concluded president Horace Fraser in 1964, showing a touching solicitude for the welfare of Le Nickel.[8] Instead, hammering the theme that nickel-users should avoid dependence on a single source of supply, Falconbridge went after a share of INCO's growing U.S. market. "For years they sat quietly as a lamb," said an INCO official, "but now they're going after business hot and heavy."[9]

This turnabout was necessitated by the expiry of Falconbridge's contracts to build the American nickel stockpile. As a product of the new approach to commercial sales and a certain degree of desperation, Fraser in 1962 actually cut the price of nickel by a few cents a pound. INCO was stunned and enraged by the impudence of the gesture, recalls a Falconbridge insider, but "it was the best advertising we could have had. Two million dollars couldn't have bought us that kind of publicity." INCO followed the price down the next day, but later INCO Chairman Wingate remembered the incident regretfully. "It was wasteful," he mourned. Faced with the same situation again "we might let them nibble away for a while."[10] Its purposes achieved, Falconbridge was not so foolhardy as to tempt fate further. Once it had gained a firm foothold among U.S. nickel buyers, standard monopoly pricing resumed. Since that rare day in 1962, the only deviation has occurred when Falconbridge led a price increase. In peaceful monopoly industries, prices do not go down.

Operating in tandem Falconbridge and INCO enjoyed strong markets throughout most of the 1960s. Both expanded production in Sudbury; INCO opened a mine in Thompson, Manitoba, but demand generally ran ahead of supply. Although nickel prices rose 65 percent between 1965 and 1970, the general policy of the two companies was to allocate scarce supplies as fairly as possible among buyers and exercise restraint in pricing to prevent the intrusion of new suppliers. The nickel giants were preparing for overseas expansion of nickel production, but only under their benevolent control at a time of their choosing.

By the middle 1960s both Falconbridge and its parent McIntyre were poised for major expansion and diversification. McIntyre, once owner of Blue Diamond Coal Company, was getting ready to return to the coal business on the strength of large deposits located in the Alberta

8. "Mining new markets for nickel", *Business Week,* September 5, 1964, p. 64.
9. *Ibid,* p. 62.
10. "The Beguiling New Economics of Nickel", *Fortune,* March 1970, p. 138.

foothills area of Smoky River. It also had a large stake in the Madeleine
copper prospect in the Gaspe region of Quebec which came into production in 1969.

Falconbridge was preparing for a $45 million investment in iron
ore in the Queen Charlotte Islands of British Columbia through its
wholly-owned subsidiary Wesfrob Ltd. The most significant and
costly project on the Falconbridge drawing board, however, was its
nickel expansion plan in the Dominican Republic. The nickel potential
of the Caribbean island had been known for a long time. In fact the
Falconbridge property had previously been held by INCO which gave it
up when, in the words of an INCO executive, Dominican dictator
Trujillo demanded "too big a bribe."[11] Falconbridge incorporated a
subsidiary, Falcondo (Falconbridge Dominicana, C. por A.) in 1956,
and maintained a program of exploration and pilot smelting and refining
in the following years.

Negotiations with the Dominican government were sporadic and
inconclusive, complicated by the instability of the failing Trujillo
regime. By 1965 the prospect of nickel shortages and rising prices
finally brought the extensive Dominican ferro-nickel ores within the
range of economic feasibility; but although the economics for a large
development were right, the politics were all wrong. Leftist president
Juan Bosch had been deposed by a military coup in 1963, but an
insurrection by elements of the army attempted to reinstate him in 1965.
With the Cuban revolution and its consequences for foreign investment
still a fresh and unsettling memory, the most promising path to rapid
growth for Falconbridge in the mid-1960s seemed fraught with political
risk.

Then within a very short span of time the calculations and circumstances surrounding Falcondo were altered beyond recognition. The
United States in 1965 invaded the Dominican Republic with 20,000
Marines, crushed the pro-Bosch insurrection, and soon installed a new
dictator, Joaquin Balaguer.[12] A former Trujillo confidant, one of
Balaguer's chief qualifications was his supine outlook on the role of
foreign capital in Domincan economic life. And while Texan Lyndon
Johnson used the presidency of the United States to re-establish a
version of law and order in the wayward republic, the masters of

11. Interview with INCO executive quoted in Fred Goff, "Falconbridge — Made in the
    U.S.A.", *NACLA's Latin American & Empire Report*, Vol. VIII, No. 4, April 1974,
    p.8.
12. "Terror in the Caribbean", *Wall Street Journal*, September 7, 1971; see also Fred
    Goff and Michael Locker, "The Violence of Domination: U.S. Power and the
    Dominican Republic" in I.L. Horowitz, et. al., *Latin American Radicalism*, New
    York, Vintage, 1969, p. 249 ff.

Falcondo, that is to say the shareholders of McIntyre, were being wooed by an aggressive Texas suitor: Howard B. Keck.

A SUPERIOR SWOOP

Superior Oil's courtship of McIntyre, begun in 1965 and consumated in 1967, was both persuasive and forceful. Keck's first approach was to Maurice Strong of Power Corporation. Strong turned him away, but left the door open for further discussions at higher prices on Power's 200,000 share block, which represented nearly 9 per cent of McIntyre's outstanding shares. Keck and his advisor in Canada, James Booth, were aware that Anglo-American was interested in the Power holding too, and were able to determine about how much it would be able to offer. In the summer of 1966 Keck pre-empted Anglo's offer by a couple of days and acquired his first chunk of McIntyre from Power Corp for a reported $100 per share, well over the prevailing price of $85.[13] The Texan was clearly prepared to pay a premium for control, and three years of waiting had proved quite rewarding for Power which nearly doubled its original investment.

Keck moved swiftly according to plan, sending Booth to London to make an offer on the 110,000 McIntyre shares held by Gold Fields of South Africa. A rude surprise awaited him. Anglo-American held first option on the Gold Fields shares, and exercised it. The battle was joined in earnest, but Keck was in some danger of suffering the same fate as Power Corporation three years earlier. There were no further breaks in the struggle until the spring of 1967.

The only avenue remaining open to the Superior Oil magnate was to split the Canadian shareholders away from their British and South African allies. The Canadian Imperial Bank of Commerce and National Trust between them controlled over 300,000 shares, enough to make either Keck or Anglo-American the dominant interest. But Keck's hopes were further shaken when Anglo-American's biggest wheel, Harry Oppenheimer, was made a director of the Canadian Imperial Bank of Commerce.

What happened next is a dark secret which none of the principals are willing to discuss beyond James Booth's hint that "Anglo-American played a wrong card."[14] In an effort to salvage his position Keck held a private meeting with Neil McKinnon, president of the CIBC, to emphasize Superior Oil's interest in bidding on the bank's

13. Frank Kaplan, "Is giant McIntyre Porcupine takeover target again?", *Financial Post,* August 13, 1966; and "McIntyre 'defenders' keeping their cool", *Financial Post,* August 20, 1966.

14. Conversation with James Booth, December 1974.

15. Conversation with Frank Kaplan, December 1974.

trusteeship holdings of McIntyre. One analyst claims Keck suggested the possibility of legal action against the bank if it failed to act in the best interest of the Bickell, McLaughlin and other trust beneficiaries. [15] One might also imagine that the preeminent role of the United States of America in Latin America and the Pacific, both areas vital to Falconbridge's future growth, played some part in the negotiation between the Canadian banker and the well-connected U.S. industrialist.

In any case Keck entered the meeting seeking a chance to compete equally with Oppenheimer. He emerged 90 minutes later with a deal sewn up. Not only had Superior Oil bought the CIBC-controlled shares, but the sale was conditional on delivery of the National Trust holdings as well. The price: $101 per share. It had been a $30 million conversation. [16]

Winning the Canadian shares made Keck's interest in McIntyre larger than Anglo-American's but not as great as the combined Locana group. This set the stage for a meeting between Superior Oil and Anglo-American, with each intending if possible to buy the other's interest. Asked about the possibility of a stalemate, Keck is reported to have grinned: "We might have to flip a coin." No coins were tossed. Superior Oil laid out another $30 million for Anglo-American's 300,000 shares and the takeover was complete. [17]

For an overall outlay of about $90 million it had captured 900,000-odd shares, a 36 percent interest in McIntyre. Putting the best possible face on defeat, Norman D'Arcy of the now-decimated Locana group commented: "I would have expected perhaps a little higher percentage figure, nevertheless this represents effective control. From Locana's point of view as straight investors this is not a bad thing . . . A tough, efficient, honest administration (to use our friend's words) is precisely what we ask. Mr. Keck has continuously kept us informed on all matters." [18]

Anglo-American's decision to break ranks with its partners in the Locana group was, as with the decision of Power Corporation, a profitable one. Perhaps the large capital gain inherent in the Keck offer met the company's need for unfrozen North American capital to pursue its interest in Hudson Bay Mining and Smelting and a new potash mine in Saskatchewan, Sylvite of Canada. Whatever the reason for its action, the withdrawal of the Oppenheimer company left Howard Keck with a

---

16. Conversation with James Booth, December 1974; see also "Who will make next move in McIntyre chess game?", *Financial Post,* May 13, 1967.

17. Frank Kaplan, "Here's how Keck got control of McIntyre", *Financial Post,* June 10, 1967.

18. *Ibid.*

free hand over McIntyre, Falconbridge and their combined assets of about $700 million.

The two major sales occurred within a month of each other in May and early June 1967. Keck celebrated his triumph with a rapidfire reorganization of the boards of directors and senior management of his new possessions. Howard Keck himself took a seat on the executive committee of both boards. His brother William Keck Jr. and other officials of Superior Oil and Canadian Superior Oil were assigned multiple directorships to create a tightly-centralized decision-making structure.

The Canadian most central to the plans of the new regime was Marsh Cooper, partner in the company James Buffam and Cooper, consulting geologists. Cooper had been a director of McIntyre since 1962, and his partner James a director of Falconbridge since 1953. For them the American takeover proved highly congenial. Keck appointed Cooper president of McIntyre in place of J.D. Barrington, and president of Falconbridge in 1969 upon the death of Horace Fraser. Marsh Cooper sums up the relationship between himself and the new owner quite pithily: "Howard Keck and I, in that order, run Falconbridge."[20] (Before tears are shed for Jack Barrington, the deposed McIntyre executive who fought against all these changes, it should be noted that he sold 15,000 shares of McIntyre in May 1967 at $101 and another 15,000 in December at $90 for a total consolation prize of $2.8 million.)

The personal benefits to Cooper for becoming Howard Keck's loyal Canadian lieutenant are considerable. His salary must be large, although Falconbridge reveals only the payments to senior executives and directors as a group: $1.2 million in 1973.[21] Salaries, however, are taxable and therefore not a preferred method of receiving income among members of the managerial elite. There are more loopholes to play with if wealth is received as a capital gain. The *Insider Trading Report* of the Ontario Securities Commission shows that Marsh Cooper purchased 30,000 treasury shares of McIntyre at a stock option cost of $83.25 per share in January 1970. Seven months later he sold 16,000 shares at a market price of $160 per share, enough to recapture his original outlay with $63,000 to spare. The 14,000 shares remaining to him clear and free had a market value of $2.2 million at that time.

20. James Beizer, "New Nickel capacity in oversupply period?", *Iron Age,* July 27, 1972.
21. Falconbridge Nickel Mines Limited, *Annual Report 1973* notes remuneration to director and senior officers at $1,166,000 (p.19).

NEW POLICIES AND PROJECTS

The Keck takeover brought a new dynamism to McIntyre, which for years had been a moribund holding company doing little to develop new productive activity. The new vigour has not always produced wise decisions, however, from the point of view of outside shareholders or the Canadian public. The tendency for Falconbridge companies to go into joint ventures with Superior Oil companies, for example, must be disturbing to investors who realize the Keck ownership interest in Superior Oil is much larger even though he controls the management of both.

This pattern of cooperative action has become pervasive. In Australia, Canadian Superior Oil took over the management of two uranium joint ventures from McIntyre Mines. In New Zealand the two organizations are engaged in joint exploration activity. Alminex, a Falconbridge subsidiary, is exploring with Superior Oil in the Gulf of Mexico for oil and gas, while in the Yukon the Minto copper deposits are being studied by Falconbridge's United Keno Hill and Canadian Superior Explorations. In Africa, Falconbridge and Superior Oil share a 49 percent interest in Western Platinum, and they have an agreement whereby Superior earns a 50 percent interest in any Falconbridge discoveries in South Africa or Namibia. Whether these arrangements contain the potential for conflict of interest is, of course, a matter for McIntyre and Falconbridge outside stockholders to ponder.

Of greater interest to the general public of Canada are the big development decisions the companies have made under Howard Keck's direction. The most dubious undertaking was McIntyre's move to get back into the coal business in which it had been active through the Blue Diamond Coal Co. during the 1920s and 1930s. Prior to the change in its ownership McIntyre had acquired extensive coal deposits estimated at 1.25 billion tons in the Smoky River area of the Alberta foothills, about 100 miles north of Jasper. The incredible Smoky River saga should help dispel the mystique of efficiency and competence cultivated by big business, and at the same time illustrate the pathetic subservience of governments, this time Alberta's Social Credit, in their dealings with large corporations.

The Smoky River project was announced with considerable fanfare late in 1968 when McIntyre signed a 15 year contract for delivery of 30 million tons of coal to a Japanese steel consortium headed by Nippon Kokan Kabushiki. As the coal was in a remote wilderness area, the plan required the creation of an entire new community, Grande Cache, and a railroad in addition to a $47 million investment in the mining complex. Total private investment amounted to nearly $100 million, but an even larger part was reserved for government.

Ernest Manning's Social Credit government rose to the bait of jobs and development, and bit hard. It commited $150 million to construction of infrastructure including $130 million for the Alberta Resources Railway and the balance for the new Grande Cache townsite. In return its revenues were to include 10 cents per ton royalties on the coal, and $1.50 per ton rental on the rail service. Calculated against the 2 million ton per year Japanese contract this would produce a modest $3.2 million annually, hardly enough to make a dent in the interest on the public investment of $150 million. As it worked out though, not even this pittance was collected. By September 1973, the Alberta government had received only $500,000 in royalties from the company.[22]

McIntyre had run into serious trouble and was unable to fulfill its contracts. The underground operations proved trickier than the company could handle, although it chose to blame these difficulties on inexperienced labour. There were also problems with the quality of the coal and these unexpected difficulties meant the contract price was insufficient to cover production costs. With operating losses mounting over $15 million by early 1973, the company announced heavy layoffs and began abandoning its underground operation in favour of surface strip mining. To help out, the government had already dropped the railroad tariff from $1.50 to $.40 per ton.

The move to lay off 150 employees from the workforce of 670 came after repeated company denials of shutdown rumours during 1972, and triggered an angry response from the miners and the community. The population of Grande Cache was about 2500, all dependent on the mine for their livelihood. The workers had been lured from all over the world—Korea, Japan, Nova Scotia, Great Britain—with promises of guaranteed work for fifteen to thirty years. They had come to Alberta to make homes, not to join one more temporary mining camp.

The Lougheed government appointed a commission of inquiry under the former CPR president N.R. Crump to delve into the mess. His report, released late in 1973, was devastatingly critical of both McIntyre and the government of E.C. Manning. The company's decision to proceed on such a large scale project was "a result of over-confidence outweighing prudence. The company lacked internal expertise and failed to give proper assessment to perils which the successful execution of the contract had to overcome." Manning's government had "agreed

22. *Liberation News Service*, No. 514, April 7, 1973.
23. "Commission tells Alberta to keep mine going for 10 years", *Financial Post*, Jan. 19, 1974, p.15.

to participate in this venture *without any realistic or independent investigation of its feasibility.''* [23] (our emphasis)

The Crump report vindicated the position of the union, the United Steelworkers of America, which had earlier accused McIntyre of serious mismanagement. Anxious to preserve stable employment for its members, the union had argued for nationalization of the mine. To leave Alberta coal in the hands of private enterprise was, it suggested, "simply to cheat the people,'' and it asked the provincial government to "create a new Crown corporation to develop and sell Smoky River coal.'' [24]

Encroaching on the domain of private profit to this extent was not Crump's style, but his report did recommend that the mine should be kept in operation, the royalty rate and railroad tariffs increased, and the sales contracts renegotiated, by creating a provincial coal board if necessary.

Following this public humiliation, J.K. Godin who presided over the debacle as president of McIntyre was kicked upstairs to vice-chairman of the board under Marsh Cooper, and later downgraded to ordinary director status. Keck apparently attached no blame to Cooper, who had been president when the contracts were signed.

The Social Credit government had already received its reward at the polls in 1971, suffering a massive defeat at the hands of a smoother pro-business politician, Conservative Peter Lougheed. Ex-premier Ernest Manning, for his part, has done better than other Socred members. After his retirement from electoral politics in late 1968, he joined the board of McIntyre and is still a director of the company.

LYNDON JOHNSON'S LEGACY

A second and even more ambitious project of Howard Keck's new Canadian companies and their subsidiaries has been far more successful. This is the Falcondo nickel installation in the Dominican Republic, which got the green light in 1968, the same year as Smoky River. The Balaguer government, installed by the Americans in 1966, was perfect for Falconbridge's purpose. President Marsh Cooper spelled out the company's thinking:

> We have to diversify into lateritic sources (of nickel) and that trend will increase in the years to come. Laterites occur in the subtropical equatorial belt, and many deposits have been found in politically less stable countries. Hence, Falconbridge deems itself fortunate to have located in the Dominican Republic which not only has a stable government but which actually has played and

24. "Union urges takeover of coal mine", *Toronto Daily Star*, June 27, 1973, p.42.

continues to play an important and effective part as a co-worker
. . . of Falconbridge Dominicana.[25]

By 1973 the $195 million complex was running at capacity,
adding about 65 million pounds of contained nickel to Falconbridge's
100 million pound Canadian output and confirming its status as the
world's number two nickel producer.

While Falcondo potential was by no means the sole attraction of
McIntyre and Falconbridge, it is an important one which Keck considered prior to making his takeover bid. Two conditions for success of
Falcondo, in addition to an increase in the price of nickel, were apparent
even then: outside financing and an American-incorporated partner for
the nominally Canadian Falconbridge. Such a partner would qualify
Falcondo's potentially huge fixed assets for insurance from the U.S.
Overseas Private Investment Corporation (OPIC) against war, insurrection, revolution, expropriation or currency inconvertibility, any or all of
which were possibilities not be overlooked in the Dominion Republic.

ARMCO Steel, of which Howard Keck is also a director, neatly
filled the bill on both counts and was brought in as a 17.5 percent partner
on the equity financing of Falcondo. With large operations in Texas and
elsewhere in the United States, ARMCO is the world's leading supplier
of hardware to the oil and gas industry. Principal control rests within the
First National City Bank of New York group, with some participation
by Rockefeller's Chase Manhattan, the Mellons of Gulf Oil and the
Houston group.[26] Falconbridge was the dominant partner in Falcondo
with 65.7 percent of the common stock, while the obliging Dominican
government of Balaguer settled for 9.5 percent and other private investors took the balance.

One of the notable features of Falcondo's financing is the high
ratio of debt to equity capital. The shareholders named put up only $15
million, turning to investment bankers Dillon, Read and the First National City Bank to raise the other $180 million. Dillon, Read, for a fee
in excess of $1 million, arranged the following package: $114 million in
long term securities from three important U.S. insurance companies,
Metropolitan Life, Equitable and Northwestern Mutual; $25 million
from the World Bank, a creature of American foreign policy headed by
former Ford Motors executive and Secretary of Defense Robert
McNamara; and short term revolving credits of $21 million from the
First National City Bank and $20 million from the Canadian Imperial

25. "New nickel capacity in oversupply period?", *Iron Age*, July 27th, 1972, pp. 50.
26. S. Menshikov, *Millionaires and Managers*, Moscow, Progress Publishers, 1969, pp. 275, 283.

Bank of Commerce. Dillon, Read and the two banks are now represented on the Falconbridge board of directors.[27]

The large debt structure served two important purposes. It spread the undeniable risks of the Falcondo investment among some of the most powerful financial interests in the United States, guaranteeing maximum response from the United States government in the event of any unwelcome political developments in the Dominican Republic. It also built very heavy interest charges into the cost structure of the company, allowing most of the surplus wealth generated by the mine and refinery to be tapped without being subject to Dominican profit taxes. In 1973, for example, out of revenues of $91 million, Falcondo paid $17 million to its foreign creditors and only $3.3 million in taxes and dividends to the Dominican government. The flow of funds is further controlled by Falconbridge which, for a fee, sets prices and acts as the exclusive selling agent for Falcondo, depositing the funds in trust with the Chase Manhattan Bank.

GENERALLY ACCEPTED BUSINESS PRACTICES

A consistent pattern emerges from the welter of acquisitions, mergers, stock manipulations, interlocking directorships and government boondoggles sprinkled generously through Falconbridge's corporate history. All these activities were normal, garden variety big business practice. The company was drawn into ever larger resource empires as it, like many other companies, fell under the sway of larger and more powerful aggregations of finance capital.

This process was intertwined with decisions of the military and government, because the affairs of powerful financial groups are inseparable from the affairs of government: both are involved with managing and determining the course of society. When it fell under the control of Superior Oil in 1967, Falconbridge was being integrated more securely into the plans of one of the world's largest private financial groups, centering on the First National City Bank of New York. Its affairs have since been managed by people with ready access to the government of the world's single most powerful military and imperial power: the United States of America.

27. Business International, *Nationalism In Latin American: The Challenge and Corporate Response,* New York, B.I., 1970, pp. 78, 79; also Falconbridge Dominicana, C. Por A., 1973 Annual Report, pp. 10-12.

CHAPTER FIVE

Unholy Matrimony: The Marriage of Business and Government

"It's the first time in recorded history that a rat has swum toward a sinking ship," a former Texas senator observed on John B. Connally's conversion to the Republican party in 1973. Connally was rushing to the barricades as the Watergate scandals began to burst around his close political ally, Richard M. Nixon. At the time it seemed that Big Bad John might be able to succeed Nixon in the White House in 1976, but by 1974 he was under indictment for a number of alleged criminal offenses. While he was still flying high in '73, though, Superior Oil's Howard Keck recognized Connally's services past and future by making the flamboyant presidential hopeful a director of Falconbridge Nickel Mines.

Connally's appointment to the board of a major Canadian mining company like Falconbridge could not have been more appropriate or symbolic. His multiple connections at the highest levels of American politics and finance epitomize the contempt for the public interest which characterizes the private corporate business system so well entrenched on both sides of the U.S.-Canadian border.

Scrutiny of the Connally connections and the "Texas Nexus" of which Howard Keck is a part is difficult to limit. As indicated by Watergate, once investigation is begun there is no logical end; the circle keeps widening until it engulfs not just a few bad apples but the whole barrel. Our Canadian apples in business and government have been cross-pollinating with those American ones for a long time, with the predictable result. It's hard to tell them apart.

The problem in both countries is in large measure the same. Representative government has not turned out to be democratic government. The various political parties function as wings of one all-embracing formation, the Property Party.[1] Massive concentrations of private wealth finance a political process which facilitates the accumulation of ever-greater private wealth in the hands of a small elite. Economic growth has triumphed over economic equality as the accepted road to the good society, and the millions left out are supposed to be patient.

In this Alice in Wonderland world nothing is as it seems. The promise of progressive taxation is more honoured in the breech than in the observance. The answer to every economic problem is lower taxes and more privileges, discretely called "incentives", for the wealthy and the corporations they control. Public resources are regularly turned over to private interests, and their profitable exploitation is heavily subsidized from the public purse. The whole travesty is rationalized by continuous appeals to freedom, democracy, and in many cases, national defense. Another favoured twist is the claim that jobs are being created, on the assumption that working people have only two options: tolerate privilege and exploitation, or starve. That Canadians or Americans for that matter might work and produce wealth on terms and for purposes other than the existing ones is dismissed as a fantasy by the ideologues of private enterprise.

Free enterprise in the world of large, privately owned corporations which by now dominate the world economy does not mean the competition familiar to farmers and small businessmen. For transnational corporations and their wealthy owners freedom of enterprise refers to their unbridled right to inherit, set prices, buy politicians, bust unions, lobby for tax exemptions and otherwise dip into government treasuries and other people's pockets in their pursuit of private wealth and power. It's a brand of freedom they are prepared to defend to the death.

Although Big Money rules the United States, the governing coalition is not constant. New tycoons have appeared to take their place beside the old plutocracy. The super-rich and powerful like the Rockefellers, Mellons, DuPonts, Pews, Fords, Harrimans and holders of other gigantic fortunes founded in earlier periods of American history were joined by upstarts like the Kennedys, Getty, Hughes, Hunt, Richardson, Murchison, Bechtel, Dillon, Keck, Brown, Kaiser and more. Many of the new fortunes, usually inferior to the combined family holdings of the old rich, have been built on construction, defense

---

1.   For an extensive study of private wealth and how it endures and grows in the U.S.A. see Ferdinand Lundberg, *The Rich and the Super-Rich,* Bantam, New York, 1969. Lundberg elaborates the concept of the "property party" with devastating effect.

contracting and oil, areas of profit generation which require constant and intimate dealings with governments.[2]

The new rich have been dubbed the Cowboys of American capitalism to distinguish them from the older Yankee establishment. In the last twenty years the Cowboys have risen to great prominence in the councils of Wall Street and Washington but the Falconbridge-Superior Oil saga shows just how well the Yankees and Cowboys can get along when they try. If the Cowboys' style is sometimes a little cruder, the objectives are the same.

THE TEXAS NEXUS AND ROBERT ANDERSON

Both Presidents Nixon and Johnson were known as champions of oil, but in an earlier day it was Dwight Eisenhower who was described as the best friend oil had in Washington.[3] Ike, the fatherly, cheerful and seemingly ingenuous hero of the second World War presided for eight years over a cabinet drawn from the highest ranks of big business. He appointed men like George Humphrey and later Robert B. Anderson to the key post of Secretary of the Treasury. Humphrey was president of the Hanna Mining Company and later of National Steel, both beneficiaries of the extensive U.S. stockpiling and armaments programs of the 1950s. Anderson, as Secretary of the Navy, Deputy Secretary of Defense and then Secretary of the Treasury was a representative of Texas oil and also an important supporter of big armaments programs, stockpiling, and huge tax and tariff subsidies to the oil industry. He took time out from these endeavours to manage Ventures Ltd. and Falconbridge during the key 1955-57 period when Thayer Lindsley's control was broken.

A man like Robert Anderson is a shining example of the large group of politicians, civil servants, military brass and top businessmen who move frequently and easily back and forth between public and private service, leaving the impression that in spirit they never leave private service at all. They are bound together by more than common ideology. The regular and potent incentive of the direct payoff plays a larger part in explaining political decisions than most of these establishment figures will ever admit. As a case in point, Ovid Demaris' book *Dirty Business* reveals that Anderson's boss Dwight Eisenhower received more than $700,000 during his years as president in aid of the maintenance of his farm estate at Gettysburg. The donors were three

2. *Ibid.*, pp. 35-112.
3. Ovid Demaris, *Dirty Business*, Harper's, Boston, 1974, pp. 177-198 describes relations between the Eisenhower administration and the oil industry. This book is a most instructive compendium of white-collar crime.

friends in the oil business the Eisenhower administration treated so well.[4] The president, naturally, was not acting alone. The necessary manipulations require effective and understanding servants in posts like the Treasury.

Robert Anderson, by all accounts a man of considerable if misdirected abilities, was born and raised in the Lone Star state, becoming both a lawyer and a Democratic member of the Texas state legislature in 1932 at the precocious age of 22. After holding such important posts as assistant attorney general, state tax commissioner and chairman of the unemployment commission, in 1937 he took a job with the $300 million Waggoner estate. Four years later he was the general manager at a salary of $60,000, and he continued to operate in the milieu of Texas oil with men like John B. Connally and Lyndon Johnson for another ten years.

With a full 20 years training in the politics of cattle, oil and the Texas-style Democratic party behind him, Anderson in the early 1950s made a political switch more significant in form than substance; he headed up the Texas organization of Citizens for Eisenhower. With the Republican victory of 1952 he moved quickly to take up a post in Washington on the recommendation of Sid W. Richardson, an influential oil millionaire and friend of Eisenhower's.[5] After a brief stint as aide to the secretary of the Army, landlubber Robert Anderson was appointed by Ike as Secretary of the Navy. This plum usually goes to an oil man, as the Navy is one of the world's largest consumers of oil, and also disposes of vast tracts of public oil lands on lease to private companies.

Navy Secretary Anderson was an enthusiastic advocate of increasing U.S. seapower. He improved the Navy's status within the interservice Pentagon rivalries and pushed through authorization of a new super aircraft carrier and the biggest shipbuilding program since Korea. He was also very sympathetic to the opening of public lands in Alaska to private development. On the question of arms procurement he took the position that more expensive is better, arguing "the higher costs of keeping more defense companies in production at a slow rate were offset by the strategic gains," and he won battles favouring "premium prices to keep certain producers going."[6]

4.   The three men, all of whom are now dead, were W. Alton Jones, chairman of the executive committee of Cities Service; B.B. Byars of Texas, a close friend of Sid Richardson and Clint Murchison; and George E. Allan, a heavy investor in oil and a Washington superlawyer. Demaris, *op. cit.*, pp. 188-189.

5.   Robert Sherrill, *The Accidental President*, Grossman, New York, 1967, p. 144 gives an account of the first meeting and budding friendship between Ike and Richardson.

6.   "Keeping out of headlines," *Business Week*, June 18, 1955.

After little more than a year with the Navy, Ike moved Anderson to Defense. A soft-spoken, relatively colourless figure, 33rd degree Shriner, practising Methodist, Anderson was known as an effective backroom operator and administrator who got things done. Eisenhower, already looking for a successor, held the Texan in high esteem: "I firmly believe that the smartest man in this whole nation is Bob Anderson. He would be perfect for the job (President of the United States). Golly, that fellow can reduce the toughest problem to its bare essentials like nobody else I've known, and in damned short order too."[7]

Politician Anderson, explaining his reasons for coming to Washington, told *Business Week:* "I felt it was an opportunity for me to discharge an obligation."[8] His greatest obligation was not to public service, but to big oil. As the administration's top man from the oil lobby's American Petroleum Institute, he took time away from his military responsibilities to help the State Department deal with Premier Mossadegh of Iran in 1953 after that country nationalized foreign oil interests. Mossadegh was overthrown with CIA intervention, and in the ensuing realignment of property American companies, including Cities Service, gained a share of the Iranian oil fields at the expense of British interests.[9] One of Eisenhower's illicit Gettysburg patrons was W. Alton Jones, chairman of Cities Service. Furthermore, Eisenhower's last act before leaving office in 1961 was to sign an executive order juggling oil import quotas in favour of several companies including Cities Service. Three months later W. Alton Jones was killed in a plane crash on the way to Palm Springs to visit the retired president. In his suitcase was $61,000 in cash and traveller's cheques for which no official explanation was ever required or given.[10]

Recently revealed evidence indicates Eisenhower not only talked about the erstwhile Anderson's suitability for high office, but took steps to set Anderson up for a run at the presidency. The plan was to drop

---

7. Demaris, *op. cit.,* p. 82. See also "Robert Anderson to head world mining empire", *New York Times,* Sept. 14, 1955, p. 49.

8. "Keeping out of headlines", *op. cit.*

9. The coup against Mossadegh was masterminded by a grandson of Theodore Roosevelt, Kermit Roosevelt, who after gaining greater access to Iranian oilfields for U.S. corporations quit the CIA and went on to become a vice-president of Gulf Oil. See David Wise and Thomas Ross, *The Invisible Government,* Random House, New York, 1964, pp. 110-111. Another CIA operative in Tehran at the same time was Richard Helms, later CIA director and presently U.S. Ambassador to Iran. Cities Service gained concessions in Iran for the first time after the coup (see Michael Tanzer, *The Political Economy of Oil and the Underdeveloped Countries,* Boston: Beacon Press, 1969, p. 326, and footnote 16 pp. 417, 418).

10. Drew Pearson and Jack Anderson, *The Case Against Congress,* New York: Pocket Books, 1969, p. 450, cited in Demaris, *op. cit.,* p. 198.

Richard Nixon from the Republican ticket in 1956 and replace him with
Anderson, a notion which drew hearty approval from Texas oil millionaire Sid Richardson and others. Anderson told Ike and Richardson
he was tired of modest federal salaries and that he would need about $1
million to make four more years of public service financially worth-
while.[11] This is related to his retreat from Washington in 1955 to the
$100,000 post with Ventures-Falconbridge and also the recent revela-
tion that Anderson was in this period the beneficiary of an $84,000
"loan" from Nelson Rockefeller.[12]

In the effort to provide Anderson with funds Eisenhower and
Richardson set in motion a complicated set of transactions involving
certain Richardson oil properties on lease to Standard Oil of Indiana and
other companies. To avoid the appearance of a direct transfer from
Richardson to Anderson, the other oil companies were asked to assign
certain royalty interests to a go-between, who sold them to Anderson for
one dollar. Anderson collected $70,000 in royalties and sold his new
rights for $900,000 to another of Richardson's friends who resold them
back to the Richardson family in the person of a nephew, Perry Bass
(then law partner to John Connally). "Thus the property went full circle
with Anderson grabbing his $970,000 as it went past."[13] Actually only
half the payoff was in cash: the rest depended on future American oil
prices, which Anderson later influenced in a strong upward direction.

While Anderson collected the laundered money, the plans to
advance him politically foundered on Richard Nixon's tenacious struggle to keep the vice-presidency. This by no means ended Anderson's
usefulness to the oil lobby. Ten days after the payoff from Richardson
was completed in 1957 Anderson was confirmed as Eisenhower's
secretary of the Treasury. In this capacity, working hand in glove with
old friend and Senate Majority Leader Lyndon Johnson, he introduced
the oil import quota system which generated windfall gains estimated at
$1.5 billion per year to the largest American oil companies between
1959 and 1973. The suggestion that the import licences might be put up
for auction rather than be passed out by administrative fiat, with the
windfalls accruing to the U.S. Treasury instead of the oil companies,
was quashed by Anderson and Johnson.[14]

11. Robert Sherrill, *op. cit.*, p. 145.
12. See *Toronto Star*, October 30, 1974; for a look at the role of Rockefeller and his
    companies played in arranging for Anderson's new wealth see *The Nation*,
    November 13, 1974; also see M. Mintz and J. Cohen, *America, Inc.*, New York:
    Dell, 1972, pp. 242-244.
13. Sherrill, *op. cit.*, p. 271.
14. *Ibid.*, p. 147.

Anderson's influence as a political heavyweight continued beyond his cabinet years. Following the Kennedy assassination Lyndon Johnson spent a considerable portion of his first two days as president conferring with his fellow Texan.[15] Their informal and almost clandestine connection attracted little public notice, but occasionally Anderson was described by insiders as one of Lyndon Johnson's most important pipelines to the business community and his "number one financial adviser."[16] That Johnson was a Democrat and Anderson by then a Republican was of little consequence; both were loyal stalwarts of the Property Party.

The significance of these American political relationships and practices for Canadian affairs, while difficult to measure, is substantial. By bringing in Anderson in 1955 Ventures Limited-Falconbridge, with a major nickel contract to the U.S. stockpile, was performing an important favour for a man who might become president of the United States. This could do the company's nickel business no harm and perhaps a great deal of good as resistance to the corporate welfare aspects of the stockpiling program was growing south of the border. Anderson's hiring backfired for Lindsley and hastened his downfall, but it strengthened the position of the corporation.

That an ostensibly Canadian company even in the mid-1950s found itself looking to Washington rather than Ottawa for its most vital political connections was a powerful indicator of the real patterns of power in Canadian economic and political life. In the history of Falconbridge the Anderson appointment presaged by a decade the formal American takeover of the company and the simplification of the command structure which now ties it so firmly into the American political and economic decision-making process.

MORE OILY POLITICS: BIG BAD JOHN CONNALLY
The arrival of John B. Connally on the Falconbridge board in 1973 created an uncanny aura of deja-vu, as if 17 years later Robert Anderson

15. *Ibid.*, p. 142.
16. *Ibid.*, p. 142; As recently as 1973, Anderson was still close to the Washington power elite. In that year Richard Nixon appointed him chief negotiator for the President in the revision of the Panama-U.S. canal treaty. Anderson has also continued to be involved in dubious business deals. Recently he was promoting a company selling cemetery plots in Latin American on the installment plan ("a little bit down and a whole lot to come" was the way one former company official described the plan). The company begain turning sour and one investor took Anderson to court charging "fraud and deceit" in his sales pitch. Anderson had also been involved with Bernie Cornfeld and his ill-fated I.O.S. Ltd. Anderson's latest wheelings and dealings have centred around his struggle to control Clinton Oil. See *New York Times*, April 3, 1973.

had been dusted off, retreaded and brought back under a new name. If Anderson were dead, Connally would be his reincarnation.

More than one student of the seamier realities of American politics has found significance in the parallels of the Anderson and Connally careers in business and public life. Both were bootstrappers, ambitious middle class lads on the make.

> Both Anderson and Connally are Texans, attorneys and graduates of the University of Texas. Both have been oil lobbyists and have held high state offices. Both have been close to Lyndon Johnson. Both have served as Secretary of the Navy and Secretary of the Treasury in Republican adminstrations, in that order, and both have received nearly a million dollars through the kindly auspices of the late Texas oil millionaire Sid. W. Richardson.[17]

Connally's rise began in 1938, when as a law student he worked in a Lyndon Johnson election campaign. In 1940 he managed another Johnson campaign, and in 1948 took charge of LBJ's first successful bid for the U.S. Senate, a recount victory produced by ballot-box stuffing with which Connally was associated.[18] He went to Washington as Johnson's administrative assistant and then returned to the backyard of big oil, acting as an attorney for Sid Richardson.

Wheeler-dealing and fixing have always been the hallmark of Connally's practice of law. In 1955, for example, Lyndon Johnson was piloting a bill through the Senate designed to release the U.S. natural gas industry from federal price regulations. Connally spearheaded an intensive $1.5 million lobbying campaign on the bill, although he hadn't taken the trouble to register as a lobbyist as the law required. The whole corrupt exercise nearly came to disaster when two employees of Howard Keck's Superior Oil were accused by Senator Case of South Dakota of offering him a $2500 bribe in return for a vote in favour of the gas bill.

In the Congressional investigation which followed it was obvious that large amounts of money had changed hands over the gas bill, with Keck's men the only ones to get caught. Connally and Howard Keck's attorney and lobbyist Elmer Patman were known in Washington as the Gold Dust Twins.[19] Patman reluctantly testified that for eight years Keck had been handing him thousands of dollars at a time to distribute among politicians, but he couldn't remember how much or to whom it had been given.

17. Demaris, *op. cit.*, p. 83.
18. See Walter Stewart, "The Tough Texan who is telling Canada to pay up", *Toronto Star*, February 26, 1972; also see Charles Ashman, *Connally: The Adventures of Big Bad John*, New York: William Morrow, 1974, pp. 65, 66.
19. James Conaway, "Oil: The Source", *The Atlantic*, March 1975, p. 67.

He gives it to me in cash . . . I tell him what I have done with it.
. . . I never render a written account. . . . I see the boss occasionally at his pleasure, sir . . . and I tell him what I have done with his
personal money. And if he has got anything else that he wants me
to do over and beyond my official duties he will give me some
money or he might say 'Are you out?' . . . There are no norms . . .
It is a relationship. I think he trusts me and I know I have been
honest with him.[20]

In brief testimony Howard Keck told the committee that he had a
man who expedited all "charitable contributions, the Community Chest
and things like that" and that he himself took no active part in such
matters.[21] Although the bribe to Senator Case was clearly only a tidbit
in Superior Oil's bag of goodies, and Superior only one of many actors
in a giant industry lobbying campaign, Lyndon Johnson and vice-
president Richard Nixon steered the investigation into safe hands and
nothing much came of it. Patman and the other errand boy were given
one year suspended sentences for failing to register as lobbyists,
Superior Oil paid a $10,000 fine, and the matter dropped from sight.[22]

John Connally reportedly "sat white-faced for hours in his May-
flower Hotel room" in Washington the day Senator Case blew the
whistle, and then skipped town. He was not called to testify, although
he was "one of the most brazen lobbyists . . . the mainspring of that
lobby and masterminded the battle on Capital Hill."[23] The bill, incidentally did not become law right away. It passed the well-oiled Congress,
but Eisenhower withheld his signature in election year 1956. He signed
it through in 1957 when the heat had died down.

During this same period Connally, always a very busy man, made
the arrangements for Sid Richardson's previously described $970,000
payoff to Robert Anderson. Rolling up to his eyeballs in oil, he became
executor of the Richardson estate and manager of the Richardson
Foundation upon the death of his sponsor in 1959, a chore which
entitled him to $1.2 million in cash and deferred payments. Just like

20. "That $2,500 Gift . . . ", *The New Republic,* March 5, 1956, p.8.
21. *Ibid.,* p. 8; Harold Morton, Howard Keck's lawyer at the time, told *Newsweek* (March 19, 1956): "People in business have to make contributions. They tapped Howard $5,000 for this Salute to Eisenhower dinner here in January. You got to be on everybody's sucker list." Keck was also a 'sucker' for Senator Joe McCarthy ($2,000) and Lyndon Johnson ($200,000 in 1960 alone). See Sherrill, *op. cit.,* p. 171.
22. Demaris, *op. cit.,* p. 193 and Fred Goff, "Falconbridge — Made in U.S.A.", *NACLA's Latin America & Empire Report,* Vol VIII, No. 4, April 1974, p. 9.
23. Drew Pearson quoted in Ashman, *op. cit.,* p. 83; also see Ronnie Dugger, "John Connally: Nixon's New Quarterback", *The Atlantic,* July 1971, pp. 82-90.

Anderson his oil connections made him for a brief stint in 1961 Secretary of the Navy under Kennedy; but he soon left Washington again to run for governor of Texas, a job he won and held for three two-year terms.

Governor Connally's political fortunes soared inestimably when he was struck by a bullet from the volley which killed John F. Kennedy in Dallas in 1963. Although he was, in the view of more than one critic, "the worst, most reactionary and vicious governor in Texas history" and no friend of Kennedy, he cultivated the image of faithful wounded companion to the martyred president.[24] Four years later the *Baltimore Sun* had to remind him "the black arm sling that Governor Connally is fond of wearing is getting frayed."[25] While playing top gun in Texas state politics Big John easily weathered scandals over his illegal deferred income from the Richardson estate and his acceptance of an airplane from an oil company.

Tiring of the governorship, Connally withdrew from elected politics in 1969 to become a leading partner in Houston's most powerful law firm, Vinson Elkins Searls Connally and Smith. This firm and the closely controlled First City National Bank of Houston are the heart of the Texas Nexus, representing and coordinating the activities of such powerful interests as construction giant Brown & Root, the Texas Eastern Transmission Corporation and a number of oil companies including Superior Oil.[26] While consolidating his personal wealth and business connections, the restless and ambitious Connally was becoming part of Richard Nixon's southern strategy for the Republican party. In 1971 Democrat Connally, in a move reminiscent of Anderson's switch to Eisenhower 20 years earlier, joined Nixon in Washington as Secretary of the Treasury.

Regarded as a "Lyndon Johnson with couth", Connally was a solid right-winger on policy matters. Nixon was fascinated by the Texan's crass bully-boy approach to the affairs of state, and the two rapidly became an intimate "coach" and "quarterback" combination in the Imperial Bowl. Together the dynamic duo gutted social programs and defended military spending and tax concessions to special interests. They blamed U.S. trade problems on their NATO allies who weren't, in their opinion, pulling their weight in America's imperial adventures in defense of the free world.

24. Former U.S. Senator Ralph Yarborough quoted in Ashman, *op. cit.*, p. 24.
25. *Ibid.*, p. 15.
26. Our analysis of the Texas Nexus is based on the work done by Fred Goff (*op. cit.*) and the North American Congress on Latin America (NACLA); for a recent overview of the Texas elite see Conaway, *op. cit.*, pp. 60-70.

The Nixon-Connally alliance was based on Nixon's need for southern votes in 1972 and Connally's desire to be president in 1976, a hope he could never realize through his own party. Connally was too obviously in the camp of big business to be acceptable to organized labour and the more liberal wing of the Democrats. His only rapport was with wealth, and he spared no distortion to prove the point many times over. "I sit before Congressional committees and without fear, embarassment or shame say," he once boasted, "that I think profits are too low in this country. I think Congress has gone too far in reducing individual income taxes . . . while raising corporate taxes. . . . "[27] In fact the share of corporate taxes in federal government revenue had declined from 30 percent in 1952 to 16 percent by 1972. A Nixon man commenting on Connally's ability to brush aside inconvenient facts observed: "He's full of the old crappo. On the Hill they are too, and they love him."[28]

Following the game plan, Connally resigned from the cabinet before the 1972 election to form the "Democrats for Nixon" and campaign full time for the president.[29] In 1973, as Watergate threatened to disqualify the whole Nixon team including its Texas recruit, Connally officially joined the Republican party and returned to Washington to advise the beleaguered Nixon. "Watergate is a sordid mess, but it was a silly, stupid illegal act performed by individuals," he bravely assured the American public. "The Republican party didn't do it." When the collective corruption of the whole administration was being dragged into view, a bewildered Connally warned "There is an element of hatred in this controversy, the smell of a vendetta, and if wise and cooler heads in both political parties don't take control we are in for a much greater national trauma than we have heretofor experienced."[30]

The contained bi-partisan rivalries of the Property Party indeed took an unfamiliar twist, and John Conally was on the casualty list. The usually tame establishment press declared open season on any number of well established political practices in 1973 and 1974 during the campaign to dump Richard Nixon, producing a rich harvest of damning revelations. A review of Big John's record indicates how extensive his political influence really was. Among his exploits:

27. Demaris, op. cit., p. 400.

28. Ibid., p. 80.

29. Upon hearing of Connally's decision to head up "Democrats for Nixon" Liz Carpenter, Lady Bird Johnson's former press secretary, referred to him as a "political transvestite who, at the battle of the Alamo, would have organized Texans for Santa Ana". Quoted in Ashman, op. cit., p. 8.

30. Stewart, op. cit.

*bulldozing through Congress a $250 million loan guarantee for the failing Lockheed L1011 Tristar airbus program in 1971 in response to pressure from the major banks — Bank of America, Bankers Trust, Chase, Citibank, Morgan Guaranty — which had huge loans out to Lockheed, its suppliers, and the airlines slated to buy the craft. The banks were important contributors to the Republican party.[31]

*stern defense of the incredible oil depletion allowance against pressures to reduce it in 1971.

*big export subsidies under the DISC program in 1971. In defense of this measure, aimed largely at Canada, Connally trotted out the old crappo: "The truth of the matter is that we permitted others to take advantage of us over the last several years. Now that day is gone."[32]

*introduction in 1971 of the investment tax credit and 20 percent accelerated depreciation, two additional business tax loopholes worth $80 billion over ten years, with $64 billion of that likely to accrue to the largest one-twentieth of one percent of all American corporations.[33]

*a major role in suppressing anti-trust action against ITT, another important contributor to Republican coffers.[34]

*prime engineer of the economic blockade of Chile after the election of Salvador Allende. Connally as Secretary of the Treasury was also U.S. representative to the World Bank and the Inter-American Development Bank and controlled the U.S. Export-Import Bank. All these institutions participated in the economic strangulation of the new government by withholding credit and encouraging other governments to follow suit. [35]

*promotion of a $45.6 billion natural gas deal with the Soviet Union at prices 500 percent above prevailing rates. Among the planned beneficiaries: Brown & Root, Texas Eastern Transmission. Despite revelations in 1973 that executives of Texas Eastern gave $30,000 to Nixon's re-election committee just before the campaign finance law went into effect and that Texas Eastern employees passed on an additional $30,000, the gas deal is still alive.[36]

31. Demaris, *op. cit.*, p. 72.
32. Stewart, *op. cit.*
33. Demaris, *op. cit.*, pp. 86-87.
34. *Ibid.*, pp. 60-62.
35. Ashman, *op. cit.*, p. 219; Richard Fagen, "The United States and Chile: Roots and Branches", *Foreign Affairs*, January 1975, p. 305. While in the Cabinet, Connally was also a member of the National Security Council — better known as Kissinger's Committee of 40 — which approved CIA policy. After leaving the administration Connally became a member of the President's Foreign Intelligence Advisory Board, the so-called CIA watchdog committee.
36. Conaway, *op. cit.*, pp. 65-66.

*personal advisor to Richard Nixon on energy matters during the phony 1973 energy crisis. This assignment was worth plenty. "Everyone wants to hire him," said one of his law partners "because everybody wants to get acquainted with John Connally."[37] A full description of the national security-energy crisis game appears in Ovid Demaris' excellent book *Dirty Business* and James Laxer's *The Energy Crisis*.

*arranging postponement of $1.3 million in overdue taxes from Dave Beck, former Teamster union president, as part of an elaborate entente between the Teamsters and the Nixon administration. Nixon also commuted the jail sentence of former Teamster president Jimmy Hoffa. Frank Fitzsimmons, the current president of the corrupt Mafia-linked union, joined Connally's Democrats for Nixon campaign in 1972 and channelled $50,000 into the political warchest.[38]

*allegedly arranging an increase in milk support prices in response to a promise of $2 million from the Associated Milk Producers Inc. for the campaign to re-elect the president in 1972.[39]

In this last case Connally has recently been aquitted of a charge of accepting a $10,000 personal bribe to influence milk prices. *Newsweek* reported, however, that the jury was less than enthusiastic: "Our verdict meant not that we had found necessarily that John Connally was innocent, but rather not guilty based on the case presented to us."

Before Watergate and related controversies were unleashed John B. Connally was a hot, potentially-presidential property. All the while maintaining his close relations with Nixon, he accepted invitations to join the boards of Brown & Root, Texas Eastern Transmission, the First City National Bank of Houston, Pan American World Airways, the American General Insurance Company and a string of other corporations including Howard Keck's Falconbridge Nickel. Given the patterns of political decision-making highlighted by Watergate, his popularity as a business advisor was not difficult to understand. Access on a friendly basis to the top levels of government is worth tens and hundreds of millions of dollars to large corporations.

INSIDE THE WHITE HOUSE

Where politics is concerned, the wealthy are not inclined to put all their eggs in one basket. Using the example of Howard Keck, Superior Oil and Falconbridge to delve a little further into the byzantine wonders of

37. "Connally, Hailed By Nixon, Reported to Look to 1976", *New York Times*, March 5, 1973, p. 21.
38. Demaris, *op. cit.*, pp. 330-331.
39. *Ibid.*, pp. 359-364; *New York Times*, July 30, 1974.

the White House, we find other connections which were undoubtedly useful. Roger E. Johnson, for 27 years an attorney and vice-president of Superior Oil, was one of Nixon's special assistants supplying advice on the moods and needs of the business community. "My responsibility," explained Johnson, "is to keep in personal contact and communication with the good friends of the president he would like to see but doesn't have time to."[40] Roger Johnson's relationship with Nixon was of long standing: he and his wife were in the small party which accompanied Nixon on his Florida-Caribbean recuperation following his defeat by John F. Kennedy in 1960.

An even more potent ally of Keck interests was Peter Flanigan, assistant to the president (some said mini-president) and fixer par excellence for big business. Flanigan, himself a millionaire, came to the White House as the ambassador from Wall Street where he was vice-president of the influential Dillon, Read investment house. He served Nixon at the highest level, orchestrating the suppression of the ITT anti-trust case, marshalling the bureaucracy against impulses to tax reform at the expense of business, and acting as a troubleshooter on other such vital matters.[41] Flanigan is believed responsible for the appointment of over 300 individuals to important posts in the Nixon administration.[42]

One of Peter Flanigan's stabs at personal enrichment was thwarted when, in the name of national security, he tried to relax a regulation of the registry of vessels engaged in coastal shipping. The proposed change would have, with a stroke of the pen, added $6.5 million to the value of a $4.5 million tanker owned by his company, Dillon Read. The plot was hastily abandoned when the obvious conflict of interest became public. Among Flanigan's successes, however, was the shepherding of millions of dollars in brokerage fees on U.S. Post Office bonds to Dillon Read and other friendly investment houses. The legal fees of nearly $1 million went to Richard Nixon's Wall Street law partners, Mudge Rose.[43]

What is of particular interest here is that Dillon Read is the company Howard Keck chose to handle the $180 million financing of Falconbridge Dominicana, a project which by virtue of its size could not have escaped Flanigan's attention. Keck had appointed F.H. Brandi,

---

40. *Washington Post,* February 23, 1971.
41. Demaris, *op. cit.,* pp. 24, 55, 56, 57, 154, 155.
42. Walter R. Gordon, "The Flanigan Affair", *The New Leader,* October 28, 1974, p. 4.
43. Demaris, *op. cit.,* pp. 112-114, 365.

chairman of Dillon Read, to the Falconbridge board in 1968.[44] In these circumstances the White House could be expected to be highly sensitive to political developments in the Dominican Republic. Through Dillon Read Howard Keck had purchased the most effective political insurance available for his Dominican investment. The whole apparatus of the United States government would be ready to guarantee its security in every possible manner.[45]

CONTINUITY IN U.S. WEALTH AND GOVERNMENT

Superior Oil's numerous and intimate connections with the levers of American state power provide a useful insight into the mechanisms of expansion of American-based transnational corporations. The hopelessly and deliberately leaky American tax structure, created by decades of persistent lobbying by these very corporations in the manner already described, provides American corporations with the enormous capital resources to finance takeovers like Keck's seizure of McIntyre-Falconbridge. The confidence American capitalists have in their ability to dominate the policies of their government makes far-flung assets like Falconbridge's more valuable to them than anyone else, explaining the willingness they combine with their ability to pay top prices. Resources corporations in particular through the power of the United States gov-

44. F.H. Brandi has been caught abusing his powers as a director in the past. When Dillon, Read was dominant in the affairs of Union Oil it directed the company to buy tankers, pipelines and gas stations from small companies controlled by Dillon, Read. In the scandal which followed the public discovery of these arrangements Brandi had to resign his directorship in Union Oil. See S. Menshikov, *Millionaires and Managers*, Moscow: Progress Publishers, 1969, pp. 289-92 for a summary of Dillon, Read influence.

45. Another highly influential Dillon, Read man in Washington is C. Douglas Dillon, one of the firm's founders and a former Undersecretary of State and Secretary of the Treasury. Dillon has been in the charmed circle supervising the activities of the Central Intelligence Agency (CIA), and in early 1975 was appointed to Nelson Rockefeller's panel charged with investigating the domestic activities of the invisible arm of government. Dillon, a member of the CIA's predecessor, the Office of Strategic Services (OSS), during the Second World War, is known as a friend of the agency. In 1960 as Undersecretary of State Dillon helped to fabricate the cover story for the illfated U-2 flight of Francis Gary Power over the Soviet Union. Dillon also chaired the meetings of the Council on Foreign Relations' Discussion Group on Intelligence and Foreign Policy at which Former CIA Director of Clandestine Services Richard Bissell briefed some of the U.S.'s most influential foreign policy advisers on the entire CIA philosophy on covert operations. Victor Marchetti and John Marks reprinted the minutes in their book *The CIA and the Cult of Intelligence*, New York: Dell, 1974, pp. 357-376; also see *Counter-Spy*, Vol. 2, No. 2, Winter 1975, p. 28.

ernment can reduce the risks inherent in exploiting less developed countries.

The resignation of Richard Nixon and the disgrace of John Connally in 1974 will compel a reassessment of political strategy for Howard Keck's Superior Oil complex as well as for dozens of American corporations which had built up intimate relations with the Nixon administration and the heir-apparent. The change at the top isn't likely, however, to produce disturbing new policies. Gerald Ford and Nelson Rockefeller are both from the conservative wing of the Property Party. and can be expected to govern in the interests of big business as did their predecessors. The Rockefeller family contributed heavily to Nixon's two successful election campaigns. With family interests in Exxon, Standard Oil of Indiana, Standard Oil of California and dozens of other companies in the Chase Manhattan group, Nelson Rockefeller can be expected to favour big oil and strongly support America's foreign investment interests.

This continuity in basic U.S. policies, regardless of the appearance of new political faces, is rooted in the impressive continuity and concentration in the structure of American wealth and power. In 1962, for example, when "peoples' capitalism" was the favoured official description of the American system, 20 percent of the population held 97 percent of all public corporate stock, and *one* percent of the population held 62 percent. The top twenty percent derived more than half its income from realized and unrealized capital gains. [46]

Ownership of productive assets is only an indicator of power, since concentrated ownership usually, as in the example of Howard Keck, provides control over assets far in excess of those owned directly through the magic of minority control, holding companies, control of financial institutions and other methods of indirect leverage. In the modern world the scale of industry and the size of corporations has made single-person and even single-family ownership impractical in all but a few cases. Elaborate alliances and financial groups have become the effective instruments of economic control.

This system of high finance is described in the useful book by Soviet sociologist S. Menshikov, *Millionaires and Managers: The Structure of the U.S. Financial Oligarchy,* in which he attempted to define the major U.S. financial groups in the mid-1960s. [47] Although the lines of separation between financial power blocks were by no means neat and clean, he placed the Morgan Guaranty Trust group at the head of the list with control over $69 billion in financial and industrial

46. Demaris, *op. cit.*, p. 84
47. Menshikov, *op. cit.*

assets. The Rockefeller-Chase Manhattan group was second, controlling $62 billion, and the First National City Bank-Ford-Dillon, Read-Harriman group third with control of $38 billion. The Texas group which embraces so many of the characters linked with the Falconbridge story controlled only $18 billion in financial and industrial assets, an indication of their secondary status and need for the Dillon-Read Wall Street connection. It might be said that a secondary financial group has been allowed control of a secondary nickel company.

In this world of high finance Canadian names seldom appear. Ferdinand Lundberg's compelling study of North American wealth, *The Rich and the Super Rich* picks out only two individuals with personal assets in excess of $75 million: Sam Bronfman of Seagrams and food magnate George Weston (although John David Eaton would likely qualify).

Menshikov's analysis of financial groups did identify eighteen subordinate regional power groups in the United States in addition to eight centred in New York: Boston ($24 billion); Cleveland ($18 billion); Chicago ($38 billion); Minneapolis ($10 billion) and so on. The groupings around Canada's main chartered banks including large corporations like Canadian Pacific, Noranda, Power Corp, MacMillan-Bloedel and Argus have not been analysed in the same manner as the American regional complexes. If this were done treating Canada as one more region it would probably have compared favourably with California ($48 billion).

A KIND OF CANADIANISM
The Falconbridge case suggests that Canada has very little independent existence within the broad U.S. imperial scheme. Falconbridge's principal bank in Canada is the Canadian Imperial Bank of Commerce, the company head office is located in the bank's Bay Street office tower, Commerce Court, and an officer of the bank is on Falconbridge's board of directors. All this only makes the CIBC a useful junior ally in the larger financial combination, mobilizing the savings and natural resources of Canada to pursue policies determined south of the border. Frank and Libby Park's pioneering study of the Canadian business elite, *Anatomy of Big Business,* is replete with similar examples of the subordinate role of Canadian financial institutions.[48] The accumulated evidence provides little indication of any significant urge for independence among Canada's men of wealth, who seem to be generally satisfied with their share of the take under traditional arrangements.

48. Libbie & Frank Park, *Anatomy of Big Business,* Toronto: James Lewis & Samuel, 1973.

Perhaps the strongest corroboration of this conclusion is to be found in the political arena, where first the Liberals and finally the Conservatives have come comfortably to terms with the presence of massive foreign investment in Canada. Our own review of the nickel industry contains evidence reaching back to Sir Wilfrid Laurier that the Liberal party views Canada as little more than a playground for American capital. Laurier allowed his affinity for the type of development represented by Colonel Thompson and INCO to outrun public opinion, and was defeated on the reciprocal trade issue in 1911. His attitudes were resumed by the next Liberal leader, MacKenzie King, who served an apprenticeship with John D. Rockefeller in the United States before moving to the helm of the Liberal party in 1919.

The apologetic role King adopted in Rockefeller's service is interesting for the light it sheds on the thinking and attitudes of a man who led Canada for 21 years and strongly influenced its politics for three decades. Acceptable to Rockefeller, King was apparently quite acceptable to Canada's business class as well.

On October 7th, 1913 the U.S. National Guard staged a surprise attack on a camp of United Mine Workers who were striking the Colorado Fuel and Iron Company, a Rockefeller enterprise. The troops, mostly company guards in militia uniforms, killed five men and a boy with machine-gun fire and set fire to shacks and tents, burning eleven children and two women to death. It was one of the bloodiest incidents in American union history and came to be known as the Ludlow massacre.

John D. Rockefeller denied any knowledge of the labour policies of his Colorado company, although contrary evidence was presented, and sought to absolve himself of any responsibility for the murder of his employees. MacKenzie King was brought in by the Rockefeller Foundation to do a whitewash study of labour conditions and head off the adverse publicity. The project had to be dropped when King's efforts on behalf of his employer proved too crude and embarassing. In his visit to the Colorado coalfields he had neglected to interview any members of either the United Mine Workers or the State Federation of Labour.[49]

King's compliant attitudes toward private enterprise and American capital established the dominant tone of his Liberal governments in the 1920s, 1930s and 1940s, during which time American corporations became a dominant influence in Canadian life. The King tradition was maintained by his successor Louis St. Laurent and the powerful C.D. Howe who served under both. Howe, minister in charge of war production and later minister of Industry, Trade and Commerce, was the chief

49. Demaris, *op. cit.*, p. 277.

architect of Canada's modern economic development strategy based on continental integration and serving American markets. One of his crowning achievements was the defense production agreement of 1950 which provided that Canada and the United States would co-operate "in all respects practicable, and to the extent of their respective powers, to the end that the economic efforts of the two countries be coordinated for the common defense and that production and resources of both countries be used for the best combined results."[50]

The "common defense" was an all-embracing concept, since the Liberal governments shared in its entirety the official American Cold War view of the world. This view held that the war-shattered and impoverished Soviet Union was in fact an aggressive imperial power moving purposefully to occupy every unclaimed corner of the earth. "Our foreign policy, therefore, must be based," said St. Laurent in 1948, "on a recognition of the fact that totalitarian communist aggression endangers the freedom and peace of every democratic country, including Canada."[51]

The perpetual threat of communist conspiracy was used to blur any useful distinction between peacetime and war economics, and served as the justification for expensive and profitable military spending programs on both sides of the border. C.D. Howe's vision required that Canada capture a minor portion of the American military spending in return for an open door policy on U.S. investment in Canadian industry and resources, which is what happened.

Howe's connections with Canada's business elite were extensive, and he played an important role in furthering numerous careers. During the war many of the up-and-coming served as dollar-a-year men in the administration of war production, all of them united in support of an Allied victory but not at the expense of conscripting capital. To these men conscription was a concept perfectly appropriate to organize the expenditure of human life, but not the expenditure of private wealth. Among those serving with Howe in the war years were E.P. Taylor, Wallace McCutcheon, W.E. Phillips, H.J. Carmichael and Wilfred Gagnon, all future directors of Argus Corporation; Henry Borden (Brazilian Traction); Jack Barrington (Polymer, McIntyre Porcupine); W.J. Bennett (Eldorado, Atomic Energy of Canada, IOCO, Investors Syndicate); V.W. Scully (Stelco); and H.R. MacMillan (MacMillan-Bloedel). [52]

50. Percy Bidwell, *Raw Materials,* New York: Harper's (Council on Foreign Relations), 1958, p. 163.

51. Philip Resnick, "Canadian Defence Policy and the American Empire", in Ian Lumsden (ed.), *Close the 49th Parallel,* University of Toronto Press, 1971, p. 99.

52. Park, *op. cit.,* pp. 58-60.

This group managed the war departments in a way that would "raise the minimum number of problems for big business, interfere least with the pursuit of the largest possible profits, and leave the big companies in the best possible position after the war," as a by-product placing themselves in very good positions as well.[53] A high American official described the dollar-a-year men on the U.S. War Production Board as "crawling maggots looking out for their private interests," also an apt description of the Ottawa clan in view of their subsequent record.[54]

Reflecting on Howe's role as czar of Canadian industry, Mitchell Sharp says that he "knew every important business man in Canada, and they seemed to have made a practice of talking to C.D. whether they wanted anything from the government or not."[55] David Lewis in *Louder Voices; The Corporate Welfare Bums* traces the growth of the corporate welfare state back to those Howe-dominated post-war years when he claims the web of tax concessions and subsidies began. Although this ignores earlier giveaways, Lewis is right in emphasizing that the magnitude of corporate welfare has expanded greatly since the war, particularly in the defense-related industries and resources extraction which are so closely linked to American requirements. With each succeeding triumph of special interest lobbies in the U.S. Congress on tax questions, Canada's Liberal governments have rushed to match the ripoff in the Canadian tax system, and sometimes even upped the ante. All this is done to create a favourable climate for business and keep Canada competitive. Thus when the indefensible U.S. oil depletion allowance was 27.5 percent, Ottawa decided 33 percent had a better ring to it. In a more recent example, Finance Minister John Turner boldly met John Connally's U.S. export subsidies under the DISC program by cutting the corporate tax rate in Canada.

The C.D. Howe cabal intersects significantly with Falconbridge history in 1956. J.S.D. Tory, that most versatile of Canadian corporation lawyers, was looking for new talent in his capacity as Chairman of McIntyre Porcupine. Howe recommended Jack Barrington, president of the federal Polymer Corporation, and Tory appointed him to the McIntyre board. At the time Howe, acting as executor of the James Dunn estate, was overseeing the sale of Algoma Steel to McIntyre and A.V. Roe, a company which had received nearly $1 billion in contracts from Howe's department of Defense Production. The multiple conflict

53. *Ibid.*, p. 59.

54. Demaris, *op. cit.*, p. 175.

55. John Porter, *The Vertical Mosaic*, Toronto: University of Toronto Press, 1967, p. 430.

of interest led to demands for Howe's resignation, which he naturally ignored.[56] His protege Barrington left the public service to manage McIntyre and play an important part in the previously described acquisition of Thayer Lindsley's Ventures Ltd. and with it Falconbridge.

THE CENTRALIZATION OF POWER

The pattern evident in the modern period of Falconbridge history is one of the company falling by steps into the control of larger financial groups with increasingly powerful political connections. Although Thayer Lindsley's work patterns involved almost weekly trips to New York, Washington and Ottawa, he was not in the heavyweight division. The sale of shares to McIntyre, achieved against his will, linked the company with the Barrington-Tory-C.D. Howe group, a potent entree to the cabinet in Ottawa, and with the financial resources of the Locana-Anglo-American group. The hiring of Robert Anderson promised high-level good will in Washington. The Keck takeover pushed this logic to a higher stage of development in view of the Texan's multiple relations with Connally, Anderson, Lyndon Johnson, Richard Nixon and the whole Texas-Wall Street Nexus.[57]

The underlying dynamic of this trend is that men of great wealth and their large corporations which are capable of financing takeovers and the growth of monopoly tend to have extensive dealings and good relations with the highest levels of government. It is also true that these good relations produce large and tangible financial results which provide the wherewithal to finance further takeovers and concentration of economic power. It is no accident that the resource industries like oil,

---

56. *Debates of the House of Commons,* Ottawa: Queen's Printer, April 12, 1957, pp. 3472-3476.

57. A new firmly integrated member of the Texas Nexus elite is Marsh Cooper, Falconbridge's president. Cooper's corporate directorships have become so numerous as to give rise to concern in the United States. According to the March 12th 1974 *New York Times,* Cooper was among twenty-five executives under investigation by the U.S. Justice Department, Federal Trade Commission, Securities and Exchange Commission, and Congress for possible anti-trust violation as result of sitting on several oil company boards simultaneously. Cooper is on the following boards: Texas Eastern Transmission Corporation (La Gloria Oil), Home Oil Company, Alminex Limited, and Superior Oil. The *New York Times* found Cooper reticent:

> Asked in a telephone interview how many directorships he held in oil companies, Mr. Cooper said: "I don't know, I haven't counted lately." Asked if he considered it ethical to sit on more than one, he answered: "I have no comment whatsoever."

Also under investigation are a number of other members of the Texas Nexus, including John Murchison and Perry Bass. Bass, a close friend and former partner of Connally's, figured in the scheme to make Robert Anderson a millionaire.

with their extravagant and unjustifiable tax advantages, have generated so much of the surplus capital involved in the corporate merger movement of which Falconbridge has been but a small part.

The unsavoury dealings around Falconbridge have not been confined exclusively to the political realm. An interesting sidelight to the company's affairs appeared in 1972 when it was announced that its shares of La Luz Mines in Nicaragua were being sold to companies represented by Lou Chesler.[58] Chesler is a well-known investor and stock promoter closely associated with Mafia chieftain Meyer Lansky and Trigger Mike Coppola, and has been described as one of the conduits by which the Mafia's profits are laundered and reinvested in "legitimate" business. Chesler's diverse array of friends in the investment and political world includes Robert Anderson, the former president of Ventures and top advisor to both Eisenhower and Lyndon Johnson.[59]

The distinction between legitimate and criminal business activity, as these connections and the behavior of so many of the respected men linked to Falconbridge suggest, is rather arbitrary and difficult to make. A former U.S. Secretary of the Interior, Harold Ickes, once observed that "an honest and scrupulous man in the oil business is so rare as to rank as a museum piece."[60] The problem is by no means confined to oil. In all big business the stakes are enormous and the personal gain to men at the top beyond the imagination of most people.

As long as the pursuit of private wealth and ownership of the productive system is the name of the game, the corrupt and corrupting relationship between big business and government is inescapable, and reform cannot reasonably be expected to go beyond the cosmetic level. In a colourful analogy even *Newsweek* allowed itself to recognize "the relationship between money and politics is so organic that seeking reform is tantamount to asking a doctor to perform open-heart surgery on himself."[61]

58. Chesler's option to purchase La Luz (see Falconbridge Nickel Mines Limited, *Press Release*, January 17, 1972) was eventually passed on to Security Capital Corporation (*Wall Street Journal*, February 11, 1972). More recently Chesler has been involved in a battle to assert his control over Security Capital. See *Toronto Star*, November 29, 1974, p. C8 and *Globe & Mail*, December 6, 1974.

59. The *Wall Street Journal*, June 1964, referred to in Ed Reid, *The Grim Reapers*, New York: Bantam, 1972, pp. 107-112, 116-118, 121-122. The *Wall Street Journal* eventually won a Pulitzer Prize for its exposés on the Lansky-Mafia-Gambling operations in the Bahamas.

60. Demaris, *op. cit.*, p. 175.

61. "The $400 Million Election Machine", *Newsweek*, December 13, 1971, quoted in Demaris, *op. cit.*, p. 373.

In both Canada and the United States, relatively wealthy societies, it has been possible for a majority of the population to accept the continuing rape of the public interest by private interests with a certain resignation. Although power is still exercised in a highly un-democratic manner in both countries, the economic system has spread its benefits widely enough to pacify a substantial portion of the citizenry and leave the most disadvantaged in a state of general disorganization and cynicism.

These salad days of the capitalist system are now coming to an end. As we enter harsher times the injustice, human suffering and distorted priorities inflicted on us by our free-wheeling corporate and political masters will be subjected to a much closer scrutiny. The record will show, as it does in the case of the Falconbridge group, that Canadians have paid a high price for allowing such a free hand to the corporations and their owners. It will also show that, whatever price Canadians have paid, it cannot begin to compare with the misery, exploitation and oppression occasioned by the overseas activities of our good corporate citizens.

CHAPTER SIX

Canada's Wasting Heritage

*A One Horse Town obviously suits the man that owns the horse just fine.
If you want to use his horse, you have to be nice to him. And when he
decides that there are greener pastures elsewhere, the poor old town
doesn't have any horse left at all.*
    —Michael Nash, Sudbury Environmental Law Association,
        1973

*For several years past I have referred to the problems of maintaining a
profitable nickel industry in Canada. Although this country was for
many years the world's leading source of nickel production, that
position has been sharply eroded. . . . If governments continue to
increase restrictions, taxes and royalties and move toward an all-
pervasive part in the industry, the risk money and the expertise available up to this time . . . will seek opportunity in other parts of the world.
. . . Unless the investment climate is attractive, exploration will gradually decline.*
    —Falconbridge president Marsh Cooper, 1974 Annual Meeting

Canada Counts on Mining.
    — catchy slogan of the Mining Association of Canada

For seventy years now, thanks mainly to the natural riches of the
Sudbury Basin, Canada has occupied a position of overwhelming
dominance in supplying world nickel markets. The Canadian preemi-
nence in nickel, in terms of market share, has vastly exceeded the
position the Arab states now enjoy in world oil supply, yet Canadian
nickel has never been used in like manner as a lever of national foreign
policy or national economic development. On the contrary, this great
national resource has been harnessed under American ownership to the

industrial and military requirements of Western Europe, Japan and the United States. Now that Canada's monopoly is rapidly weakening and the end of our low cost nickel reserves is in sight, the time to review past management of this strategic asset is overdue.

THE REPUBLIC OF NICKEL

The main legacy of Canadian nickel is Sudbury, the Nickel Capital of the World and Canada's largest company town. With an urban population of 90,000 and another 65,000 people in the surrounding area,[1] metropolitan Sudbury owes its existence almost entirely to the International Nickel Company and Falconbridge. About one-third of the paid labour force is directly employed by the two huge companies, and most other economic activity revolves around them.

As a community Sudbury reflects in every aspect of its social life the enormous power of its economic overlords and the pattern of development which has evolved to suit their needs. Its nickel-copper export economy makes the Sudbury district a resource colony within Canada, displaying many of the symptoms of other transnational enclaves in less developed countries around the world. It is a city of migrants and tenants, pulsing to the boom and bust cycle of primary metal markets. In 1971, with the mines operating full tilt, the vacancy rate for apartment accomodation was three-tenths of one percent, the lowest in Canada. Two years later, with INCO pursuing a major investment program and simultaneously slashing 6,000 jobs, the vacancy rate was 10.7 percent, the highest in the nation.[2]

Both wages and living costs in the nickel capital are above the Canadian average. In 1974 the minimum basic weekly wage at INCO and Falconbridge was $167, but employment opportunities for women are extremely limited in the one-industry city, resulting in a per capita income lower than the Canadian average.[3] Over the decades INCO and Falconbridge have resolutely resisted the oft-voiced wish of politicans and union officials that their profits be channeled into the industrial diversification of the region. Both companies have been in the business of servicing foreign growth patterns, and consequently ninety years of hosting the highly profitable nickel industry have not made Sudbury a prosperous community.

1. *1971 Census of Canada: Population,* Statistics Canada, Ottawa, 1972.
2. *Vacancy Rates in Apartment Structures of six units and over: 1963-1974,* Canadian Mortgage and Housing Corporation statistics, mimeo, 1974.
3. *Design for Development — Northeastern Ontario Region: Phase I, Analysis,* Department of the Treasury and Economics of the Government of Ontario, Toronto, January 23, 1971. Also see: David Lewis, *Louder Voices: The Corporate Welfare Bums,* James Lewis & Samuel, Publishers, Toronto, 1972 for a chapter on Sudbury as "one city, two worlds".

The social impoverishment of Sudbury showed up markedly throughout most of its history in the city's underfinanced public services. Surveying this situation as recently as 1971 one commentator observed:

> Sudbury does not have a sewage treatment plant. Raw sewage is dumped directly into Kelley Lake, the effluent of which eventually flows into Lake Huron. The roads in Sudbury must rate as the worst in any city of comparable size anywhere in Canada. (Sudbury) does not even have its own city hall. . . . The hospital which serves the large French-speaking population resembles something from before the turn of the century, with poor facilities and crumbling plaster falling off the walls.[4]

The inadequacy of public services was not due, the same writer pointed out, to any deficiency in civic pride or community spirit. The homeowners of Sudbury for years carried a property tax burden 21 percent above the average for 29 Ontario cities,[5] steep enough to have driven many citizens of the Sudbury region into the welter of unincorporated communities which dot the surrounding district. A 1970 report of the Ontario Municipal Board (OMB) on the regional underdevelopment of Sudbury indicated the unsatisfactory state of affairs in these settlements:

> There is municipal water in Lively, Levak, Onaping, Falconbridge and Coniston but none in Waters, Drury, Denison and Graham, Dowling, Rayside, Valley East or Balfour. . . .[6]

The OMB report noted that except for Copper Cliff, Lively, Levack, Onaping, Coniston, Falconbridge, Chelmsford, Capreol, Neelon and Garson, there were no sewers in other municipalities, and observed further:

> In some ways it is surprising that in Copper Cliff, Lively, Onaping, Levack, Falconbridge and Coniston in which mining companies are large landowners and dominant corporate citizens there is no official plan or land use control by-law in force.[7]

At the root of this planner's nightmare were INCO and Falconbridge. For decades they were immune from municipal taxation, and

4. Allan Rimmer, "INCO's Policies of Underdeveloping and Overpolluting Sudbury", *Canadian Dimension,* February 1971, p. 26.
5. Brief submitted to the Government of Ontario by the City of Sudbury, 1964 cited in *The Mucker,* Vol. 1, #4, Sudbury, 1971.
6. J.A. Kennedy, *Sudbury Area Study,* report to the Hon. Darcy McKeough, Minister of Municipal Affairs, May 27, 1970, p. 10.
7. *Ibid.,* p. 14.

only in the early 1970s did the lethargic corporation-dominated Ontario Conservative government begin to intervene. The modest provincial mining tax, part of which used to be turned over to the hard-pressed municipalities, is now supplemented by a municipal assessment on the assets of the two corporations in conjunction with the new regional government program. This belated development has overtaken the Republic of Nickel 72 years after the formation of INCO and 46 years after the appearance of Falconbridge. Still, only above-ground buildings and land, not machinery and equipment or below-ground improvements, are taxable. INCO is assessed at $70 million and Falconbridge at $14 million,[8] when recent balance sheets show Falconbridge's physical assets in its integrated nickel operation at $74 million, and INCO's worldwide physical plant assets, the majority in Sudbury, at $1.4 billion. While the nickel companies were slipping through grossly underassessed, a civic official estimated Sudbury's revenue shortfall in 1972 at $7.7 million.[9]

Corporate power in a company town manifests itself in other important ways. As many as three of five members of the police commission have been INCO management personnel, helping to assure appropriate law enforcement at critical times, especially during labour disputes. An INCO management official, Dick Dow, sits at the right hand of Mayor Joe Fabbro on city council. Falconbridge president Marsh Cooper, a resident of Toronto, is on the board of governors of Sudbury's Laurentian University. In these and other community activities Falconbridge, whose main facilities are located 15 miles east of Sudbury, plays a subordinate supporting role to INCO.

THE ENVIRONMENT AS FREE GARBAGE DUMP

The corporations' impact on community life in Sudbury is not restricted to the invisible sphere of civic finance and power relations. One of the most obvious and unpleasant effects is their fouling of the very air people breath. Falconbridge and INCO, with three and six smokestacks respectively, together in 1969 spewed 2 million tons of sulphur dioxide as well as nickel and other heavy metal particles into the atmosphere, which the companies have been allowed to treat as a free garbage dump throughout their history. The effluent, which afflicts the environment for 50 miles in all directions around the smelters, combines with water to form sulphurous or sulphuric acid, to the detriment of buildings, machinery, vegetation, fish, animals and people. The visual evidence of decay is striking:

8. MPP Elie Martel reported in *Northern Life,* Sudbury January 15, 1975.
9. Elie Martel, *Debates of the Ontario Legislature,* Queen's Printer, Toronto, June 22, 1972, p. 4092.

> The veteran traveller is generally satisfied to wonder why people might actually choose to live there, for the area immediately around Sudbury is one of almost absolute desolation. Stunted vegetation, jagged outcroppings of weathered rock and air tainted with the sulphurous fumes of the smelters make up the picture. . . . Towering above all this are the belching smokestacks. . . . [10]

It was this aspect of Sudbury which made it suitable as the training site for the U.S. Apollo moon landing missions, a dubious honour under the circumstances.

INCO and Falconbridge, in defense of their Sudbury operations, point out that the whole area was first ravaged by the logging industry during the 19th century, particularly to rebuild Chicago after the great fire of 1871, and that the Sudbury terrain was subsequently swept by bush fires. Falconbridge also takes refuge in the fact that much of the devastation dates from the early practices of INCO's forerunner, the Canadian Copper Company, which used huge quantities of timber for "heap-roasting" its ores, simply piling them on open fires and burning off the sulphur.[11] In this view of things the area had been desolated already and the effects of more recent pollution should not be exaggerated.

The corporate outlook, however, is not shared by many residents of the region. The continuing evidence of dying white pine stands and the persistent decline in fish populations, apparently caused by the sulphur dioxide-induced acidity of lakes within the fall-out zone, is impossible to ignore. There are even more fundamental warning signs in human health statistics: the death rate for people over the age of 55 in Sudbury was in 1961 a frightening 33 percent greater than the figure for all Ontario.[12] Given that Sudbury is not a retirement haven for the nation's aged, some explanation for this alarming phenomenon must be sought either in the mine and smelter working environment, general environmental conditions, or a combination of the two.

The inevitable corporate apologies and obfuscation, which sometimes extend to citing the beneficial effects of extra doses of sulphur, must be measured against other negative trends in the district which have recently come to light. The agricultural labour force declined between 1951 and 1966 from 1,529 to 630, reflecting general trends in agriculture but also a response to declining productivity of the soil.[13]

10. Allan Rimmer, *op. cit.*, p. 23.
11. *Globe and Mail,* November 8, 1974, letter to the editor from W. Taylor, Falconbridge Technical Services.
12. J.R. Winter, *Sudbury: An Economic Survey,* Laurentian University, Sudbury, 1967, p. 13.
13. 1971 Census of Canada: Population, *op. cit.*

As the years go by, fewer and fewer farmers can carry on; their soil becomes more acidic and their crops are burned. Some of them have tried to get compensation from International Nickel in the past, and when they managed to succeed the company extracted from them a smoke easement as their price for settlement. . . . From the moment the smoke easement is purchased by INCO the holder of the land, whoever he may be . . . is forever barred from claiming compensation for crop damage. . . . Many square miles have been effectively ruined for farming and a whole class of people have been uprooted over the decades. . . . We have to pay higher food prices as a result of the decline of farming.[14]

The lumber industry has suffered a parallel injury. In the 720 square mile inner fume zone around the smelters the government of Ontario estimates the annual loss of white pine through death and stunted growth at $117,000 based on 1953-63 data.[15] The study made no estimates for the broader area affected by the polluters, nor for the negative impact on species hardier than white pine, which constitutes only about 10 percent of the forest cover.

The tourist industry too has been a victim of the side effects of nickel production in the INCO-Falconbridge style. Neither trees nor fish, the basic ingredients of the call of the wild, have weathered the sulphur dioxide onslaught well. According to a report of the Ontario Water Resources Commission, of 30 lakes in the area once known for their fishing six now have no fish at all, 18 have no lake trout and the rest have all shown marked signs of decline. The report says 25,000 acres of pickerel water and 17,000 acres of lake trout water have been completely lost. "One would not expect," the civil servants cautiously conclude, "a change of this magnitude due to angling pressure alone."[16]

This judgement is confirmed by tourist operator Peter Peloquin, whose fishing camp 38 miles northeast of Sudbury is in the path of prevailing summer winds from the smelters. Beside stands of of tell-tale dead white pine lies Chiniguchi Lake "which used to jump with trout and smallmouth," says Peloquin.[17] In 1971 Ontario natural resources officials netted for 58 hours without catching a single fish in the

14. Michael Nash, "Pollution control and Unemployment in the Sudbury Area", Sudbury Environmental Law Association, mimeo, 1973.
15. Samuel Linzon, "Economic Effects of Sulphur Dioxide on Forest Growth", Ontario Ministry of the Environment.
16. "Preliminary Report on the Influence of Industrial Activity on the Lakes in the Sudbury Area", Ontario Water Resources Commission, Sudbury, 1970.
17. "The slow souring of a paradise: Pollution ended the fishing", Toronto Star, January 13, 1975, p. C3.

high-acidity waters. "It's a hell of a heritage we leave our children, the country around Sudbury and what's been done to it," laments the long-time woodsman whose livelihood has been ruined. A Falconbridge spokesman defending the company in late 1974 said he could not agree to "allegations of the effects of industrial pollution . . . which have been hypothesized but to my knowledge are as yet unproven," noting that if compensation were paid to Peloquin "we could hardly deny similar assistance to everyone who might request it no matter how nebulous their claims might be."[18]

Another "nebulous" category of pollution damage is the accelerated depreciation of buildings, metal corrosion, leather and rubber damage to furniture and clothing and the costs of cleaning clothes and buildings subject to heavy air pollution. Based on calculations from the Ontario government's 1969 Zerbe report on the cost of air pollution, Michael Nash of the Sudbury Environmental Law Association estimated these losses in the Sudbury airshed to be in the order of $20 million annually, a sum comparable to Falconbridge's profits from its nickel operations. [19] The losses are suffered mainly by people who are not on the receiving end of Falconbridge or INCO dividend cheques.

The many indirect effects of Sudbury's massive air pollution problem are difficult to pin down in the kind of neat, definitive causal analysis which might stand up in a court of law. This allows INCO and Falconbridge to scoff at "hypotheses" which point the finger in the obvious direction, and carry on pretty much as they please. The combined pollution damages, undoubtedly very large, mount every day.

> It is clear that sulphur dioxide can irritate or damage sensitive tissues of the respiratory system, cause coughing, chest pain, and irritate the eyes and throat. The pollutant has also been linked with heart and respiratory diseases, as well as lung cancer, but evidence to this effect is not conclusive. . . . (However) the fact that it does no good is well known. Various studies have been completed by both federal and provincial governments on the effects of sulphur dioxide on the health of Sudbury residents, but none of these have been made public.[20]

Such a longstanding situation demands government intervention for the protection of the nickel company employees, the people of Sudbury, the tens of thousands who at one time or another find themselves downwind, and the flora and fauna over at least 2100 square

18. *Ibid.*
19. M. Nash, *op. cit.*
20. "INCO and Pollution: the Facts", Sudbury Environmental Law Association, mimeo, June 28. 1973.

miles within range of the companies' poisonous byproducts. The government of Ontario has met the challenge with all the lethargy it can muster. In 1970 the Minister of the Environment finally decreed a pollution abatement program under which Falconbridge was to cut back its 1969 emissions of 959 tons of sulphur dioxide daily to 55 percent of that level by 1975. INCO, which completed a 1250 foot superstack in 1970 at a cost of $25 million apparently with the objective of dispersing its effluent over a wider area, was told to cut emissions from the giant pipe from the original estimated 5200 tons daily to 4400 tons by 1974 and 750 tons by 1978.

The extent to which these rather lenient clean-up timetables will actually be met is difficult to ascertain. A terse note from the Financial Post Corporation Service casts some doubt on INCO's progress.

> Plans for construction of a $32 million sulphuric acid plant with a capacity of 700,000 tons a year designed to reduce the quantity of sulphur dioxide emitted into the air by the iron ore recovery plant were cancelled in 1971 due to inflationary costs.[21]

INCO's profits, $208 million in 1970, had indeed dropped to $94 million in the recession year 1971, still well short of destitution.

Falconbridge, which in the business community is considered stronger in the political and financial spheres than in technology and production, suffered a severe setback in the early 1970s which affected its abatement program. The company in 1972 declared a $65 million writeoff on a nickel-iron pellet refining complex and related sulphur recovery plant it had been developing over the previous two years. The loss to Falconbridge was cushioned by the Canadian taxpayer, about $30 million of it being financed by a reduction in deferred income taxes, but it was a traumatic experience for Falconbridge management and shareholders.

The Ontario government demonstrated its solicitude in 1973 by granting Falconbridge a four-year extension to 1979 on its pollution targets, and the company announced planned revisions to its smeltering processes including the construction of a sulphuric acid plant at an estimated cost of $65 million. This program, according to the most recent announcements, is now scheduled for operation in 1977 with costs escalated to $95 million.[22]

Symptomatic of the type of dickering that has taken place between the provincial government and Falconbridge for the past several

21. Financial Post Corporation Service, *INCO,* April 12, 1972, p. 7.
22. Financial Post Corporation Service, *Falconbridge Nickel Mines Ltd.,* current information card, November 26, 1974, p. 2.

years is the widely-publicized Happy Valley episode. Once a cluster of 23 houses located less than a mile from Falconbridge's smelters, Happy Valley has become, according to *Sudbury Star* reporter Neil Stevens, "the first community to be wiped from the map of Canada to make way for continued air pollution."[23] The Ontario Department of the Environment in 1971 installed an air pollution monitor among the scattered houses and on a number of subsequent occasions obtained record high readings. With an index of 32 marking the limits of acceptability, the monitor hit 94 in August 1973, and on one day in 1972 apparently reached 141 before climbing off the scale. These and other excessive readings in an area of human habitation required production cutbacks at the Falconbridge smelter, leading Energy and Resources minister George Kerr to conclude it would be better to move the families than to interrupt production.

Falconbridge has since contributed $230,000 and Ontario $130,000 to buying out the homeowners, a number of whom have resisted the attempt to evict them because the compensation will not provide them with equivalent accomodation. At this time most of the dwellings have been removed; people who lived in the shadow of death for so many years because it was what they could afford have been overruled in their calculated risk of their health.

Happy Valley is representative of many long-term industrial pollution situations, where simple common sense indicates a likely danger to human health but its full extent is likely to become apparent only over a long period of time. The general corporate response is to adopt the low cost or higher profit approach, and wait and see what happens. The guinea pigs, after all, are only "uninvolved" citizens or employees who can be replaced, and corporate management's first responsibility is not to them, but to its shareholders who are not part of the experiment.

The countervailing force in these circumstances is supposed to be government, but the Ontario government's performance in this case is distinguished by inadequate legislation and weak enforcement. It is as if INCO and Falconbridge owned the government in addition to their other extensive assets. Everything is arranged by private discussion and agreement. In the five years since the new air quality standards were established, neither of the companies has faced a single prosecution. Pollution abatement is taking place only as the companies, in their own sweet time, modernize their facilities in connection with their own

23. Neil Stevens, "The Solution? Wipe out the town, not the pollution", *Canadian Dimension*, November 1974, p. 10. In addition see: "Who Killed Happy Valley?", *Weekend Magazine*, October 19, 1974.

schedule for increasing production in Sudbury. The government, incredibly, has even relied on the companies for its information on how much pollution is taking place.

Falconbridge and International Nickel have argued that it would be folly to force them into hasty and expensive pollution control measures which might quickly be rendered obsolete by additional research.[24] On the other hand, regular stiff fines which provided adequate compensation to the general public for the continuing abuse of employees, citizens and the environment of the area might have produced some miraculous technological ''discoveries'', and their introduction at a much earlier date. As long as the environment is a free dump, and the companies face only the occasional chat with friendly government officials, pollution will keep winning the war on pollution.

In Sudbury's environmental conflict between the public interest and private profit, the Ontario government has come down squarely on the side of profit. If this conclusion seems too severe, the reader might try to imagine what would be happening if a representative amount of sulphur dioxide and heavy metal particles could be daily pumped into the homes and offices of members of the Ontario cabinet, the top management of INCO and Falconbridge, and leading shareholders like Howard B. Keck until their mess was cleaned up. Would these people tolerate the same treatment as Happy Valley and the rest of the Sudbury population?

LABOUR RELATIONS: DIVIDE, LAY OFF, AND CONQUER
Falconbridge's production workers are represented by the independent Mine Mill and Smelter Workers Local 598, a union whose history is unmatched in the Canadian labour movement for sheer tenacity in the face of the most persistent and sophisticated attacks from every imaginable quarter.[25] Local 598, certified in 1943, is all that is left of the International Mine Mill and Smelter Workers Union. It has survived Mine Mill's expulsion from the Canadian Congress of Labour, relentless raiding by the United Steelworkers of America well into the 1960s, gross injustice at the hands of the Ontario and federal labour relations boards, intense persecution by the U.S. Justice Department, the established press and the Catholic Church and vigorous opposition from the

---

24. L.S. Renzoni (INCO vice-president), ''The fight to curb pollution'', *Mining and the Environment,* published by INCO, 1972.

25. For this section on labour history in Sudbury, and particularly for the history of the Mine Mill union, we have relied extensively on John Lang's unpublished work, *A Lion in a Den of Daniels: A History of the International Union of Mine, Mill and Smelter Workers in Sudbury Ontario 1942-1962,* M.A. thesis, University of Guelph, 1970.

CCF. This massive and concerted opposition to its survival, most of it rationalized by the Cold War hysteria against Communism, finally led to the dismemberment of most of Mine Mill's jurisdiction with the exception of the Falconbridge local.

In its day Mine Mill was a powerful, militant and radical continental organization. It was born of the atrocious conditions in North America's mining industry and a long tradition of labour struggle reaching back to the Western Federation of Miners, the Industrial Workers of the World, the One Big Union movement, the Communist-led Workers Unity League of the 1930s, and the great CIO organizing drives of the late depression and World War II era. Former INCO president J.F. Thompson in his history of the nickel monopoly refers nostalgically to the days when Sudbury miners worked 12 hour shifts for $1.75 a day and "preferred to walk along the railroad tracks" between their homes and Copper Cliff rather than pay the stiff 25 cent streetcar fare.[26] The very tyranny and paternalism of INCO, and later Falconbridge, which mirrors INCO's labour policies, guaranteed the emergence of a militant trade union loyalty among their workers.

Mines and smelters are among the chief battlegrounds of industrial production, and as in military warfare the men in the front lines run the risks and suffer the gruesome injuries to life and limb, physical health and psyche. Describing depression conditions in Sudbury when the basic wage was 52 cents an hour, William Kon wrote that the companies drafted only the healthiest men from the long lines of hungry applicants, thus keeping the workmens' compensation premiums down. That these men would be lucky enough to stay healthy was doubtful, Kon advised:

> You go either to a mine or the smelter. It doesn't matter because they both rate near the top for accidents and near the bottom for insurance risks. In the mines the loose nickel oxidizes and the heat rises in wet steamy clouds. And when you drive a shovel all day into rock that is heavy with ore the water drips from your body and in two weeks your clothes rot from never being dry. And if you stay there long enough the dust goes in your lungs and forms scabs and one day you stop breathing. This is technically known as silicosis. But you really don't have to worry about that too much. Every six months you get another medical examination. If you look a little rocky they find they are overstaffed for the time and you are laid off.[27]

26. J.F. Thompson and N. Beasley, *For the Years to Come,* Toronto, 1960, p. 76.
27. W.E. Kon, "Boom Town Into Company Town: The Story of Sudbury", *New Frontier,* 1937, p. 6.

Kon catalogued the other company practices which workers finally banded together to combat through the Mine Mill union: intense speed-ups, forcing badly injured men to report for work to hold down the lost-time accident statistics, and so on. Many men didn't live to see the union come: the *New Frontier* article described how horrible death could be, detailing the agony of a smelter worker who fell into a cooling tank which lacked protective railing:

> The hot water bit his skin and it all puffed off his flesh and he screamed and tried to crawl out and his hands slipped and he fell back screaming. The water ate into his peeled flesh and he screamed and they pulled him out by the arms, tight because under the shirt the skin was soft and sliding like wet chamois . . . he just lay and twitched and screamed until the ambulance came and took him to the hospital and he died. . . . You can't be a rugged individualist . . . if you have to testify (at the inquest) and not say much about the chain that John Smith tripped on and hear the verdict that John Smith died from falling into a tank of hot water and that he shouldn't have been in the tank.[28]

By World War II the long history of low wages, little job security and the companies' callous disregard for their health and safety had prepared Sudbury mine and smelter workers for industrial unionism. In 1942 INCO, which as recently as 1972 relied on professional labour spies,[29] spent $68,000 promoting a company union, but the employees recognized the ploy for what it was. Instead they responded massively to the efforts of former Workers Unity League organizers to bring in the CIO and Mine Mill. Almost overnight the union became such a potent force in Sudbury that its local president, Bob Carlin, was elected to the Ontario legislature as a CCFer in 1943. The first contracts with INCO and Falconbridge were signed in 1944, and Mine Mill moved triumphantly from its victory in Sudbury to certify locals throughout the mining towns of northeastern Ontario.

The labour unity established by Mine Mill in the Ontario mining industry was short-lived. After the union was won, internal power struggles broke out pitting CCF loyalists against the Communist Party members and sympathizers who had played instrumental roles in organizing Mine Mill. Similar conflicts were brewing in other CIO unions

28. *Ibid.*, p. 9.
29. Marc Zwelling, *The Strikebreakers,* Toronto, 1972, p. 131. According to Zwelling, the company that INCO has recently used for labour-spy activities is William R. Brock & Associates, based in Toronto. In general, Zwelling's book shows that the age-old tactics of spying, provocation and disruption that have been used by companies against union movements are still very much in currency today.

and in the Canadian Congress of Labour. At the same time the United Steelworkers of America were increasing their influence in the CCL and casting an envious eye at the extensive Mine Mill jurisdiction.

On the employer-government side of the fence there was growing anxiety over Mine Mill's strength and radicalism. In their view it was disastrous to have the Free World nickel supply vulnerable to a union well-sprinkled with Communists, but at the same time they were also concerned about the rising influence of the CCF's democratic socialism in the working class of northern Ontario. These potential challenges to the status quo were soon dissipated however by a debilitating rivalry between the competing socialist philosophies and the labour organizations in which each was strongest.

In 1949, with the Cold War well launched and the McCarthyist witchhunts building in both the United States and Canada, Mine Mill was expelled from the Canadian Congress of Labour. This was the signal for raiding by the United Steelworkers, who spent an estimated $2 million in pursuit of the Mine Mill jurisdiction during the following 13 years. The Mine Mill leadership became enmeshed in a narrowing circle of legal harassment by the U.S. government, which had equated Communism with treason. The left-wing labour men were faced with incessant character assassination and attacks on their motives as trade unionists, in which every organization and institution which stood to gain by their destruction gleefully participated. CIA penetration of the American labour movement during this period is a matter of record.[30]

Mine Mill's record of effective trade union action and constructive participation in community affairs in Sudbury made it more difficult to dislodge than its labour and CCF opponents anticipated. New jurisdictions like the uranium mines of Elliot Lake went to the Steelworkers, who were clearly favoured by the labour relations boards in Toronto and Ottawa, but the raids on established Mine Mill locals in Ontario were largely unsuccessful throughout the 1950s. In 1955, with its American section crumbling under the anti-Communist onslaught, the Canadian section of Mine Mill became formally autonomous within the international union.

The turning point in Mine Mill's defensive battle for survival in Canada came in 1958 when it ventured into its first strike against INCO. The company, faced with the loss of its U.S. stockpile contracts and rapidly rising inventories, laid off 1,000 workers in Sudbury and 300 in Port Colbourne and challenged the union to strike. Judge D.C. Thomas,

30. George Morris, *The CIA and American Labour,* International Publishers, New York, 1967.

chairman of the conciliation board, admitted to union representatives "that he felt the company had not even come to the conciliation session to bargain but rather because of the statutory obligation on them to do so."[31]

Local 598, which at that time included both INCO and Falconbridge workers, rashly met INCO's dare head-on, after 82 percent of 13,000 members voted in favour of strike action. Faced with an offer of no wage increase whatsoever, Mine Mill walked out in September 1958 and stayed out nearly three months. The result was a serious defeat with the workers returning to the job under a humiliating three year contract providing wages increases totalling only six percent.

In the wake of this setback a "reform" executive under Don Gillis was elected, with one of its pledges being closer liason with the Canadian Labour Congress. This was later interpreted to encompass negotiations for a merger of Mine Mill with the United Steelworkers, precipitating a terrible internal struggle which tore Sudbury apart and finally brought the Steelworkers to town.

The stage for the Steelworkers' takeover of most of Mine Mill's nickel jurisdiction was set during the reelection campaign of the Gillis executive in 1959, when the anti-Communist campaign in Sudbury was intensified by the Roman Catholic Church, the *Sudbury Star,* and Mayor Joe Fabbro among others. At a massive family life conference attended by 8,000 people at the Sudbury Arena in October 1959, Archibishop Berry lectured his audience on the dangers of totalitarianism. Lest anyone think INCO or Falconbridge was under attack, Mayor Fabbro sharpened the point:

> Sudbury is reputed to be the hotbed of Communism for all the North American continent. It appears incongruous for such a condition to exist in an area where the inhabitants are better than 60 percent Catholic denomination. It is time we proved ourselves and rid ourselves of a dubious honour. . . . [32]

The Sudbury Star also gave prominent coverage to the activities of university extension lecturer Alexandre Boudreau, who was influential in organizing the Gillis forces. Boudreau termed the 1959 union elections "the last ditch fight between Christianity and Communism." Gillis and his slate won over traditional left-wing candidates led by Nels Thibault in the heaviest voting turnout in years.

By 1961 it was apparent to many members of Mine Mill that the Gillis executive was arranging a merger with the United Steelworkers

31. J. Lang, *op. cit.,* p. 267.
32. "Must Prove Sudbury Communist Area", *Sudbury Star,* October 10, 1959.

without a membership mandate and in violation of the union constitution. Attempts to suspend the executive including a petition by 6,000 members were frustrated by lengthy court injunctions, which had the effect of paralyzing local 598 while Steel mobilized for its most determined raid ever.

A well-orchestrated series of events in 1961 once more created extremely bad press for Mine Mill. In Washington the Subversive Activities Control Board, which had harassed Mine Mill throughout the 1950s, reopened hearings on the union with six Steel organizers as its chief witnesses. Late in the year Mine Mill was publicly attacked by two U.S. cabinet officers, Arthur Goldberg and Robert Kennedy. In Canada the Commissioner of the RCMP, George McLelland, warned of penetration of organized labour by the Communist Party and urged support of the Gillis faction of Local 598, remarks which were endorsed in the House of Commons by Justice Minister Davey Fulton. The rumour spread that Don Gillis, who was on cordial terms with John Diefenbaker and became a Progressive Conservative federal candidate, was being groomed as a potential Minister of Labour.

The deck was thus heavily stacked against Mine Mill as the recertification vote between it and the Steelworkers approached in February 1962. The last two months of open campaigning produced a blizzard of advertising, a number of near riots, and a legacy of bitterness among the working people of Sudbury which in some ways continues to the present day. For all the effort expended in discrediting the Mine Mill union, the attempt very nearly failed. When the results of the INCO vote were finally announced in June 1962, the Steelworkers counted 7,182 supporters and Mine Mill 6,951 out of 14,333 eligible. Steel won the right to represent INCO workers by the narrowest imaginable margin, 15 votes more than the required absolute majority. Mine Mill retained its Falconbridge stronghold when Steel withdrew from the vote after numerous forgeries and irregularities in its application for certification came to light.

Subsequent developments in 1967 suggest that the individual left-wingers were acceptable as long as there was no left-wing union. While local 598 continued at Falconbridge as an independent union, the Mine Mill national office merged with the United Steelworkers. Former Mine Mill officers who had been villified as subversives and a menace to freedom and democracy were absorbed into the Steel staff, a belated recognition of their long and effective service to the trade union movement in Canada.

The losers in this inglorious chapter of Canadian labour history were the miners and smelter workers of INCO and Falconbridge. Beset by the interminable raids, which by law were concentrated near the expiry of collective agreements with the companies, Mine Mill was not able to concentrate its full energies on the struggle with the nickel monopolists over wages, working conditions, or in the political domain. During the savage conflict of 1962 and the changeover to the Steelworkers alone, INCO employees went 19 months without a wage increase.

That the mining companies found advantage in labour's internicine warfare was revealed as early as 1949 when Mine Mill was expelled from the Canadian Congress of Labour. The *Globe & Mail*, long a voice of the Ontario mining industry, reversed its editorial attacks on Mine Mill and defended it against the action of the CCL, to the mild embarrassment of the union's leaders. This demonstrated no sudden affection for the left-wing union, but a growing fear of the CCL and the CCF, which also posed potential difficulties for the mine owners. Divide and conquer is the time-tested strategy, and it proved quite effective throughout the 1950s and early 1960s.

OWNING IS EASIER THAN WORKING FOR A LIVING, AND SAFER TOO

The two trade unions have slowly squeezed modest pension benefits, better paid holidays and other fringe benefits out of their reluctant employers INCO and Falconbridge. In the crucial area of wages, the range of basic rates for various skills has risen from $.65-$.95 an hour in 1945 to $4.17-$5.78 negotiated for 1974. These gains are not as substantial as they appear at first glance, a 1967 Laurentian University report points out:

> Until recently it was widely supposed that wages paid in Sudbury were higher than those of other Ontario centres. This cherished belief was more apparent than real when allowance was made for the different conditions. First there is evidently higher mortality and much shorter working life in the Sudbury area. In addition people require payment to offset geographical isolation and the lack of other . . . amenities of life. The cost of living is undoubtedly greater, not only in terms of actual prices but as regards extra expenditures that are necessary because of the climate and other conditions peculiar to the area. . . . It is hardly likely that wages on a comparable basis were ever much superior here than elsewhere.[33]

The report also showed that real wage rates in Sudbury, after taking account of inflation, stood still between 1957 and 1964, a period encompassing the unsuccessful strike of 1958 and the intense battle

33. J.R. Winter, *op. cit.*, p. 31.

between Mine Mill and the United Steelworkers. It also stated that real wage rates increased 40 percent more in all of Ontario than they did in Sudbury between 1951 and 1964, a substantial decline in the relative wage status of the Nickel Capital.

In non-wage issues, although Mine Mill and Steel have had some success in improving working conditions, the mining industry continues to be physically very dangerous. In the words of a 1972 federal government report:

> Mining as a whole and each sub-sector of it, including surface mining, have some of the highest accident rates in industry, ranging from 1.5 to 10 times those for 'all industries' in the U.S. and Canada.[34]

The civil servants state that "miners are still quite unjustifiably exposed to accident and disease."[35] Since 1945 over 900 Ontario miners have died from accidents on the job, and the impact of industrial diseases is only now being more fully recognized.[36] INCO's sintering plant, which before its closure in 1963 had long been dubbed "The Black Hole of Calcutta" has been linked with lung cancer among 30 men who formerly worked there, three-quarters of them now dead.[37]

In addition to the outright deaths there have been 80,000 non-fatal compensible accidents in Ontario mines and smelters since 1945, and INCO and Falconbridge have accounted for a considerable portion of this human wear and tear. Between 1960 and 1972, 65 men died from work accidents in the service of INCO and 19 died toiling for Falconbridge, four in 1972 alone. At Falconbridge another 135 to 185 were maimed one way or another each year, while at INCO with its larger work force the non-fatal injuries reported ranged from 1,240 in the strike year of 1969 to 1,990 the following year. The non-fatal accident rate at Falconbridge appears to be about half that at INCO where it runs steadily at about one accident per year for each ten employees, but Falconbridge has a poorer record of fatalities in relation to labour force.[38]

In testimony before Ontario's Ham Commission on mine safety

34. D.B. Brooks and D.R. Berry, *Mine Health and Safety as an Analytic Problem*, MR 125, Department of Energy, Mines and Resources, Ottawa, 1972, p. 1.
35. *Ibid.*, p. 19.
36. Mines Inspection Branch, *Annual Reports*, Ontario Department of Mines, Toronto and Mines Accident Prevention Association of Ontario, *Annual Reports*, 1967-73, Toronto.
37. "Lethal dust and a union that didn't care", *Globe and Mail*, September 28, 1974.
38. Mines Inspection Branch, *op. cit.*, and Mines Accident Prevention Association of Ontario, *op. cit.*

Sudbury union representatives identified intense heat in the deeper mine workings and inadequate ventilation as the major threats to worker safety, due to both long term effects and immediate stress and fatigue which render men prone to accidents. One INCO worker claimed that underground temperatures on occasion reach 130 degrees F. at the 7200 foot level of the Creighton mine, and that a government health official on an inspection tour collapsed and had to be carried from the shaft.[39]

Mine Mill Local 598 at Falconbridge has called for an end to overtime, shorter working hours, compulsory transfer of underground workers to other jobs with no pay loss after a maximum of 15 years, and the inclusion of rheumatism and arthritis as compensible industrial diseases. The unions are also critical of the production bonus schemes which encourage dangerous working practices.

Mine health and safety, like environmental pollution control, is an area of responsibility in which the provincial government has been lethargic and ineffectual. It relies heavily for its safety programs on the Mine Accidents Prevention Association of Ontario, a voluntary group staffed by the mining companies and paid for by the Workmens' Compensation Board. In the civil service a pro-employer atmosphere prevails. Of 19 district and chief engineers in the engineering branch of the department concerned with mine regulation, in 1972 no less than 16 were former mining company employees.[40] To rise in government service, or to keep open the alternative of returning to the private sector, these people avoid any risk of being labelled crusaders. The result is something less than stern and vigorous inspection and enforcement, with powerful circumstantial evidence indicating that government mine inspectors tip off mining companies to allow them time to clean up before inspection of work areas takes place.[41]

Ontario goverment performance on health and safety is typified by the response of Allan Lawrence, then Minister of Mines, to a complaint by the United Steelworkers about INCO's roaster department in 1970. Lawrence rejected the union's description of dangerous gas and dust conditions, thereby implying that a government inspection had revealed no problem. His letter brushing off their warnings, union officials later discovered, was based *word for word* on a letter from INCO's superintendent of safety, to whom the government had referred

39. "Inspector collapsed, safety probe told", *Toronto Star*, January 30, 1975.

40. "An *Alternatives* interview with Elie Martel, MPP", *Alternatives*, *Vol, 2*, #3, Spring 1973, Peterborough. Also see: *Debates of the Ontario Legislature*, Queen's Printer, December 14, 1972, p. 5734-5738. This Ontario Hansard gives a list of names and employment histories.

41. *Alternatives*, *op. cit.*

the complaint. In his own addendum to the INCO-ghosted correspondence, Lawrence rejected charges that he was in collusion with the
company. ''The accusation is so ridiculous no comment is necessary,''
the minister wrote indignantly.[42] What is ridiculous is that anyone can
still be asked to believe that Conservative government policies are not
tailored to the needs and demands of the mining corporations.

   In addition to continuing health and safety problems, the nickel
workers and their unions have faced a great deal of instability in their
employment with INCO and Falconbridge. INCO, which sets the
pattern in labour relations, has repeatedly hit the labour force with
substantial layoffs coinciding with collective bargaining. A gross example was the company's performance in 1958, the fateful year for
Mine Mill. But in 1962-63 the Steelworkers had to bargain from
scratch, fighting for such an elementary provision as the union check-
off, and INCO further strengthened its hand by laying off 2200 employees in September 1962. Falconbridge also laid off 530 men as its big
U.S. stockpile contract terminated.

   The Sudbury workers were further stifled in their collective
demands in 1966 when wildcat walkouts exposed the Steelworkers to
threats of a multi-million dollar lawsuit by INCO, withdrawn as part of
a more modest than hoped for settlement. Not until 1969, eleven years
after the crunch of 1958, did the unions make major gains and then only
after a seven week strike while nickel was in strong demand. The record
seems to indicate that the now-traditional pattern of three-year contracts
gives INCO and Falconbridge greater maneuverability than the unions
across the bargaining table. The companies have at their disposal not
only their normal power to build inventories in anticipation of a strike,
but also the possibility that bargaining will take place during a cyclical
downturn in sales during which a strike causes little damage. It may
even be welcomed as a means of trimming expenses and reducing
inventory.

   The resulting contracts guarantee no work stoppages for three
years when sales may be strong and profits high. This happened again
prior to the 1972 negotiations. Both Falconbridge and INCO cut back
severely between August 1971 and April 1972 when faced by soft
markets, with INCO laying off 6,000 employees, fully one-third of its
labour force. Falconbridge deferred its Sudbury development projects
late in 1971.[43]

---

42. *Ibid.*, p. 12-15, for full reprints of the INCO letter and its reproduction on
    Lawrence's letterhead.
43. Financial Post Corporation Service, *Falconbridge Nickel Mines Ltd.*, June 12,
    1974, p. 5.

INCO signed its collective agreement with Steel in July, 1972 and Falconbridge reached an almost identical contract with Mine Mill a month later. The Falconbridge development activity resumed in February 1973, while INCO hired back more gradually as it was embarked on a major reinvestment program which eliminated many jobs.

Prior to the 1972 negotiations Falconbridge President Marsh Cooper issued dire warnings about rising costs and declining ore reserves and grades in the Sudbury mines, possibly with a view to softening labour's bargaining position. Falconbridge and INCO both experienced a sharp reduction in profits in 1971, but once again the conjuncture was more favourable for them than for the employees. With the new collective agreements safely in hand and markets strengthening, the companies resumed expansion in Sudbury and initiated a series of price increases for nickel totalling 54 percent between 1972 and 1974, restoring a healthy margin of profitability.

The 1972 contract provided an across-the-board increase of 80 cents an hour spread over three years, a 23 percent gain over 1971 wages for the lowest classification and 16 percent for the highest. Inflation was so severe that the companies agreed to reopen the wage clause in 1974. Mine Mill president Jim Tester reported to his members that in spite of the extra increase, their real wages in 1975 would still be slightly lower than they had been at the beginning of the contract.[44]

The 1975 labour negotiations will again take place in a climate of business recession, layoffs and large inventories which will make a strike potentially suicidal. On balance the unions have experienced great difficulty in capturing for their members either a large or a stable slice of the monopoly profits INCO and Falconbridge enjoy.

CANADA DOTES ON MINING

During 1974 the debate in Canada over the role of extractive industries in the national economic life gained drama as the oil crisis focussed attention on resource prices, supplies, profits and taxation. The Mining Association of Canada, the official industry lobby, deluged the country in advertisements proclaiming "Canada Counts on Mining", and wondering in those unforgettable full page ads, "Does Anybody Out There Give a Damn if the Mining Industry is *Taxed* to *Death?*" (original emphasis). This campaign was part of a highly-visible upsurge in institutional advertising conducted by several large resource corporations — Noranda, Imperial Oil and CPR, which were clearly concerned that public opinion might be turning against their methods of operation and their highly favoured tax status.

44. "Buying power declines despite allowance", *Northern Life*, November 20, 1974.

These companies defend themselves with slick ads and some not-so-slick arguments. They claim to be operating in a high-risk environment, particularly in the search for new mineral deposits. They claim to be a major and beneficial contributor to Canada's foreign trade. And while the employment they generate is small in relation to capital investment, they claim to create jobs far in excess of the number directly involved in mineral extraction. The indirect employment multiplier has been bloated as high as 10 in some of their propaganda, but in other places a factor of three additional jobs for each of the 150,000 people actually on their payrolls in all of Canada, is mentioned. [45]

The self-serving rationalizations of these corporations and their owners have come under intense scrutiny in recent years. The Carter Royal Commission on Taxation, the NDP under David Lewis, and Liberal ex-cabinet minister Eric Kierans,[46] among others, have subjected the industry defenses to withering criticism which has somewhat influenced the provincial governments of British Columbia, Saskatchewan, Manitoba and even Ontario to attempt stiffer taxation of the resource sector. Unfortunately the political and economic clout of the large companies has largely thwarted this tendency.

The tax privileges of the major resource corporations are truly amazing. During the 1965-69 period studied by Kierans in his *Report on Natural Resources Policy in Manitoba*, the metal mining industry in Canada racked up profits of $3.1 billion. Because of pathetic tax laws only $591 million of this was taxable and the people of Canada through their government received only $366 million in taxes, about 12 percent of total profits. These breaches in the tax system are not just loopholes, but gaping wounds.

Kierans' data also indicates that in the same period the mining industry was experiencing galloping monopoly: the number of companies declined through failure, takeover and merger from 852 in 1965 to 272 by 1969. This number had declined further to 198 by 1971. By 1971 forty-one mining companies with assets over $25 million controlled 92 percent of all metal mining assets in Canada, while 14 of them with assets over $100 million, including INCO and Falconbridge, controlled fully 73 percent of the industry's assets.[47] The main risk in the industry seems to be that of being gobbled up by these giants as they expand their control using untaxed earnings and unpaid taxes.

45. "More for Canadians from Canada's Mining Industry", *The Falcon,* July-August 1974, p. 5.

46. Eric Kierans, *Report on Natural Resources Policy in Manitoba,* McGill University, 1973.

47. Statistics Canada, 61-207, *Corporation Financial Statistics, 1971,* and 61-208, *Corporation Taxation Statistics 1971,* Ottawa, 1974.

"The risk image," says Kierans, who was once president of the Montreal Stock Exchange and knows whereof he speaks,

> . . . stems from the association in the public mind of two fringe activities, mining stock speculation and individual prospecting, that have only the barest connection with today's mining industry. Stock promoters armed with leases sell probabilities, "properties lying adjacent to", "geological surveys indicate", "exploratory drilling is planned for", etc. This is simply trafficking in paper and is unrelated to the mainstream of the industry. . . . The search for paper gains involves risk, like bingo, racetrack betting or gambling at Las Vegas, but this has little to do with the realities of the extractive industries.[48]

In the age of monopoly mining corporations and scientific exploration on a continuing, large scale basis, the chief risks in mining are not born by the companies. They are born by their hourly-rated employees, who as we have seen are subject to massive recurrent layoffs, frequent physical danger and steady erosion of their health.

Two of the very largest mining corporations are INCO and Falconbridge. INCO's global assets by 1973 had reached $2.2 billion, while the Falconbridge Group showed assets in excess of $700 million. In the period 1967-73, INCO reaped after-tax profits of $1,041 million but paid only $341 million in taxes for an effective rate of taxation of 25 percent. By 1973 its deferred taxes, an interest-free loan from the government of Canada, had reached the stupendous total of $274 million, approaching in value the company's entire inventory of refined metals. This dodge is worth about $25 million annually, and led David Lewis to dub INCO one of the largest corporate welfare bums.

Falconbridge, operating on a smaller scale, played the tax-dodging game even more skillfully. Between 1965 and 1971 its after-tax profits on its integrated nickel operation were $91 million and it paid only $9 million in income taxes, an effective tax rate of nine percent. Its deferred taxes by 1971 were $25 million, more than the company's inventory of refined metals. Far from being taxed to death, these corporations are being heavily subsidized through low taxes and interest-free loans at the expense of the general public.

As for the degree of risk inherent in their operations, the numbers speak for themselves. In the profit-and-loss private enterprise system, losses for monopolies are almost unknown. INCO has shown a profit in every year since it incorporated in Canada in 1928, with the single exception of 1932. Its profits, without adjusting for inflation, totalled more than $2.8 billion by 1973, with retained earnings over $1 billion

48. E. Kierans, *op. cit.*, p. 15.

and shareholders' equity of $1.2 billion. In the period of 1952-73 Falconbridge and later the Falconbridge Group showed a profit in every year but one, with the total mounting to $363 million including retained earnings of $205 million. Shareholders' equity was about $290 million by the end of the period.

The significance of the high-level tax avoidance engaged in by these corporations with the blessing and encouragement of a cooperative federal government cannot be emphasized too strongly. The situation may be getting worse. Certainly ever-larger sums escape the government with each passing year, as an Ontario NDP research study of the treasury raid of 1970 indicates:[49]

CANADA METAL MINING 1970

	$ million
Book profit before tax	883
Deduct:	
Exempt mine income	180
Other (including Canadian dividends)	135
Total non-exempt income	568
Deduct:	
Accelerated depreciation	106
Exploration, development, depletion	175
Charity, provincial mining tax, other	54
Taxable profit (after adjustment for losses)	218
Income tax paid (federal and provincial)	115

In 1970 the industry as a whole paid income taxes of 53 percent on taxable profit, but only 13 percent of book profit. These figures indicate how small the public benefits from the mining industry really are in relation to the economic surplus it produces. It is in this manner that corporations have become the principal savings mechanism of Canadian society, and through reinvestment of their retained earnings decide what it will, and what it will not, become.

The behavior of INCO and Falconbridge in this latter respect embodies a dual strategy. On one hand they have constantly increased the rate of exploitation of Canadian ores, particularly in Sudbury, and continue to do so in step with the long-term increase in industrial

49. "Revenue from Mining Industry", Ontario New Democratic Party Research office, mimeo, July 17, 1974.

demand. On the other hand a rapidly growing proportion of new investment is being shifted by these transnational companies to new mining areas outside Canada, as exemplified by INCO in Guatemala and Indonesia and Falconbridge in Africa and the Dominican Republic.

At 1973 rates of production the stated Canadian reserves of Falconbridge and INCO will last 20 years. These reserves have risen over the years as discovery outpaced the growth in mine production, but the quality of the reserves has been declining and the cost of exploiting them rising as the mines are driven ever-deeper under the Sudbury basin. Many of the shafts are 3,000 and 4,000 feet deep now, with a few down to 6,000 and 7,000 feet. Canadian nickel, like Canadian oil, is a fast-wasting asset which has been used to build vast corporate empires and private wealth with minimal returns and little lasting benefit to its nominal owners, the people of Canada.

The consequences for Sudbury are not encouraging. The Nickel Capital of the World will enter a period of economic decline within the next decade, as the companies put Sudbury on a maintenance basis after the current round of investment to provide for the final 10 to 15 years run. The figures indicate they will find it necessary to gradually depreciate their fixed investment in the area and transfer the liquid funds to their newer expansion projects, some in Canada but most overseas. The fruits of corporation-dictated Canadian and Ontario government policies which have allowed rapid exploitation of the resource at give-away tax rates and modest prices are now ripe.

The reluctance of governments in Canada to impose economic policy on the corporations parallels the deficiencies of environmental and health and safety policies earlier described. Falconbridge, for example, has not only been slow with its pollution abatement program. It has shown no haste in complying with another Ontario law passed in 1969 requiring refining in Canada of 51 percent of ores mined in Ontario by 1975. At one point Falconbridge envisaged a $150 million refinery with a nickel capacity of 40 million pounds annually to be located in Becancourt, Quebec, but it postponed the project in 1971 "pending improvement in the company's financial position."[50]

The problem for Falconbridge in this case was that its 100 million pound Norwegian refinery is geared to handle the entire Sudbury ore production, and extensive new refining capacity in Canada would create supply problems for the European facility. The company could conceivably have resolved this dilemma by bringing into production the rich but remote ores of its subsidiary, New Quebec Raglan Mines in the

50. Financial Post Corporation Service, *Falconbridge Nickel Mines Ltd.*, November 26, 1974, p. 2.

Ungava district, which contain nickel reserves equal to one-third of the company's other Canadian properties. The Ungava ores would go to Norway, freeing a portion of the Sudbury output for refining in Canada.[51]

Despite the Ontario legislation Falconbridge rejected this alternative, favouring instead the combination of expansion in the Dominican Republic and an acceleration of its exploitation in Sudbury. Combined nickel-copper deliveries from Sudbury increased from 130 million pounds in 1969 to 153 million in 1973, a rise of 18 percent, while the volume of ore mined leaped a startling 48 percent between 1969 and 1970 and has continued at the higher level since. Those were the years in which Ontario announced both new pollution control standards and the Canadian refining requirement.

On February 21, 1975 the government of Ontario amended the Mining Tax Act to disallow deductions from income for the cost of offshore processing. Falconbridge announced that the change, which affected its Norwegian facility, would cut $8 million from its estimated 1974 profit of $30 million and said the change was "completely unexpected".[52] Apparently the company had not believed the government was serious about its refining policy, or expected to be granted an exemption. While Falconbridge made "continuing representations" to have the tax measure modified, the Conservative government continued its preparations for what was expected to be a tough re-election fight in 1975.

RESOURCE COLONIES GET LEFT IN THE LURCH
The rapid exhaustion of Sudbury reserves practised by INCO and Falconbridge has been encouraged by Liberal governments in Ottawa through the extensive tax favours previously outlined. Structurally the Canadian economy has become wedded to the process, as the Mining Association of Canada is quick to remind us:

> Canada is the third largest mineral producing nation in the world. . . . Mining and mineral based products account for 26 percent of Canada's commodity exports. They are one of the mainstays in our efforts to pay our way in the world.[53]

The MAC tries to refute critics of Canada's mining taxation subsidies

51. "Falconbridge: l'usine de Becancourt couterait $150 millions", *Le Devoir*, October 8, 1974, p. 32.
52. "Falconbridge learns tax change will reduce profit by $8 million", *Globe & Mail*, March 7, 1975.
53. Advertisement, *Financial Post*, August 3, 1974, p. 4.

by arguing that overall industry return on assets is comparable to other industries; 7.6 percent from 1969-73 compared with 7.1 percent for manufacturing and 6.8 percent for all industries, according to their figures. This in itself is a significant difference, but it ignores the basic contention of the industy's critics who maintain that far too much of the nation's scarce capital resources have been pumped into extractive industries because of their privileged tax status. Total assets in metal mining in Canada rocketed from $3.6 billion in 1965 to $6.1 billion in 1969, a 70 percent increase in only four years fueled by the absurdly low rates of taxation.[54]

Eric Kierans, who has forcefully pointed out that by such policies Canada relentlessly squanders its non-renewable public wealth without laying the groundwork for a sound economic future, poses the larger problem in this way:

> If Canada cannot break out of its developing nation status, i.e. heavy reliance on staple exports, it is because our federal policy makers have so decided. They cling to the image of a Canada whose growth depends on the export of its wealth. They fail to see that their policies work against the real development that comes from the transformation of raw materials by human skills into final products.[55]

Other Canadian writers have elaborated on this dilemma.[56] The overdevelopment of capital-intensive extractive export industries has major negative consequences for the evolution of Canadian society. It simultaneously restricts the availability of capital for other purposes, and blocks the possibility of exporting processed goods embodying greater labour content.

The situation, which is largely the result of extensive foreign ownership of the Canadian economy, is constantly made worse by that same foreign ownership. The Ontario legislature's Select Committee on Economic and Cultural Nationalism reports that in 1968 sixty-three percent of all mining industry assets were owned by non-residents of Canada.[57] Much of the economic surplus from Canada's short-sighted resource policies not only escapes the tax man, but escapes the country altogether.

54. E. Kierans, *op. cit.*, p. 15.

55. *Ibid.*, p. 9.

56. See: Robert Laxer ed., *Canada Ltd.: The Political Economy of Dependency*, McClelland and Stewart Ltd., Toronto, 1973.

57. Kates, Peat, Marwick & Co., *Foreign Ownership and the Mining Industry*, prepared for the Ontario Select Committee on Economic and Cultural Nationalism, 1973, p. 16.

The resource sell-out policy has a corollary in Canada's now-customary high level of unemployment, and the weaknesses of the country's unbalanced economic structure will be further revealed in the current economic crisis. That the resource-export economy is increasingly incapable of fully utilizing the talents and energies of Canada's working population will soon be apparent to growing numbers of citizens.

Eric Kierans and others of similar liberal persuasion, having perceptively detailed these symptoms of economic folly and illness, assume that rational understanding will lead governments to administer the cure. In the case of mining this is supposed to involve higher taxation and a rechanneling of economic surplus from mining companies to the public purse. Unfortunately this scenario takes little account of the monopolization of the industry, the enormous political power of the owners of monopoly capital, and their unshakeable determination to defend their privileges regardless of the consequences for the majority of the population.

Pierre Trudeau described this reality in the phrase later picked up by David Lewis and the NDP during the 1972 federal election. Rationalizing his government's failure to enact basic tax reform, the Prime Minister confessed:

> . . . it's likely we heard more from the vested interests than we did from the little taxpayer who didn't have . . . the high-paid lawyers to speak for him. . . . I suppose in participatory democracy there will always be some whose voice is louder than others.[58]

Canada's leading politician was corroborating the argument advanced in chapter five, that large transnational corporations are not regulated by independent governments, but are the single most important factor in determining both the composition of governments and their policies.

Unmistakably one of the "louder voices" to which Trudeau referred is the Mining Association of Canada, which was and continues to be vociferously opposed to reduction of the industry's tax privileges and rapid exploitation practices. To drive home their views the mining corporations have used both carrot and stick on wavering politicians. The public is treated to only an occasional glimpse of the carrots as they pass between corporations, political parties and individual elected officials, but the stick is often waved in plain view for all to see, as in the recent MAC publicity campaign.

58. CTV, December 28, 1971, cited in David Lewis, *op. cit.*, p. iv.

It's time for governments—federal and provincial—to end their squabble over tax revenues from the mining industry and reverse the trend towards increasing interference and management of this vital industry. Already exploration and development activities are being drastically curtailed in certain provinces and mining companies are being forced to accelerate their exploration efforts outside Canada since they must maintain supplies for their customers. That's a basic fact of business life. . . . The hard fact is Canada has already become a much less attractive place for the large amounts of risk capital required for mining. Mining, you see, is your business too. Let's not destroy it.[59]

This thinly disguised blackmail by large corporations which have already received hundreds of millions in tax concessions and interest-free government loans is an interesting mixture of fact and fancy. Companies like INCO and Falconbridge are already proceeding with overseas investment of their Canadian-generated profits despite this country's lax tax structure. But it is true, as the oil companies have recently proved, that this process can be accelerated if governments attempt to corral some of the fabulous resource revenues for the public domain. Capital can and does go on strike, and in the hands of transnational corporations it is considerably more mobile than labour.

Falconbridge, which ranks behind only INCO, Alcan, Noranda and Cominco among Canadian mining giants, plays a leading role in the lobbying and public opinion-moulding activities of the Mining Association of Canada. One of its men, D.R. DeLaporte, is a member of the executive committee and second vice-president of the MAC, and serves Falconbridge as vice-president for the western minerals division, president of Wesfrob, president of United Keno Hill, and president and managing director of Giant Yellowknife Mines, the company associated with the arsenic pollution of the Yellowknife water supply. Five other Falconbridge men sit on the 41 member board of the MAC: R.B. Fulton (McIntyre president); G.P. Mitchell and D.R. Lochhead (Falconbridge vice-presidents); W.A. Moore (managing director of the Manitoba Manbridge Mine); and W.J. Tough (retired vice-president of Wesfrob). Three of these gentlemen are doing double duty. Lochhead is president of the Ontario Mining Association, Moore of the Manitoba Mining Association, and Tough holds the same post with the Mining Association of British Columbia. With this all-star lineup in the field, the interests of American multi-millionaire Howard B. Keck are well and truly represented in the councils of the Canadian mining industry and in the formation of Canadian mining policy. The industry's giant

59. Advertisement, *Financial Post, op. cit.*

corporations appear to have achieved a far more effective and highly-coordinated united front than the various provincial governments attempting to impose a fairer tax burden on them.

Still, the poor record of mining giants like Falconbridge on pollution, on municipal financing, on health and safety conditions, on employment stability, on legalized income tax avoidance, on processing in Canada, on over-rapid resource extraction, and on manipulation of the political process will continue to generate opposing pressures in Canada for much-needed changes. These pressures will be heightened by an increasing revulsion over the role such companies play in their rapidly expanding imperialist activities in the Third World, as described for Falconbridge in the following two chapters.

The Kierans concept of expanding the role of crown corporations in mining as a means of controlling the industry, breaking the blackmail power of the corporations, and capturing more of the economic surplus for public benefit will seem logical, sensible and vitally necessary to more and more Canadians. When this happens, we will begin to see the ugliest side of gigantic private wealth and corporate power. For an understanding of how corporate citizens and their owners respond to democratic decisions of which they disapprove, Canadians will do well to keep in mind the lessons of Chile and of another field of Falconbridge operations, the Dominican Republic.

CHAPTER SEVEN

The Caribbean Crews: Falconbridge Dominicana

Many Dominican politicians . . . see the Dominican problem as if it were circumscribed by our frontiers. And they despair because they think there is no solution within the Dominican Republic. But the country is on the battlefront of a world-wide struggle. In this struggle things will happen rapidly and will have very profound effects on our own situation. . . . The Dominican Republic is not a country which makes its own history. Others have always been making our history for us. First the Spaniards; later the English, the French, the Dutch, the Haitians; still later the North Americans. The United States made our history for us when it invaded us in 1965. And it continues making it for us today, when in fact we are still occupied by the United States although the forces of occupation are not visible.

     — Juan Bosch, former president of the Republic, speaking in 1971.

The truth of the matter is that the Dominican people have benefitted far more than the shareholders of Falconbridge from (our) operation. . . . I cannot comment on the widening gap between the rich and the poor in the Dominican Republic. That is something over which we have no control.

     —Marsh Cooper, president of Falconbridge, December 6, 1974.

To meet the rapidly growing industrial demand for nickel and pioneer the new supply strategy of the nickel monopolists, Falconbridge has added 65 million pounds to its overall capacity with the construction of an integrated mining-reduction ferro-nickel complex on the Caribbean island of Hispanola in the Dominican Republic. This technically sophisticated and highly efficient installation, begun in 1968 and completed in 1972 at a capital cost in the neighbourhood of $195 million, represents the largest single expansion of the nickel industry to date in the 1970s.

According to Falconbridge, as it ventured into the troubled political climate of the Caribbean, the vast project of its subsidiary Falconbridge Dominicana (Falcondo) would be of great benefit to the Dominican Republic. The massive infusion of investment would provide the Dominicans, in return for the surrender of their nickel resource, a substantial bounty of foreign exchange earnings, tax revenues, jobs, new skills, new technology, and extensive improvements in local housing, municipal services, education and medical services. In short Falconbridge made the shopworn pledges of progress and mutual benefit which are the habitual litany of transnational corporations.

A LAND OF STARK CONTRASTS

If these promises were true, their realization would be a godsend to the Dominican people. The overwhelming majority of the population of 4.5 million lives a harrowing existence, unable to maintain even the minimum standards of good health. The life expectancy of a Dominican peasant is 40 years. The per capita income in 1969 was $323, a figure which masks one of the most unequal income distributions in the world: the poorest 40 percent of the population receives only 12.2 percent of the income pie, while the richest 20 percent hog 57.5 percent.[1] Wage levels are pathetic, with agricultural workers earning as little as $1.50 to $2.00 per day when they can work. Social statistics are hard to come by, but in an adult male work force of 800,000 the unemployment in 1971 was estimated at 300,000.[2] Many of the dispossessed gravitate to the cities in search of sustenance. The barrios of the capital city Santo Domingo with its population of about 600,000 are teeming concentrations of misery.

The social and economic structure of the Dominican Republic which permits and perpetuates this human sacrifice displays similarities with other Latin American countries. Living off the suffering of masses of impoverished Dominicans is a small, parasitic elite fond of its Mercedes Benzs, palatial residences and other accoutrements of wealth. Less than 500 latifundists, the traditional landlord class, control over 30 percent of the country's limited supply of cultivable land. They

1. *Finance and Development*, IMF and World Bank Group, Sept. 74.
2. C.M. Gutierrez, *The Dominican Republic, Rebellion and Repression*, Monthly Review Press, New York, 1972, p. 13.

employ only a tiny fraction of the rural population, a major factor in the forced migration of rural Dominicans to the urban areas.

In addition to the traditional landed oligarchy, Gulf and Western Corporation and the Dominican government itself are heavily involved in the export-oriented sugar, coffee and tobacco plantation economy producing primarily for shipment to the United States. The "enclosure" of most of the Dominican land base in this manner is at the root of the high food costs and malnutrition which most Dominicans must endure.

The stunted industrial sector, by a quirk of history, is largely state-owned. The dictator Rafael Trujillo assembled at least 65 percent of the entire economy under his personal and family ownership prior to his assassination in 1961, including portions of the cane sugar industry previously held by American interests. The amazing extent of personal control Trujillo achieved during his 30 year reign of terror is detailed in the *Hispanic American Report*:

> Official sources revealed that Trujillo's share of the national wealth had amounted to the following: bank deposits 22%; money in circulation 25%; sugar production 63%; cement 63%; paper 73%; paint 86%; cigarettes 71%; milk 85%; wheat and flour 68%; plus the nation's only airline, its leading newspapers and the three principal radio and television stations. According to the Swiss daily *National Zeitung*, the Trujillo family had deposited no less than $200 million in Swiss banks in the name of fictitious companies.[3]

Trujillo's assassination opened the way for succeeding governments to sell off some of these state holdings to their friends, but many of them are still under the management of CORDE, the state corporation. The huge investment by Falconbridge has also brought in its wake a substantial influx of foreign capital to develop the tourist potential of the island. All this has produced a certain diversification of the ownership statistics but no substantial change in social conditions, which remain abominable.

AMERICAN DOMINATION: THE TRUJILLO ERA
A social and economic structure which so disastrously fails to meet the basic needs of most of its subjects cannot be maintained by consent, but

3. *Hispanic American Report,* cited in Goff & Locker, "The Violence of Domination: U.S. Power and the Dominican Republic" in I.L. Horowitz, et. al., *Latin American Radicalism,* New York, Vintage, 1969, p. 254.

only through coercion. The history of the Dominican Republic is an almost unbroken chain of rebellion countered by violence, terror, repression and death administered since the turn of the century by the United States and its client Dominican governments. An excellent description and analysis of this brutal saga appears in an article by Fred Goff and Michael Locker, "The Violence of Domination: U.S. Power and the Dominican Republic".[4]

In the early decades of the 20th century direct intervention and gunboat diplomacy were in vogue. American troops first landed briefly in the Republic in 1904 to protect a sugar estate and take sides in a dispute over control of the government. One thing led to another:

> In a dozen years from 1904 to 1916, the United States moved from the Roosevelt Corollary to full-scale Marine occupation of the Dominican Republic. First we collected customs, then we forbade insurrection in order to maintain stability, then we held elections with warships in the harbor and sailors or Marines at the polls, then we demanded full control over internal revenues and expenditures as well as over customs, then we demanded the disbanding of the Army and the establishment of a Guardia National (Constabulary); then we sent the Marines.[5]

The direct U.S. occupation lasted from 1916-24, during which time the Marine-trained National Police became the most powerful force on the island. In 1928 the police were reconstituted as an army under the command of Rafael Trujillo. Within two years he engineered a fake uprising and, with the approval of his former U.S. superiors, took command of the Dominican government "to preserve order and prevent bloodshed."[6] In the following thirty years Trujillo built an all-pervasive one-man government and economy on terror, bloodshed, blackmail, an astute distribution of the spoils internally and effective bribery and lobbying in Washington.

> The army was his private instrument of coercion and terror; the oversized officer corps benefitted materially and enjoyed privileged status. . . . Political opposition was erased or manipulated by co-option, imprisonment, exile or murder.[7]

The estimates of murders and executions during Trujillo's reign of terror run to 500,000 including the slaughter in one day of October

4. Goff and Locker, *op. cit*.
5. John B. Martin, U.S. ambassador to the Dominican Republic under president Kennedy and president Johnson in his book *Overtaken by Events: The Dominican Crisis from the Fall of Trujillo to Civil War*, New York, 1966.
6. Goff & Locker, *op. cit.*, p. 252.
7. *Ibid.*, p. 253.

1937 of nearly 25,000 cane-cutters from neighbouring Haiti who were literally hacked to pieces by the Dominican Army. Trujillo was also a torturer par excellence, maintaining numerous dungeons around the country. "I still shudder," wrote one senior *Look* magazine editor, "about Snowball, a dwarf . . . whose specialty was biting off men's genitals." Snowball was only part of the torture apparatus of Trujillo's Military Intelligence Service which also made extensive use of slow-shock electric chairs, electrified rods known as "The Cane", nail extractors, whips, and water tanks full of bloodsucking leeches. [8]

The United States government supported Trujillo partly because of his devout diatribes against Communism, and also because of his influential U.S. business connections. In addition to protecting the interests of South Puerto Rico Sugar, the large plantation controlled by the powerful Kuhn-Loeb banking house and the Rockefeller group, Trujillo made other friends: Joseph Davies (General Foods); Herbert May (the Pittsburgh Mellons, ALCOA); and the Kaplan brothers, molasses dealers with strong influence in the liberal wing of the Democratic party. [9] The Kaplan Fund was exposed in 1964 as a major conduit for CIA funding of various liberal organizations and publications.

Toward the end of the 1950s "The Benefactor's" luck ran out. The crude terror and immense suffering he inflicted on the Dominican people for more than three decades with U.S. collaboration was increasingly an invitation to social revolution and this problem preoccupied American foreign policy planners, especially after the successful Cuban revolution overthrowing Batista in 1959. The U.S. took steps to isolate its long-time Dominican ally economically by manipulation of the sugar quota and politically by encouraging opposition to him within the Dominican army. Trujillo, having outlived his usefulness, was assassinated by army officers in 1961. [10]

THE DESTRUCTION OF DEMOCRACY

Restabilizing the country following the dictator's murder presented the United States with difficulties. Trujillo's extended political and economic monopoly had pre-empted the development of a modern industrial and financial class capable of presenting effective but moderate political leadership. President John F. Kennedy, summarizing the American dilemma, said there were "three possibilities, in order of decreasing preference: a decent democratic order, a continuation of the

---

8.   All reported in John Gerassi, *The Great Fear in Latin America,* Collier Books, New York, 1973, p. 196.

9.   Goff & Locker, *op. cit.,* p. 256.

10. *Ibid.,* p. 261.

Trujillo regime, or a Castroite regime. We must strive for the first, but we cannot really exclude the second until we are sure we can avoid the third."[11]

The U.S. dealt itself a complete hand to cover all contingencies. It temporarily maintained the Trujillo family in power while trying to round up a new conservative coalition to take office by popular election. At the same time it infiltrated the most important opposition force, the social democratic Partido Revolucionario Dominicano (PRD) led by Juan Bosch, with CIA agents. One of the covert operatives, Sacha Volman, played an important part in organizing a large peasant league in support of the PRD and became a trusted advisor to Bosch.[12]

The elections of 1962 produced what was for the army, the conservative oligarchy and the U.S. a worrisome result. Freed from the bondage of Trujillism the people expressed their desire for radical reform by giving the PRD 60 percent of the suffrage in support of its program: profit sharing for workers in industrial and agricultural enterprises, the prohibition of large landholdings, restrictions on foreign ownership of land, redistribution of excess holdings to the landless peasantry, and other social democratic reforms.

The PRD government, as Bosch had feared and publicly predicted prior to the election, was not allowed to survive long. U.S. influence within the PRD was too weak for effective control, and most U.S. aid during his short time in office was channelled to the armed forces. With major U.S. property interests, particularly in sugar, threatened by the land reform, Bosch's support within the Kennedy administration evaporated. The PRD government was overthrown by a military coup in September 1963. The Dominican Republic, which was to have been a model of the Alliance for Progress and a democratic alternative to the Cuban revolution, became once again a U.S.-supervised dictatorship.

11. Cited in Gutierrez, *op. cit.*, p. 145.
12. One time CIA Operative Philip Agee refers to Sacha Volman in his book (*Inside the Company: CIA Diary*, Penguin 1975, pp. 419, 611, 623) as the CIA contract operations officer who in Costa Rica set up the Institute of Political Education (cryptonym ZREAGER). The Institute was used by the CIA to give political training to young reformist hopefuls in Latin America. Agee also attributes the organization of the present vote in favour of Bosch to Volman. Goff & Locker (*op. cit.*, pp. 267, 268, 272) give a more detailed account of Volman's activities including a description of his relationship with the Institute of International Labor Research (IILR) and the J.M. Kaplan Fund. See also Gutierrez *op. cit.* pp. 24-27. According to a group of former intelligence officers who now research and publish information on 'technofascism' the current CIA Chief of Station (COS) in Santo Domingo is Thomas A. Clayton (born February 14, 1927; graduated San Jose State 1951; joined CIA 1956; served in Argentina, Peru, Venezuela, and Bolivia). See Fifth Estate Security Education *Counter-Spy*, Winter 1975, Vol. 2, No. 2, p. 24.

   Contributing to the PRD downfall, Bosch's political base in the peasantry structurally disintegrated with the withdrawal of effort by Volman and his CIA men in the peasant league. PRD support in the working class also suffered from divisions introduced by the "non-political" AFL-CIO labour central in conjunction with the U.S. government-financed American Institute for Free Labor Development. The organizations of those forces which might have sustained the elected government against the coup were too seriously infiltrated to act decisively when the need arose.[13]

   The succeeding government of Reid Cabral was hopelessly corrupt and inefficient. Despite large infusions of U.S. aid the national debt soared to $200 million, unemployment rose near 40 percent, and the country approached economic collapse. The crisis culminated in another coup in 1965, with several army factions vying for power including one supporting a popular uprising in favour of the return of Bosch. Distributing arms to large sections of the population of Santo Domingo, the Constitutionalist forces held their own and began to drive their opponents from the city.

   At this point the U.S. launched its decisive intervention. Announcing that American lives were in danger, President Johnson ordered 20,000 Marines into Santo Domingo.* As it turned out, not one American was killed before or after the invasion, and Johnson later altered the reason for the invasion, saying the revolt was dominated by Communists. This claim too was unprovable, but the basic objective of

13. In recent years there has been a wealth of material published on the penetration and manipulation of the Latin American trade union movement by the United States, its agencies and transnational corporate interests. For information about the American influence in the Dominican Republic see Suzanne Bodenheimer, "The AFL-CIO in Latin America. The Dominican Republic: A Case Study" in Viet Report, Sept.-Oct. 1967: by the same author see also, "U.S. Labor's Conservative Role in Latin America" in The Progressive, Nov. 1967. A research guide on the American Institute for Free Labor Development (AIFLD) can be found in "CIA Labor Operations in Latin America" in Counter-Spy, Winter, 1975, Vol. 2, No. 2; see also Winslow Peck, "Clandestine Enforcement of U.S. Foreign Labor Policy" in Counter-Spy, Fall 1974, Vol. 2, No. 1. Both issues of Counter-Spy contain complementary extensive bibliographies (available from Fifth Estate, P.O. Box 647, Ben Franklin Station, Washington D.C. 20044, USA). Also see: Fred Hirsh, An Analysis of our AFL-CIO Role in Latin America, 1974 (available from 316 South 19th St., San Jose, California, 95116, USA); and Agee, op. cit. for a dramatic personal account of CIA involvement in labour organizations. The North American Congress on Latin America (Box 57, Cathedral Station, New York City, N.Y. 10025, USA) has published numerous excellent articles on the AFL-CIO and AIFLD, the most recent being "Argentina AIFLD Losing Its Grip" in NACLA's Latin America & Empire Report, Nov. 1974, Vol. VIII, No. 9. Also useful is Ronald Radosh, American Labor and United States Foreign Policy, New York, 1969, Random House.

 *Other reports estimate troop strength at 42,000.

U.S. policy was achieved. The Dominican government was kept out of the hands of the PRD which was certainly by this time suspicious of the United States.

During the crisis the Canadian government relied heavily on U.S. sources of information, although it did send Michel Gauvin to hobknob with the Americans as they went about creating a new government. On April 29th External Affairs Minister Martin was able to report: "We have . . . been in touch by telephone with the Falconbridge Nickel plant . . . and we are told all is well in that quarter." On May 3rd Prime Minister Pearson told the Commons: "The Embassy is also investigating reports that the main branch of the Royal Bank of Canada (largest bank in the Dominican Republic) has been looted," while Defense Minister Hellyer admitted there was a Canadian warship in the area on standby.

When it became clear the Americans would never be able to provide proof either of serious danger to American citizens or Communist domination of the Constitutionalist forces, Pearson became very evasive during the House of Commons question period. The Liberals never criticized the American invasion, and Paul Martin apologized for it on May 28th: "It is easy enough to criticize countries which bear the brunt of responsibility when dangerous situations develop. Such criticism might best be directed at the imperfections in our international arrangements."

Only T.C. Douglas and H.W. Herridge of the NDP finally realized what had happened and had the honesty to speak out against it. Douglas on May 28th said the United States was adopting the Johnson doctrine, "namely that (it) reserves the right at any time to intervene unilaterally wherever a country has a government the ideology of which is unacceptable to the United States," and added: "We do not want some new form of colonialism masquerading as an anti-communist crusade."

Between 1965 and 1968 the United States literally drowned the Dominican Republic in money in its efforts to create and legitimize a pro-U.S. government. In a country with an annual budget of about $200 million, the Americans contributed in the three-year period $280 million in grants, $153 million in loans, and a strong contingent of police and army advisers and accompanying funds of about $11 million. This effort set the stage for new elections in 1966 in which the pro-American candidate, Joaquin Balaguer, won a victory over Bosch's PRD in a vote surrounded by charges of fraud, coercion and heavy police repression of the opposition.

Bosch, who until the events of 1965 had believed that the United States would allow social democratic reform in his country, reached a bitter conclusion:

> I believe that in the Dominican Republic Latin America has been given a lesson: the lesson is that it is not possible to establish a democracy with the help of the United States, and neither is it possible to establish a democracy against the United States.[14]

MORE PUPPETRY WITH BALAGUER

The Balaguer government claims to be democratic, and has permitted some "rights" including a relatively free press. Balaguer has had himself re-elected twice, once in 1970 and again in 1974, but both elections were boycotted by the PRD and other parties of the left in protest against the impossibility of a free vote. *Business Latin America*, a weekly report to corporate managers in Latin American, tells why:

> . . . a week before the (1974) elections, the Electoral Council changed voting regulations. The change allowed a voter to cast his ballot at any polling place within his district, rather than strictly at his registered polling station. The opposition claimed this move would lead to widespread fraud, since such votes would be difficult to check adequately. Also, the military came out overtly for Balaguer by wearing his Reformist Party banner. . . . Moreover Balaguer used the mass media extensively (his campaign manager also is the head of state TV and radio) while the opposition claimed it did not have the same access to them.[15]

Lip service to democracy by Balaguer and his government masks a still-vicious Dominican political reality. Balaguer runs a more presentable state than his former mentor Trujillo, under whom he served as the last puppet president, but the present regime is also based on terror. There are 600 or more political prisoners rotting and tortured in his jails, most in on false charges and some not having had the benefit of charges or trials at all.[16] At least 2,500 political opponents have been assassinated or have simply disappeared during his eight-year rule. During the more intense waves of repression the political murder rate is about one a day, more than enough to discourage most open forms of anti-government activity. In 1971 a gang of para-military thugs known as La Banda freely roamed the streets of Santo Domingo under the approving eye of the authorities beating and killing people it believed unfriendly to the government. The group was brought under control only after strong internal and international protest.[17]

14. Cited in Goff & Locker, *ibid.*, p. 275.
15. *Business Latin America*, May 29, 1974, p. 172.
16. Information from the *Comite Permanente por la Libertad de los Presos Politicos* in the Dominican Republic.
17. Latin American Working Group, *La Banda*, Toronto 1972.

The United States contributes to maintaining the Balaguer regime in various ways. The massive aid of the post-invasion period has been cut back, but the aid and training to army and police continue adding to the nearly 1500 Dominicans who received formal Military Assistance Program training between 1964 and 1968.[18] Economic pressures and political repression have combined to drive over 200,000 emigrants from the country since 1965, most of them to New York. This safety valve is of considerable importance to preserving the tenuous stability of the government.

Balaguerism is in effect a modernized Trujillism. The omnipresent slogans, ''God, Trujillo and the Virgin: the Three Great Ones'' are gone, and so is Trujillo's tendency to monopolize profitable sectors of the economy for himself at the expense of foreign capital. President Balaguer and his government have, as might be expected in view of their road to power, a different policy:

> In broad measure we depend on the political and economic collaboration of the native land of Washington and Lincoln and, unlike other Latin American countries, we cannot allow ourselves the luxury of shaking off the yoke of so-called U.S. imperialism to accept others that do represent a humiliating . . . satellization. . . . (a reference to Cuba). Even in the hypothetical event of the installation here of a demagogic government of patriots of the new breed that abounds in Latin America today, it would be absurd to think that our country could insanely launch itself on a course of nationalization inspired by pseudopatriotic reasons or by irresistible impulses of a socialist nature.[19]

The old butcher tactics of The Benefactor have been superceded by modern police methods developed under American tutelage. Selective and controlled terror has replaced the mass persecution of yesteryear. All the same the greatest single obstacle to progress and an improved life for most Dominicans continues to be, as in the past, their American-imposed government. Under Balaguer, as under Trujillo, the land, labour and mineral resources of the country are directed to purposes which have little to do with raising consumption standards for the majority.

THE PECULIAR NEUTRALITY OF FALCONBRIDGE
What is the role of a transnational corporation like Falconbridge in this oppressive scheme of things? Does the company by its policies and

---

18. U.S. Department of Defense, *Military Assistance Facts,* 1969, p. 21, reprinted in NACLA Newsletter, Nov. 1970.

19. Balaguer to the U.S. Chamber of Commerce of Santo Domingo, *El Caribe,* May 1, 1971.

actions support the Balaguer regime, maintain a position of neutrality, or support the potential for urgently needed social change in the unhappy, terror-ridden Republic? The corporate policy has been articulated by President Marsh Cooper:

> . . . all companies in the Falconbridge Group, wherever they operate or wherever they explore, are guided by these basic corporate policies: to conform in a responsible way to the laws of the country in which they find themselves; to take no part in and pass no judgement on the political system that prevails locally; that is, neither condone nor condemn other people's politics.[20]

This lofty statement of neutrality is impossible to put into practice even if it were a true measure of the company's intentions. In practice the company engages, as must all large corporations, in highly political behavior, going to great lengths to support its friends and weaken its enemies.

Falconbridge entered the Dominican Republic in 1955 at the height of Trujillism to explore promising nickel deposits, a decision taken when Robert Anderson was the guiding light of both Ventures and Falconbridge and the company with its stockpile contract figured prominently in U.S. nickel supply planning. The original mineral concessions were in the Maimon district near the city of Bonao, and the company's work proceeded on a small scale including the construction of a pilot plant employing about 175 people to experiment with the complex lateritic ores. For nearly a decade neither market conditions nor the political turmoil of the Dominican Republic provided much encouragement for further development of the properties.

Immediately following the army overthrow of Bosch in 1963, however, Falcondo's attitude altered markedly. Through negotiations with the corrupt and inept Reid Cabral regime the company acquired additional mining concessions and announced its intention of constructing a $78 million refinery.[21] In view of the company's desperate need for markets in North America in this period, the announcement appears to have been designed to shore up the shaky Cabral government rather than reveal any serious spending intentions. Following the Constitutionalist uprising, the U.S. invasion and the stabilization under Balaguer, Falcondo moved ahead in 1966, not with the promised refinery, but with a modernization and expansion of its pilot plant.

The pace of decision-making quickened dramatically following the Superior Oil takeover of the parent companies McIntyre and Falconbridge in 1967. The Texas Nexus provided the basis for arranging

20. President's address to the Falconbridge Annual Meeting, 1974.
21. Gutierrez, op. cit., p. 151.

financing, vital political influence in Washington, and insurance from
the U.S. Overseas Private Investment Corporation. In 1968 Howard
Keck authorized Falcondo's $195 million expansion, and the final
details were negotiated with Balaguer's government in 1969. The
contract was highly favourable to the corporation: 33 percent taxation
on profits, accelerated depreciation, no import duties, and exemptions
from some of the Dominican foreign exchange regulations. The terms
indicated Balaguer's eagerness to attract Falconbridge as a prestige
investor.

Instrumental in these developments was Falcondo general manager Ian Keith, who says the present Dominican mining laws grew out
of his negotiations with the Dominican government. A South African
who gained his first experience in metallurgy with the Oppenheimer
group's Nchanga Copper, Keith joined Falconbridge in 1954, was put
in charge of its Dominican operations almost immediately, and has
lived in the Dominican Republic ever since. John Harbron, the *Financial Post*'s leading reporter on Latin America, notes that Keith "has
become an intimate part of Dominican public life, as much as the
emerging elite of presidents and managers of rejuvenating Dominican
public and private companies who are absorbing some of Falcondo's
way of doing things."[22]

Assisted by his wife, a Spanish-speaking U.S. Foreign Service
officer he married in 1964, Keith has used Falconbridge's Canadian
incorporation and consequent immunity from anti-American sentiment
to pursue a skillful and low-profile image-building campaign. His
connections with "the emerging elite" managing the cluster of companies under CORDE (Corporation of State Enterprises) were important in gaining Dominican equity participation of 9.5 percent in Falcondo, adding a little "Dominicanization" to the controlling interest of
Falconbridge and ARMCO Steel. This same connection with CORDE
and other Dominican public and private companies "was essential in
the search for highly specialized personnel," Harbron reports.[23]

The flavour of Keith's Dominican recruiting is symbolized by the
hiring in 1972 of Gaetan Bucher as chief financial officer. Bucher, a
Swiss-born Dominican banker, had previously conducted a reorganization of the State Sugar Corporation for President Balaguer. On the legal
side Falcondo also has been well-connected with the island's right-wing
establishment.

Its legal counsel is Oficina Troncoso, whose partners are mem-

22. John Harbron, ',Falconbridge finds key to success in Latin America'', *Financial
    Post*, May 12, 1973.
23. *Ibid*.

bers of the powerful old-line Troncoso and Caceres families. . . .
The firm's senior partner, Jesus Maria Troncoso, sits on Falconbridge Dominicana's board. He is the son of Manuel de Jesus
Troncoso de la Concha, the second puppet president for Trujillo
in 1940. In the late 1950s Jesus Maria Troncoso was . . . "one of
the most intimate of Trujillo's courtiers.". . . . Another of the
firm's partners, Ramon Caceres Troncoso, was one of the principal Falconbridge representatives in the 1969 contract negotiations
with the Dominican government. . . . Ramon Caceres Troncoso
was Secretary of Finance under the . . . government which ruled
the island briefly after Trujillo's assassination and later was a
member of the (Reid Cabral) Triumvirate which took power after
the military coup against the Bosch government in 1963. During
the 1965 Constitutionalist uprising, Caceres sought asylum with
his friends . . . in the U.S. embassy.[24]

Ian Keith protests that it is pernicious to link the Falconbridge development with Trujillo and U.S. domination. His insistence on Falcondo's
political neutrality is contradicted by the very nature of its extensive
dealings with Trujillo's and subsequent governments, which with the
exception of the Bosch interlude have been U.S.-dominated, and by its
hirings of influential supporters of those governments. The company's
declarations of political neutrality are clearly inconsistent with its
behavior.

A more convincing presentation of the company's political lean-
ings was provided by Falconbridge president Marsh Cooper at the
official opening ceremonies of Falcondo in 1972:

> There have been achievements here which in my estimation
> would not have been possible anywhere else in the Caribbean,
> and in very few other places throughout the industrialized world.
> We in Falconbridge have found the environment in the Domini-
> can Republic an extremely favourable one in which to do busi-
> ness.[25]

President Balaguer returned Cooper's enthusiastic endorsement by pre-
senting him with the Order of Merit of Duarte, Sanchez and Mella,
Caballero grade, the highest decoration that can be bestowed by the
Dominican government.

Cooper pushed his mutual admiration campaign with the dictator
further in Falconbridge's 1973 annual report: "Grateful recognition is
accorded President Joaquin Balaguer, his Ministers and officials of the

24. F. Goff, "Falconbridge—Made in the U.S.A.", *NACLA's Latin America & Empire
Report*, Vol. VIII, No. 4, April 1974, p. 11.
25. *Northern Miner*, June 29, 1972.

Dominican government whose continued interest and cooperation have been vital factors in the success of the operation.'' Balaguer has used this keen support from the large ''Canadian'' company to maximum advantage. In a *New York Times* advertisement he pointed to Falcon-bridge as proof positive for the financial community of his government's staunch support of private foreign capital.

> Among the sure signs of the climate of security and confidence the Dominican Republic offers foreign investors are the installa-tion of the enormous metallurgical plant by the Falconbridge Co. of Canada for the mining and refining of nickel at a cost of $200 million.[26]

While Falconbridge may continue to deny its involvement in politics, the evidence is that its behavior is highly political. In this case the business decisions and style of operation of Falcondo have de-pended materially on the goodwill of both the Trujillo and Balaguer regimes, and appear to have made a significant contribution to the survival of the latter, reinforcing the thrust of U.S. foreign policy.

COSTS AND BENEFITS: A QUESTION OF CLASS

The economics of Falcondo are supposed to embody principles of mutual advantage. That there are large benefits to the corporation and its bond-holders is beyond doubt. The benefits to the Dominican Repub-lic on close inspection appear to be small and, given the nature of the government, badly distributed.

Of the $180 million construction cost, fully $149 million was spent outside the Dominican Republic for the import, tax-free, of machinery and equipment, with $31 million allocated for the three year construction spending within the country. Prime contractor on the project was Brown & Root, the Texas-based corporate giant whose growth has been based on U.S. military contracts from Texas to Spain to Vietnam, all linked to the political activities of Lyndon Johnson and the rest of the Texas Nexus. ''The Browns were the principal financiers of Johnson's early rise to power, and Lyndon is the man who more than anyone else made them rich,'' is the way one analyst summed up the relationship.[27]

---

26. *New York Times,* October 3, 1971.

27. David Welsh, ''Building Lyndon Johnson'', *Ramparts,* Dec. 1967, p. 52. George Brown, who with his brother built up Brown and Root, also founded Texas Eastern Transmission Corp. This company, one of the top three pipeline companies in the U.S., is involved in oil and gas development in the Canadian north. Marsh Cooper is also on the Texas Eastern board of directors.

For Dominicans there must be more than irony in the idea that the Browns, cronies of the President who authorized the military invasion of their country in 1965, should be among the principal beneficiaries of Falcondo's development. Others who have done well in bringing the new facility to readiness include, according to a Falconbridge prospectus: Dillon, Read, which received $1,150,000 between 1968 and 1970 for services as financial agent; Tilley Carson & Findlay, legal counsel in Canada which received $625,000 during the same period for services to the company and its subsidiaries; and Marsh Cooper's old firm James & Buffam, which received $70,000 for services as consulting geologists.[28] Falconbridge has retained its president's former partners for 10 years at $50,000 a year.

The financing of Falcondo, as outlined in chapter four, has created a situation in which for many years into the future the tax return for the Dominican Republic on its nickel resources will be inconsequential in relation to the value of the product. From total sales of $91 million in 1973, the first year of full production, the yield from the profit tax was only $3 million. Another $3.7 million has been left in the hands of Falcondo as deferred tax according to the accelerated depreciation provisions of the tax law. This is an interest-free loan from the Dominican people to the corporation.

Of the company's operating expenses, only about 12 percent were direct wage outlays to Dominican labour, while most of the balance accrued to foreign nationals in one way or another. Oil was the largest single item, accounting for nearly one-third of operating expenditure, and this cost rose again in 1974. Interest charges were the second largest item, eating up 20 percent of the company's expenditures. The American insurance companies and banks, with an assist from the Canadian Imperial Bank of Commerce and the World Bank, together extracted a huge payment of $17 million in 1973 on behalf of themselves and the owners of capital. In 1973 Falcondo interest payments alone were nearly double the combined wages and taxes paid in the Dominican Republic, clearly defining where the main benefits of the project lie.

Other operating expenditures include shipping and marketing, executive salaries, office and administrative overhead, and legal, financial and consulting services. All of these transactions take place at prices far greater in scale than the company's Dominican labour rates which ranged between 50 cents and $2.37 an hour ($RD) in 1973. After all these costs and taxes were paid the Falcondo profit was still $14 million, equivalent to nearly the entire equity financing put up by

28. See Dillon, Read's *Prospectus* for $50 million in Falconbridge debentures, June 9, 1971, p. 49.

Falconbridge, ARMCO and the Dominican government. The rate of profit on equity in 1973 was 93 percent, a healthy return in any league.

Capital intensity is the primary feature of the Falcondo enterprise. The $195 million investment has created direct employment of about 1900 positions, an investment of more than $100,000 per job. If benefit to the Dominican people were the primary objective, as it obviously is not, there are many more effective ways to spend $195 million. As the *Wall Street Journal* noted,

> the Dominican Republic needs more than 3,000 new jobs *a month* just to keep pace with youths entering the job market. Mr. Balaguer recently put unemployment at 400,000 or about 33 percent of the estimated job force of 1.2 million. Unemployment is thought to approach 50 percent in some neighbourhoods of Santo Domingo.[29] (emphasis added)

Faced with this kind of contradiction, transnational mining companies whether in Canada or the Dominican Republic and other less developed countries resort to specious arguments about indirect benefits and spinoffs from their activity. This exaggerated nonsense is now being rejected even in quarters where it might be expected to find strong support. For example Robert McNamara, president of the World Bank,[30] reported to the U.N. conference on trade and development that large scale capital projects in less developed countries tend to make the rich richer while the vast majority sinks deeper into poverty. Using the case of Brazil, a big recipient of foreign investment, McNamara reported that between 1960 and 1970 the share of the poorest 40 percent of the population in national income *declined* from 10 to eight percent, while the top five percent of income recipients *increased* their share from 29 to 38 percent.[31] The Dominican Republic, where the poorest 40 percent received 12 percent of national income in 1969 compared with 57 percent for the richest 20 percent, seems to be a comparable case.

The key to analyzing projects like Falcondo is not to look for a general benefit to the working people of the host country. The benefit will accrue primarily to the company and its sources of capital, with a secondary but significant benefit to portions of the ruling clique in the country being exploited. This benefit can be transmitted in various ways. INCO, which once held some of the Dominican concessions now

29. *Wall Street Journal,* Sept. 9, 1971.
30. The World Bank loaned Falcondo $25 million at 7 percent on the guarantee of the Balaguer government.
31. Cited in Lee Aspin, ''Socialism for the Rich: Underwriting the Multinationals'', *The Nation,* Sept. 14, 1974, p. 199.

operated by Falconbridge, relinquished them when Rafael Trujillo demanded ''too big a bribe.''[32] A more general mechanism for distributing the gains from foreign investment among wealthy Dominicans appears to be foreign exchange manipulation. The arrangement works this way: the official exchange rate between the U.S. dollar and the Dominican peso has been fixed at 1:1 since 1947 but in foreign exchange markets the peso is heavily discounted, trading at about U.S.$.85. Any Dominican acquiring scarce dollars in return for pesos at the official rate is in effect receiving a gift from the Dominican government equal to about 15 percent of the transaction. The earnings of exporting corporations such as Falcondo are all in foreign exchange. Its tax payments, such as they are, and its operating expenditures within the Republic, to the extent that the necessary pesos are acquired from the Banco Central at the official rate, provide the Balaguer government with foreign exchange. The government is then in a position to pursue its own import programs, or to sell the foreign currency to Dominican importers, passing on the benefit of the differential to whomever it favours. By this device the marginal benefits of Falcondo and other such corporations to the Dominican economy are concentrated in the hands of a very small class.

To the extent this surplus is retained within the state sector, much of it contributes to the maintenance of an oversized and well-paid police and military apparatus, employing between 30,000 and 40,000 people and eating up 30 to 35 percent of the government budget.[33] This is another collective service to Dominican and foreign propertied interests. The actual amount of foreign exchange turned over by Falcondo to the Dominican Banco Central is difficult to determine from public documents and calculations, because there are a number of secret protocols between the bank and the company. Expatriate employees of the company claim, for example, they receive only one-third of their salaries in Dominican pesos and the other two-thirds in foreign currency, but the Dominican portion is sufficient to cover most living costs.

The economic benefits of Falcondo to the majority of Dominicans, we conclude, are negligible. The minimal benefits to the Dominican state are largely distributed to the privileged classes.

THE PACIFICATION OF BONAO
In the community of Bonao where Falcondo's production and labour

32. F. Goff, op. cit., p. 8.
33. David Fairchild, former U.S. AID officer in the Dominican Republic, cited in NACLA Newsletter, November 1970, p. 2.

force are located, the company has cast itself in the role of enlightened modernizer. ''The philosophy that guides Falconbridge in its community relations,'' says Ian Keith, ''is to support existing or newly created institutions . . . to share their burdens, but not to stifle their initiative or dominate them.''[34] Neither the company's performance in relation to its cooperatives nor its trade union relations provide much evidence to support such claims.

Falcondo is the modern ''benefactor'' to a city which in the old days was the personal playground of Arismendi ''Petan'' Trujillo, brother of the former dictator. In the benign view of the *Financial Post*'s John Harbron, Petan ''unlike his brother . . . and most of the indulgent ruling family, was an innovator and modernizer of sorts. . . . For a single devoted decade, 1950-60, (he) gave Bonao genuine economic uplift by assuring its produce a committed share of the Santo Domingo consumer market.''[35] This view is strongly contradicted by other sources including the North American Congress on Latin America (NACLA).

> Petan set out to repeat on a local scale what his brother in the Presidency was doing on a national scale. He recreated the small town of Bonao, making it the headquarters of a personal domain that was feudal in every respect except land tenure. Protected by a private army, using terror, bribery and intrigue, Arismendi accumulated most of the city's wealth. He also asserted the right to rape any woman in the town before her marriage. To glorify himself he showered the city with his ''benevolence'': sumptuous avenues, public buildings and parks—tribute to a dynasty built on massive poverty and oppression.[36]

Falcondo managed to co-exist with this tyrant for the last five years of Trujillism, another application of the company's ''neither condoning nor condemning'' political philosophy. The depredations of Trujillo left a legacy of fear and the most pronounced authoritarianism in Bonao, which experienced heightened economic woes after 1961. By 1968 official unemployment in the city of 20,000 was 46 percent, with estimates of disguised unemployment raising this figure much higher. Only 21 percent of the population wore shoes; more than half the families received yearly incomes less than $50, and 86 percent less than $100. The mortality rate for children under four years of age was a

---

34. Quoted by John Harbron, *op. cit.*
35. *Ibid.*
36. ''A Project Camelot in the Dominican Republic'', in *NACLA's Latin America & Empire Report,* Vol. VIII, April 1974, p. 15.

staggering 60 percent, with most households lacking basic sanitary facilities.[37]

Moving into this environment to establish an ongoing profitable enterprise presented Ian Keith and Falcondo with a number of tactical questions on how to deal with the local community. This required detailed knowledge of local attitudes to pursue what the company calls "effective community relations" but which might also be characterized as "pacification." Falcondo engaged the services of the Catholic University of Santiago to perform a detailed socio-economic survey of Bonao in 1968, and "during the following two years, 130 professors, students and assistants overran the city . . . collecting information on all facets of life and providing their mentors with an encyclopedic description of the community on IBM cards."[38]

That the university, which is the centre of higher learning for the Dominican upper classes, was equipped for such a sophisticated social research project was not accidental. The United States government has for many years been keenly interested in research into the "social processes" of less developed countries to help it deal effectively with problems of "insurgency." This interest was expressed in the U.S. Defense Department's controversial Project Camelot during the 1960s when it contracted with numerous supposedly independent and objective social scientists to inquire into the likely ramifications of direct U.S. military intervention in unstable areas like Chile and Quebec.

The Dominican equivalent of Camelot, of which Falcondo was the first beneficiary, grew out of relations between the Catholic University of Santiago, the Catholic University of St. Louis, and the U.S. Agency for International Development (AID).[39] In 1966, in conjunction with the stabilization of the Balaguer regime after the U.S. invasion, AID pumped $750,000 into the Catholic University of Santiago to develop a capability for advanced social science investigation — interviewing, data analysis, and managerial skills.

Gil Medeiro Saudade, an employee of U.S. Army Intelligence from 1946-58 and subsequently a political officer at U.S. embassies in Chile, Ecuador and Brazil, was appointed project co-ordinator at the University of St. Louis. The Chairman of the political science department and director of Latin American Area Studies for the University of St. Louis, Henry Anthony Christopher Ph.D., was sent to head the project in Santo Domingo during 1967 and 1968. Christopher, who had the academic credentials Saudade lacked, also had an intelligence

37. *Ibid.*, p. 15.
38. *Ibid.*, p. 17.
39. *Ibid.*

background; he served as a political analyst to the U.S. Department of Defense from 1951-55, and then as political officer in the U.S. embassy in Madrid.

When Falcondo in 1968 found itself in need of social research, the university apparatus with a political intelligence orientation was ready for action. As NACLA concludes "few would admit that two such accomplished intelligence operatives as Christopher and Saudade would not have seen the confluence of interests between the U.S. government, the Texas-controlled Falconbridge, and these research-hungry social scientists."[40] The questionaire administered in Bonao by the university team included many items which "would have been highly inflammatory if asked by officials of the company or agents of the U.S. or Dominican governments" and allowed Falcondo to "pin-point its potential allies and enemies, elaborate a strategy of community relations and . . . channel . . . political energies into manageable directions."[41]

A sample of the questions designed to elicit information about political and class consciousness supports the NACLA assessment of the underlying purpose and use of the research. Among the more blatant:

- Is it true that in this country the rich are getting richer and the poor poorer?
- Do you think the police have the right to torture an agitator to force him to tell where he hides arms?
- What type of government do you prefer, one with freedom but with hunger, or one without freedom but without hunger?
- Do you believe Cuba today is better off, the same, or worse off than it was under Batista?
- Are you a member of a political party?
- Do you regard the installation of a North American factory or industry in Bonao as beneficial, prejudicial, or indifferent for the country?

The study for which Falcondo bore the non-salary costs revealed, despite the suspicions the respondents must have had, a fairly high level of alienation from existing Dominican social and political structures.

Sixty percent believed it was difficult or impossible to move to a higher social class, and nearly 75 percent believed that in the Dominican Republic the rich get richer and the poor get poorer. Up to 22 percent were willing to state that it is justified to use

40. *Ibid.*
41. *Ibid.*, p. 18.

violence to overthrow a tyrannical regime and 75 percent said it
was better to overthrow a bad government. Forty-one percent
regarded the 1965 U.S. invasion as damaging for the country,
while only 34 percent thought it was beneficial. Nearly 90 percent
agreed that the United States should stop fighting in Viet Nam,
while 35 percent believed Cuba was as well off or better today
than it was under Batista. One must remember that the 35 percent
answering "yes" were risking jail terms.[42]

General manager Ian Keith's responsibilities are primarily for the
political affairs of Falcondo, and his planned adaptations to the anti-
foreign sentiment in Bonao are a testimonial to his effectiveness in this
role. The decision to hire legal counsel and a number of administrative
employees connected with the circle around President Balaguer was one
product of Keith's judgement, even though some of the North American
staff have complained about the inefficiency of the patronage appointees. To handle community and labour relations Keith took another
astute tack, described thus by John Harbron of the *Financial Post*:

> A possibly precipitous move by Keith was hiring prominent
> individuals from the Dominican Trade Unions and the socialist
> Dominican Revolutionary Party. . . . It goes without saying that
> these unions and the PRD are anti-government, possibly
> even anti-business. However hiring these controversial men,
> mainly to develop employee relations, *somehow worked*. (em-
> phasis added)[43]

This is not as great a mystery as Harbron suggests. One of the
"prominent individuals" from the PRD now associated with Falcondo
is Sacha Volman, who can hardly be called anti-government or anti-
business. Volman, a Rumanian-born adventurer, was the CIA's top
man in the PRD and one of Bosch's principal betrayers when his
government was overthrown in 1963. [44] Trained by the U.S. Office of
Strategic Services in intelligence skills during World War II, he worked
subsequently for Radio Free Europe and was then transferred by the
CIA to Latin America. Volman has operated primarily in the Caribbean
as a "sociologist" and "labour expert" building "anti-Communist
centre-left political fronts." One source affirms that he created no less
than 17 political parties with funds drawn from the CIA,[45] as well as

42. *Ibid.*

43. John Harbron, *op. cit.*

44. For details on Volman's CIA career, see Gutierrez, *op. cit.,* pp. 35-37.

45. George Morris, *The CIA and American Labor,* International Publishers, New York,
1967.

founding the Institute of International Labor Research. The IILR and the Kaplan Fund were the conduits through which the CIA financed Volman's various covert plots and manipulations in the Latin American labour movement.

In Bonao Volman's task is to smooth over as much as possible the inevitable tensions arising from the creation of a privileged Falcondo enclave side by side with the old town. The 175-unit company housing complex, constructed at a cost of $3 million, is equipped with its own water supply, paved avenues, large front lawns and gardens, in striking contrast with the adjacent poverty of the mine workers and other citizens. Social life in the North American-style barrio is fairly self-contained and revolves around the private club. Built in 1972, the club features an olympic-size swimming pool, tennis courts, billiards, dance hall, movie theatre, bar and restaurant. The company's wage workers are excluded both by the $170 annual fee and a rule restricting membership to monthly-salaried employees.

The company school, administered by the Adrian Sisters, is theoretically open to all, but the academic requirements and tuition fees put it too beyond the reach of local residents. The segregation of upper company personnel extends to religion as well, with many of the Catholics preferring to celebrate Sunday mass in their own homes rather than attend the two Bonao churches.

Residents of Bonao claim that, since the construction of the Falcondo plant, very few of the city's original inhabitants have retained employment with the company. Most of the wage workers have been drawn from other parts of the country where they had already acquired skills, usually in the sugar mills. This influx of labour has created shortages and spiralling prices in Bonao, rendering the impoverishment of many of its citzens even more acute than before.

One of Volman's main devices for diffusing the tension has been the creation of a multi-purpose cooperative called Coofalcondo. Initially limited to credit union and transportation functions, it has accumulated assests of $1.6 million and is preparing to branch into pharmacy, food and housing. One of the vital activities of Coofalcondo, which remains firmly under company influence, is political education: the co-op offers courses in leadership training, democratic process, and worker-management relations, all defined in terms suitable to Falcondo. Coofalcondo in this sense provides an important two-way flow of information; even as it spreads ideas approved by the company, it places Volman and his aides in an excellent position to keep tabs on people and attitudes in the community, providing the basis for corrective intervention as required.

Among the benefits it claims to have brought the Dominican Republic, Falcondo places its training programs high on the list. It has established in conjunction with the Universidad Catolica Madre y Maestra a number of extension courses in technical specialties, some making use of the company's laboratories. These courses are designed primarily to meet the company's technical manpower needs, but the training received by Dominicans will undoubtedly be of value to the individuals involved and perhaps ultimately of service to the country.

There are, however, sections of the Falcondo plant, those which house the reputedly superior and innovative metallurgical processes, to which only a handful of trusted company personnel have access. The whole Falcondo operation, and this section in particular, are cloaked in secrecy preserved by a large security force. This reflects several fears, among them the possibility of political sabotage; industrial espionage by other companies eager to unravel the mystery of the highly-efficient process; and political espionage. Not only Falconbridge but also the United States would regret losing the secrets to the Cubans, who have extensive lateritic nickel deposits. This serves as a partial explanation of the persistent rumours about CIA men in the company's employ. But the other people who must not understand the critical aspects of the operation are the Dominicans themselves. Falcondo's ace-in-the-hole against nationalization, whatever turn Dominican politics may take, is to maintain a monopoly of essential knowledge about the production process. This provides a definite limit on how far it is prepared to push the logic of "Dominicanization" and training of local people.

TRADE UNION EDUCATION: THE FALCONBRIDGE SCHOOL

The best indication of Falcondo's view of its own future and the future of the Dominican Republic is contained in the labour relations strategy elaborated by Ian Keith and Sacha Volman. In essence it is a highly political attempt to encourage "non-political" unionism of the North American variety. "It behooves foreign investment to help the cause of bread-and-butter trade unionism," advises Business International Corporation in a report to corporate clients on methods of combatting nationalism in Latin America.[46] These international consultants have nothing to teach Sacha Volman, who has been promoting this concept in Latin America for the last thirty years. Falcondo's interests are served, in this scheme of things, by union leaders and members who ignore the general political and social tragedy of their nation, who draw no unpleasant conclusions about the relationship between the company and the government, and who think that business and work have nothing to do with politics.

46. Business International, *Nationalism in Latin America: The Challenge and Corporate Response*, New York 1970 (BI), p. 37.

The preference of a large corporation like Falcondo for business unionism is a matter of simple logic. Its overriding concern is to keep $195 million in capital working continuously. Its wage bill is a relatively small component of costs, and the company can accommodate the negotiation of higher wages for its 1500 or so wage workers with relative ease, provided only that this does not create too much unrest in the remainder of the Dominican labour market. What would be disastrous for Falcondo is a highly militant union, especially one prepared to shut down the plant on non-wage issues or the many social issues which do not relate directly to production. The management led by Keith and Volman has done everything possible to prevent the emergence of such political unionism.

Serious labour discontent first appeared at Falcondo during the early construction phase in May 1970, when practically the entire 2,000-man work force went on strike, paralyzing the job site and jeopardizing the project timetable. Not represented by a union, the workers elected a bargaining committee to put forward their demands for higher wages, job security, better working conditions and safety provisions, free transportation, improved equipment, life insurance and the rehiring of 11 men fired for strike involvement. After four days bargaining with subcontractors, the men went back to work giving the subcontractors and Falcondo a month to consider their demands.

During and after the walkout organizers from the Confederation of Christian Trade Unions (CASC) aided the Falcondo workers', and by early June a CASC-affiliated union had formed. No progress was made during the month-long moratorium, particularly on the question of job security since the company had no intention of retaining most of the employees beyond the construction phase.

The strike resumed toward the end of June, and it became immediately apparent Falcondo had decided not only to resist the union demands, but to break the strike without delay. Within hours of the stoppage Dominican government military and police units occupied the Falcondo site and violently removed the strikers. Some were beaten while others were arrested and imprisoned in the local military garrison. [47] Widespread intimidation and harrassment of the rest of the union members including the 22-man bargaining committee continued, while Ian Keith, reportedly on Volman's recommendation, fired 35 men and rumours circulated that the entire 600 who had signed the original union charter would be dismissed. In the town of Bonao, high school students

47. Accounts of the strike appear in the following articles: *Listin Diario,* June 25, 1970; *El Caribe,* June 25, 1970; *Ibid.,* June 26, 1970; *El Nacional,* June 26, 1970; *Listin Diario,* June 26, 1970.

protesting the military presence were dispersed by army gunfire and the high school was surrounded by troops and closed.

A.A. Chamberlain, Falcondo construction manager, accused the secretary-general of CASC, Henry Molina, of being a political agitator and threatened more trouble if the construction workers insisted on maintaining their negotiating team. Ian Keith, rising to the defense of the Trujillo labour code, claimed the union was not seeking better working conditions but trying to provoke a political crisis. (Strikes are illegal in almost all feasible circumstances in the Dominican Republic.) "The interests of the Dominican people lie in large scale industrial developments such as Falcondo," Keith lectured, "and consequently the project should not get involved in political conflicts of this nature." [48]

The company mounted an intensive advertising campaign to bring in strikebreakers, supplementing the pressure exerted by the armed forces. At the same time Keith further elaborated his labour philosophy:

> Falconbridge Dominicana and its construction sub-contractors are well-disposed toward dialogue and discussion with groups representing the workers' aspirations and demands. We have a great desire to maintain harmonious labour-management relations, as well as a desire to win affection and respect from the workers—the most important human element, appreciated by all good industrialists. [49]

On the eighth day the strike was broken. Military and police units, including the American-trained "Cascos Negros" anti-riot squad from Santo Domingo, broke into a meeting of 150 workers, union leaders and their lawyers, arresting and imprisoning 92 including CASC's top official Henry Molina and Dr. Gonzales Canhuete, union legal adviser and secretary of the PRD. [50] The military commander accused the group of being Communists and threatened to kill some of them. While the union bowed to overwhelming force and its members returned to work, company advertisements accused "minority groups of extremist tendencies" of using violence and intimidation against the majority of employees who wanted to work, and called on the population to remain calm so that "together we can continue to work for the development and prosperity of Bonao." [51]

48. *El Caribe*, June 29, 1970.
49. Advertisement in Dominican Newspapers, June 29, 1970.
50. *Listin Diario*, July 2, 1970.
51. *El Caribe*, July 2, 1970.

The most easily identifiable minority group of extremist tendency was the Falcondo management. "We saw no alternative but to crack down hard," Keith later told the *Wall Street Journal*,[52] and he on another occasion revealed he was concerned with "the structure and origin of union leadership" as much as with the actual demands of the workers. The gulf between this behavior and the rhetoric of political neutrality and non-paternalism is unbridgeable.

The Catholic Bishop Flores, who had tried unsuccessfully to mediate the dispute, put matters in a more balanced perspective. Criticizing the company for its refusal to negotiate, he affirmed that the leaders of CASC were neither agitators nor Communists. Flores also pointed out that the right of workers to free association without control by the company or the government had been a fundamental issue of the conflict.[53]

The remainder of the construction phase was marked by continuing tension, flareups and police intervention. Official reports admitted 138 accidents and four deaths in a six month period; social security deductions for numerous employees were not remitted to the government, resulting in denial of benefits; the housing project was struck when a sub-contractor failed to pay back wages, with 400 workers finally resorting to a hunger strike. Still, as Falcondo later stated, the nickel processing plant, power station and oil refinery were all completed in record time. By the end of 1971 the peak construction labour force of more than 4,000 had been reduced to less than 600.

After the completion of construction Falcondo behaved quite differently toward its workers, at least until late 1974. In 1971, with about 300 production workers on the job, Keith took initiatives in recognizing a bargaining unit, carefully excluding construction and office workers. Falcondo handed the union a two-year collective agreement modelled after the Aluminum Company of America (ALCOA) contract and the Dominion labour code. The preamble expressed company production objectives quite clearly:

- Worker-management harmony is an objective to be reached and maitained as the essential condition for the increase in production and the improvement of individual or collective output.

- The prosperity of the company is the best guarantee for the prosperity of the workers.[54]

52. "In Dominican Republic Murders Rise, and so Does Poverty", *Wall Street Journal*, Sept. 9, 1971.
53. *Listin Diario,* July 3, 1970.
54. *Pacto Collectivo de Condiciones de Trabajo Entre Falconbridge Dominicana, C. por A. y el Sindicato de Trabajadores de la Empresa, 1971-1973,* Santo Domingo, July 1971.

The collective agreement, which by 1973 covered about 900 of 1300 production workers was weak in many respects, but provided wages well above the Dominican average.

The 1973 renegotiation, both lengthy and difficult, resulted in some gains in the area of job security, grievance procedure and fringe benefits as well as wages. The union had disaffiliated from CASC, and Sacha Volman devoted considerable behind-the-scenes effort to prevent it from developing relationships with the more militant General Confederation of Workers (CGT). The contract, although improved, left considerable dissatisfaction among the rank and file.

Union developments in 1974 moved in the direction most feared by Falcondo. In April much of the 1973 leadership was swept away in elections favouring a more militant executive. The Falcondo miners then affiliated with the CGT to form a National Federation of Mine and Metal Workers. The union demanded that the contract be reopened to eliminate a number of retrograde clauses, including one requiring employees to work 16 and even 24 hour shifts at management command in the continuous-flow Falcondo plant.

Of even greater concern to Bonao's foreign benefactors, the new union leadership introduced education programs for its members to study not only the collective agreement, but also Falcondo's contracts with the Balaguer government. Volman is reportedly organizing a slate to oppose the current executive, and the company is resorting to the tactics of the construction period to head off undesired developments. Company propaganda has denounced the union education program as "Communist indoctrination against the company and its executives." Informed union sources report the firing of numerous employees, while newspaper accounts record 25 firings including six members of the leadership.[55]

A general meeting of the union on November 5, 1974 called to deal with the firings was broken up by Bonao police, who also acted to prevent those dismissed from reaching the meeting hall. Three visiting officials of CASC were detained and told to leave town.[56] The CGT claims these actions are part of a nation-wide campaign of repression against its members and supporters mounted at the behest of Falcondo, ALCOA and La Rosario, three mining corporations which have reason to fear the rising popularity of the National Federation of Mine and Metal Workers.

One month after the police action in Bonao, the Balaguer government announced that Falcondo would be granting a 10 to 15 percent wage increase over and above the provisions of the collective agree-

55. *La Noticia,* November 2, 1974.
56. *La Noticia,* November 6, 1974.

ment. As a palliative this is not particularly impressive, since inflation in the Dominican Republic has been ripping along at about 17 percent annually over the past three years; but the source of the announcement does indicate the close collaboration between company and government.

Despite persistent attempts to destroy the Bonao union, widespread dissent is growing at the plant, due to reported violations of the collective agreement and the International Labour Organization's Conventions on labour standards. Unjustifiable layoffs continue as well as frequent discrimination against Dominican technicians. Workers complain of serious industrial contamination in the plant, and inadequate medical assistance. In March 1975, in response to growing concern from local farmers about declining agrarian production, the Dominican government was forced to set up a commission to study the possible environmental hazards caused by Falcondo's operations in the region of Cibao, reported to be the richest agricultural area of the Dominican Republic and the "bread basket" of the Caribbean.

ALLIANCE FOR OPPRESSION

Falconbridge Nickel and Falcondo present themselves as good corporate citizens, pursuing legitimate business objectives and creating social benefits along the way in a veritable symphony of harmony and good will. Business and politics are separate spheres, and the company simply obeys laws as it finds them from one country to another without interfering in political affairs.

The truth, as the company's behavior in the Dominican Republic demonstrates, is far removed from these public relations inventions. The full extent of Falcondo's collaboration with Balaguer's police state cannot be documented, but the Dominican army and police repeatedly anticipate Ian Keith's and Sacha Volman's designs with remarkable accuracy and alacrity. The connections between company and government personnel, and Volman's links to the CIA eliminate any mystery from speculation about how these coincidences might be arranged.

Far from being apolitical, the company finds comfort in an alliance with the propertied classes of the Republic and a government which rules by terror and force. Nor are Falcondo policies in Bonao related primarily to any broad objective of improving community standards, but rather to its need to preserve stability while it extracts non-renewable resources from the country at the fastest possible rate.

As for the argument that Dominican society, in the interest of the majority, needs profound changes in social and economic relations, the company does not agree. Falcondo has done a great deal to prevent such

change, from CIA-style manipulation of the cooperative to gross interference in internal union affairs, to political firings and condoning
para-military repression of its own workers. If the corporation's plans
are realized in the next 30 years it will extract more than $3 billion from
the Dominican Republic, leaving behind to commemorate its reign in
Bonao a vast open-pit grave.

In its pursuit of profit, Falconbridge's objectives and methods are
not unique, but characteristic of transnational corporations. In the
Dominican Republic not only Falconbridge but other large foreign
enterprises, notably ALCOA and Gulf and Western, have all operated
under the umbrella of United States imperial policy, in turn helping to
shape its precise design. As the Uruguayan journalist Carlos Maria
Gutierrez wrote in 1971, these policies do more than inflict misery on
the victimized peoples: they have profound implications for the people
of the metropolitan countries as well.

> A Dominican Republic flattened by repression and the fascist
> reign of terror will be worth much as a note of caution for others
> who rebel, (but) all this exacts a price: a power with this objective
> must be disposed to go as far as necessary in being politically
> amoral. European fascism accepted that degradation for the sake
> of a like objective, and history has already felt the consequences.
> There perhaps is . . . another warning, this time for the ruling
> groups in the United States and for the new geopoliticians who
> man the computers in Washington.[57]

To this should be added a warning to Canadian leaders who are
willing junior partners in the same game. It is no matter for pride that
Falcondo's activities in the Dominican Republic are conducted in the
name of Canada and its eighteenth-largest corporation.[58] When the
people suffering under this reign of horror finally rise in judgement,
their wrath will not fall on American imperialism alone.

57. Gutierrez, *op. cit.*, p. 142.
58. Ranking by size of assets, *Financial Post,* August 3, 1974. The company ranks 23rd
    by income, and 32nd by sales.

CHAPTER EIGHT

Profits from apartheid: Falconbridge in Africa

We stand for Christian Nationalism which is an ally of National Socialism. You can call this anti-democratic principle dictatorship if you wish. In Italy it is called Fascism, in Germany National Socialism, and in South Africa Christian Nationalism.
> —Johannes Vorster, now prime minister of South Africa, speaking in 1942.

The personnel who direct Falconbridge mining and exploration activities (in Africa) are conscientious, liberal-minded people who have a record of advancement and training of indigenous people. Their demonstrated skill in this regard speaks for itself.
> —Falconbridge president Marsh Cooper, 1974 annual meeting.

You may well know apart from its mineral wealth, which is substantial, South West Africa is a poor country. This country, which is our country, is being exploited by greedy entrepreneurs, robbed of its wealth, and rendered barren for the future. Our fear is that when freedom finally comes to this land, it will be returned to us with no minerals left. Thus you will see the wonderful asset which we have for developing the land for the wellbeing of all its people will have been taken away from us. . . . We have not been consulted in all this. *We wish all foreign firms to be removed immediately; we wish to be consulted on ways and means by which our people can have a fairer share in benefitting from the wealth of the land of their birth.*
> — Clemens Kapuuo, elected chief of the Herero peoples of Namibia

The fact that we are carrying on operations through subsidiary companies in South West Africa does not involve us in any claims of South Africa to sovereignty over South West Africa. We are simply carrying on our business of developing mines, which we believe is a very useful purpose, under the existing laws of whatever country our operations are in.

— Falconbridge vice-president G.T.N. Woodrooffe, March 27th, 1973

Africa, once the exclusive domain of European colonialism, is becoming an important field of investment for transnational corporations like the Falconbridge Group. Falconbridge subsidiaries operate in Zimbabwe (Rhodesia), Namibia (South West Africa), the Republic of South Africa, and until recently Uganda. Howard Keck's corporations share this growing interest with many others for southern Africa displays, according to *Fortune* magazine, the best features of an investor's paradise:

> The Republic of South Africa has always been regarded by foreign investors as a gold mine, one of those rare and refreshing places where profits are great and problems small. Capital is not threatened by political instability or nationalization. Labor is cheap, the market booming, the currency hard and convertible. Such are the market's attractions that 292 American corporations have established subsidiaries or affiliates there. Their combined direct investment is close to $900 million, and their returns on that investment have been romping home at something like 19 per cent a year, after taxes.[1]

The same attractions exist in South Africa's illegal colony, Namibia and to a lesser degree in Rhodesia, where the foreign investor is inconvenienced by United Nations sanctions. No one can dispute that all three of these territories are organized for the most efficient possible exploitation of both mineral resources and above all, black labour.

Opportunities for great profit do not stop at the borders of the white supremacist states. For a number of years Falconbridge's biggest producer in Africa was Kilembe Mines Ltd., the largest mining enterprise in Uganda. Kilembe employed up to 4,000 people and was 70 per cent owned by Kilembe Copper Cobalt, a Falconbridge subsidiary.[2]

1.   "The proper role of U.S. corporations in South Africa", *Fortune*, July 1972, p. 49.
2.   Other shareholders in Kilembe Mines are the Uganda Development Corporation, a state owned body, with 10%, and the Colonial Development Corporation, an agency of the British government established to assist economic development in Commonwealth countries, with 20%. For further information on Kilembe see: "Kilembe mine is part of takeover by Uganda", *Globe & Mail*, May 8, 1970; "Uganda bids for an interest in a Canadian-owned mine", *Toronto Daily Star*, January 27, 1970, p. 11; "Uganda bids to buy Kilembe mine holdings", *Globe & Mail*, January 27, 1970.

The government of Uganda, until its recent expropriation of the company, held a 10 per cent minority interest. Kilembe, one of Thayer Lindsley's creations in the old days of Ventures Ltd., opened in a wilderness area of Uganda in 1956, complete with its own hydro-electric station. Since that time it has produced copper worth more than $250 million, but paid no income taxes until its capital was finally fully recovered in 1965, and generated in excess of $15 million in profit after taxes for its owners in the following five years. Since then the twists and turns of Ugandan politics first interrupted this flow of wealth and then brought it to a complete halt.

Uganda, like other newly independent African nations, is a poor country in which half the population million lives on a per capita income of $75 per year or less. The president during the late 1960s, Dr. Milton Obote, had pledged to lead his country to socialism. In 1969 he turned his attention to Kilembe, whose sales in that year reached $26 million and were the single largest item in the country's foreign exchange accounts.

By increasing the copper export tax, Obote increased the Ugandan government's take from 26 percent of Kilembe's $4.5 million profit in 1968 to 37 percent of the $9.7 million it earned in 1969. Falconbridge was prepared to live with that arrangement, but was horrified by Obote's move in 1970 in which he forced sale of majority control to the Ugandan government, reducing Falconbridge's interest to 31 percent. The parent company managed to strip out nearly $6 million in special dividend payments before this took place, more than twice its share of the entire year's profits for Kilembe.[3]

Further developments along this line were forestalled by what was for Falconbridge a mixed blessing, Obote's overthrow in early 1971 by the inimitable Idi Amin. Amin moved promptly to restore Falconbridge's 70 per cent equity in Kilembe. While this was undoubtedly a welcome gesture, it was offset by his expulsion of Asians from Uganda which decimated Kilembe's administrative ranks. Amin also raised the corporate tax rate from 22 to 40 per cent and imposed a withholding tax on dividends. By 1972, to save the country and his army payroll from disaster, Amin abruptly reversed field, rescinding the tax increase and abolishing the copper export tax altogether. Even so, Kilembe registered a combined loss of about $1.3 million during 1971-72 as its sales fell by over 30 per cent. The company continued to withdraw capital with another $1 million dividend payment in 1971. Amin's survival at that point depended on arriving at an accomo-

3. The special dividend payments were made possible through the liquidation of short term notes held in the company's treasury, accumulated there for "possible future expansion". See Ilmar J. Martens, "Falconbridge Nickel Mines Ltd. and Follow Up Report" mimeo published by Canavest House, December 17, 1970.

dation with Kilembe, and other sources of foreign capital, as his advertisement in the *Financial Times* of London in early 1972 suggests. In a personal message to the financial world he expressed "the sincere hope that since a good investment climate has been created, those intending to invest in Uganda will do so without hesitation."[4] By 1973, although production had not returned to previous levels, Kilembe again showed a $3.6 million profit and paid Amin $1.3 million in taxes. The company felt more secure about its prospects in Uganda, and restricted its dividends to one-third of 1973 profit. Kilembe's mining lease, which expired in 1973, was never renegotiated but through interim agreements the Falconbridge subsidiary hoped to continue to mine copper in Uganda.

This apparent modus vivendi between Falconbridge and the Ugandan dictator, who has executed an estimated 80,000 people since he seized power,[5] was shortlived. In late February 1975 Amin expropriated the company for a price of $2.3 million, with installments payable until 1978. Asked how the sale price related to the value of the mine a Kilembe official noted regretfully "It doesn't. It means we're through in Uganda."[6] The parting between the company and Amin, whose method of government resembles Rafael Trujillo's, occurred at the behest of the dictator, not Falconbridge.

BUSTING UNITED NATIONS SANCTIONS
The northern bastion of white supremacy in Africa is Ian Smith's Rhodesia (Zimbabwe) where 250,000 caucasians maintain political and economic domination over 5 million blacks, eighty per cent of the population ekes out its existence at incomes below the recognized poverty line, and black Africans have been allocated the least productive land areas of the country.

An international boycott of Rhodesian products and economic sanctions against the country were initiated in 1966 as part of efforts to force a recognition of the political rights of the majority. In 1967 the United Nations General Assembly condemned

> . . . the activities of those financial and other interests which by supporting and assisting the illegal racist minority regime in Southern Rhodesia, and by their exploitation of the human and material resources of the Territory, are undermining the effective

4. *Financial Times* (London), January 24, 1972.
5. Reported on Canadian Broadcasting Corporation television program *Prime Time*, February 4, 1975; see also David Martin, *General Amin*, Faber and Faber, London, 1974.
6. "Canadian firm holds fire sale of Uganda mine", *Toronto Star*, March 1, 1975, p.C8.

implementation of the sanctions imposed so far and are impeding the African people of Zimbabwe from attaining freedom and independence in accordance with the General Assembly resolution 1514 (XV), (and called upon) the Governments of the States concerned to take all necessary measures to bring such activities to an end.[7]

Judging by its past annual reports, Falconbridge appeared not to be among those "financial and other interests" condemned by the United Nations for supporting and profiting from white supremacy in Rhodesia. Only in its 1975 report did Falconbridge report holdings in Rhodesia where it has been active for some time. For years its predecessor Ventures Ltd. owned the Connemara gold mine, and in 1963 sold its exhausted workings to the Rhodesian government with the knowledge that it was to be converted into a detention camp for political prisoners.[8] Today there are still two Falconbridge mines in Rhodesia, the inactive Giant Consolidated Gold Mines Ltd. and the Blanket Mine, another gold producer, which provides needed tax revenue and foreign exchange earnings to the Smith regime. The Blanket mine's financial statistics have been a jealously guarded secret, but *Montreal Gazette* editor Hugh Nangle learned that it earned a profit of $1.3 million in 1972. The 1975 annual report shows a 1973 profit of $904,000, with 1974 earnings climbing back to $1.2 million.

Falconbridge is not simply an unhappy captive in the Rhodesian situation. In 1972 it was actively involved with the Rhodesian Mining Promotion Corporation investigating potential new mineral deposits in the Umvuma area. While Falconbridge eventually withdrew from this project in favour of the British Lonrho interests, its behavior indicates a willingness to cooperate with Smith's government in opposition to the efforts of the United Nations. British Prime Minister Ted Heath condemned Lonrho's sanction-busting activities as an example of "the ugly face of capitalism",[9] and the verdict is equally applicable to Falconbridge.

Canadian journalist Hugh Nangle visited Falconbridge's Rhodesian company in 1973 and returned with this description:

> The Blanket Mine is a disgusting example of a Canadian company exploiting black workers. It is not unfair to charge that Falconbridge is operating a slave-labour mine. Living conditions for

7. Resolution of the General Assembly of the United Nations, passed November 3, 1967, paragraph 10.
8. Hugh Nangle, "Canadians exploit blacks in Africa says Montreal editor", *Toronto Daily Star*, July 19, 1973, p. 42.
9. *Sunday Times* (London), May 20, 1973.

blacks are appalling while the white workers luxuriate over the hill in attractive homes with beautiful gardens and at least one automobile to a house. The "houses" for blacks consist of two-room asbestos corrugated sheeting. They are crowded together, one upon the other, in an area of the country where there is plenty of space. Shanties in many cases double as cooking areas and sleeping quarters.[10]

The *Montreal Gazette* editor also reported that the starting wage for black workers was about $15 a month for a six-day week, rising to between $44 and $49 a month after 20 years of service. The abysmal wages were supplemented by double food rations each week, which Nangle said were still "grossly inadequate to feed a worker and his family."[11] In contrast with the conditions of the 400 or so black labourers, some of the 11 white maintenance workers received incomes of about $810 per month and enjoyed access to the swimming pool, tennis court and recreational club. The average wages of white workers in this case were 16 times greater than those of blacks, allowing them to command tremendous amounts of black labour in support of their life-style.

The Canadian government has taken no action against Falconbridge. Officially, Ottawa pretends not to know of Falconbridge's continuing violation of resolutions on Rhodesia which Canada has supported at the United Nations. The Department of Industry, Trade and Commerce answered a YWCA questionnaire in 1973 stating that it was not aware of any Canadian-controlled investment in Rhodesia.[12] This apparent complicity in covering up Falconbridge's Rhodesian connection raises questions about the relationship between Falconbridge and the government, and about the true nature of Canadian policy on self-determination for the Rhodesian majority.

THE GREAT WHITE HOPE: SOUTH AFRICA
The core of white rule in Africa is the Republic of South Africa, where four million whites have organized a political and economic system built on the oppression and exploitation of 18 million coloured and black people. The system is called apartheid, "separation", and is predicated on the supposed biological inferiority of the non-whites, although more sophisticated rationalizations are based on theories of cultural backwardness. Either way the result is the same, a denial in the

10. Nangle, *op. cit.*
11. *Ibid.*
12. Study and Action Committee of the World Relationships Committee of the YWCA of Canada, *Investment in Oppression,* YWCA, Toronto, 1973, p. 3.

here-and-now of the most elementary political and human rights of the
overwhelming majority of the population.

Just beneath the transparent ideological veil of apartheid lurks the
naked economic reality. The privileges of whites cannot exist without
grinding down the non-white labour force, as Prime Minister Vorster
has so clearly pointed out:

> It is true that there are blacks working for us. They will continue
> working for us for generations, in spite of the ideal that we have to
> separate them completely . . . The fact of the matter is this; we
> need them because they work for us . . . But the fact they work for
> us can never entitle them to claim political rights. Not now, nor in
> the future . . . under no circumstances.[13]

South African racial policies are accordingly designed to provide a
cheap, and obedient non-white labour force, and they have succeeded to
a remarkable degree. Rates of return on investment capital run so high
"it makes a U.S. mining company's mouth water", says Sydney
Newman, the joint managing director of Falconbridge's Western
Platinum mine in South Africa.[14]

South African government policy is aimed at creating large pools
of unemployed blacks, guaranteeing a ready supply of labour at subsistence wages. Thirteen per cent of the land area of the Republic has been
set aside as black "homelands", the other 87 per cent of the land area
being reserved exclusively for white ownership. The homelands are in
effect detention areas, gripped by the most intense poverty. The High-
veld Institute recently estimated that they contain 7 million Africans,
but can provide economic subsistence for only 2.5 million.[15] The
human consequences of this iniquitous system are predictable and
terrible. UNESCO reports indicate that in 1960 between 60 and 70 per
cent of black children in South Africa suffered from malnutrition and
consequent brain damage.[16] In some homelands half the children die
before reaching the age of five.[17]

The homelands are a purgatory from which blacks must escape,

13. House of Assembly of the Republic of South Africa, April 24, 1968, quoted in Ruth
First, Jonathan Steele, Christabel Gurney, *The South African Connection: Western
Investment in Apartheid*, Penguin, 1973, p. 41.
14. *Business Week*, Special advertising section on South Africa, November 2, 1974, p.
62. Sydney Newman is joint managing director of Western Platinum by virtue of his
position as Chairman of Lonrho South Africa. The other managing director is
long-time head of Falconbridge's African operations, A.E. Pugsley.
15. YWCA, *op. cit.*, p. 11.
16. Cited in *The Times* (London), April 26, 1971.
17. Ruth First, *et.al. op. cit.*, p. 52.

but the fate awaiting them outside is little better. The South African government, with its Pass Law, Influx Control, Native Act, Bantu Act, and Terrorism Act, attempts to regulate nearly every aspect of the behavior of black Africans. All must carry identity cards and special travel documents outside the homelands. Blacks are forbidden to take up permanent residence in a white area; to organize a slowdown or strike; to organize or belong to a trade union; or to address a group of more than ten. These measures are designed to suppress the development of political organization of any kind.

The government's efforts to make Africans into pure labour without humanity know no bounds. In 1968, Mr. G. Froneman, the deputy chairman of the Bantu Affairs Commission, told the House of Assembly:

> We are trying to introduce the migrant labour pattern as far as possible in every sphere. This is in fact the entire basis of our policy as far as the white economy is concerned, namely a system of migrant labour.[18]

The same official in 1969 stated there were, in his opinion, 3.8 million superfluous Africans in white areas.[19] He was referring to the families of black wage labourers, whom he apparently wanted to ship back to the overcrowded homelands. Black families in this view have but a single function, the reproduction of labour power.

The government's attempts to confine blacks to the impossible conditions of the homelands take many forms. The Commissioner of the South African police reported that during 1969-70 a daily average of 1,794 blacks were prosecuted for infringement of the Pass Laws, a statistic which indicates the intensity of harassment outside the homelands. Where no specific law has been violated, the government can always resort to the Suppression of Communism Act. According to a former Lord Chancellor, "if you were a Communist forty years ago, you are a Communist today . . . Whether you are a Communist or not, you are a Communist if the state says so."[20]

This array of repressive legal constraints, enforced by a potent police and military apparatus, have placed black workers in a condition which is in many ways worse than slavery. In South Africa the worker is not free to bargain over the price of his labour any more than is a slave, while at the same time the employer, unlike the slave-owner, need not worry whether the worker lives or dies. There is no investment to

18. *Ibid.*, p. 45.
19. YWCA, *op. cit.*, p. 11.
20. Lord Gardiner cited in Ruth First *et.al.*, *op. cit.*, p. 56.

protect, and the homelands exist to replace broken bodies with new ones. Thus in the mining sector South African government statistics for 1971 showed 593,000 black workers earning an average $23 per month, while 62,000 whites earned an average $447, nearly 20 times more.[21] These are the labour conditions which so greatly excite transnational investors and "make their mouths water." The corporations have a vision of paradise which no decent human being can accept.

South Africa's attraction for Falconbridge and other mining corporations is a combination of this endless supply of cheap labour and the country's enormous mineral wealth which is second only to the United States in the non-communist world. The apartheid Republic produces two-thirds of the capitalist world's gold, much of its diamonds, contains 70 per cent of its platinum, chromite and fluorspar reserves, one-third of its known uranium reserves and also ample deposits of nickel, copper, tin, manganese, asbestos and zinc.[22] All this, plus tax laws which permit the complete recovery of invested capital before tax payments fall due make it an irresistible environment for profit-oriented transnational corporations.

The incentives have also produced a flowering of the corporate social imagination, as public relations men work feverishly to persuade themselves and us that investment in South Africa ultimately promotes the welfare of its enslaved black majority. Despite these apologetics, claims that black Africans are making significant progress under apartheid are unsupportable. The total denial of human and political rights condemns the argument outright. But even in the economic realm, the evidence offers little excuse for defenders of the *status quo* in South Africa. Statistics published by Johannesburg's *Financial Mail* for 1969 showed the income of the nation's whites to be $134 per month for every man, woman and child, while the corresponding figure for blacks was $10.[23] During the past sixty years the income differential between blacks and whites has been persistently widening, as might be expected in a system designed to maintain a large pool of surplus labour and hold the blacks near the margin of subsistence. In the mining sector, a study by Dr. Francis Wilson of Cape Town University indicates that the real wage rate for black gold miners remained constant between 1911 and 1966.[24] Applying the concept of economic or political progress to the condition of blacks under apartheid is an exercise best left to the advocates of white supremacy. Black Africans in due time will render their own judgement on the question.

21. *Ibid.*, p. 48.
22. *Ibid.*, p. 87, and *Business Week*, November 2, 1974.
23. Ruth First *et.al.*, *op. cit.*, p. 50.
24. *Ibid.*, p. 50.

Falconbridge, which has exploration offices in both Johannesburg and Windhoek, Namibia, is an active participant in the corporate stampede which reinforces the South African government economically even as its political position in the international arena comes under fire. The Falconbridge Group's biggest undertaking is Western Platinum, a nickel-platinum mine located 35 miles from Pretoria in the Transvaal. Falconbridge Nickel Mines Ltd. holds 25 per cent of Western Platinum's $50 million investment, while its sister company Superior Oil holds 24 per cent and Lonrho, the British company which controls more than 80 corporations in Rhodesia and South Africa, retains the controlling interest of 51 per cent.[25] The project is co-managed by Falconbridge and Lonrho in this fascinating collaboration of major American and British financial groups. The First National City Bank of New York provided an $8 million loan for initial construction activity, which suggests that the new boys have somehow persuaded the old boys to guide them around unfamiliar political turf.

Western Platinum, when it reaches full production, is expected to yield 430,000 ounces of platinum-group metals, 11 million pounds of nickel, and six million pounds of copper annually, with all refining taking place at the Falconbridge facility in Norway. It will be the third or fourth largest platinum producer in the world. While financial information is scanty, 1974 profits were $10.3 million.[26]

The Falconbridge Group's enthusiastic participation in the apartheid economy of South Africa, as well as Rhodesia, is a continuing testimony to the concept of political tolerance and flexibility so frequently articulated by president Marsh Cooper and other company spokesmen. The corporation indeed continues to demonstrate its ability to cooperate with a wide variety of right-wing political regimes.

THE ULTIMATE IN APARTHEID: NAMIBIA

While the Falconbridge Group is as yet just one transnational corporation among dozens in the Republic of South Africa, it occupies a more prominent place in the adjacent colony of Namibia (South West Africa)

25. *Sunday Times* (London), November 28, 1971. Superior Oil is no stranger to the Republic of South Africa. Despite a 1963 United Nations resolution urging member states not to supply oil to South Africa, Superior Oil in conjunction with other American oil companies moved in to help make the Republic self-sufficient in oil. Superior Oil was the first company to announce a petroleum strike, thus confirming the presence of oil on the continental shelf off Plettenberg Bay in the Cape. This sparked an even more concerted oil rush. Superior alone spent $7 million on exploration the following year. See "Oiling the Apartheid Machine", *Sechaba*, Vol. 8, No. 7, July 1974.
26. *Falconbridge Annual Report*, Toronto, 1974.

where the apartheid system has been pushed to its logical extreme. A large, arid territory, Namibia has a population of only 850,000 of which 90 per cent are blacks, but it is now recognized as a storehouse of substantial mineral wealth. Its political status a matter of intense international dispute, Namibia is becoming the principal focal point of the black African independence struggle now that Portuguese colonialism in Angola and Mozambique is in full retreat.

Nambia did not attract European colonialism until 1884, when it was invaded by Germany in its belated drive for the scraps of Africa overlooked by other colonial powers, mainly Britain and France. The nomadic indigenous peoples, especially the Hereros and Namas, resisted the foreign incursion fiercely for more than 20 years, but were finally conquered by a policy of genocide. The German Extermination Order in Namibia, which authorized the killing of every Herero man, woman and child, led to the death of two-thirds of the African peoples in the territory.[27]

During World War I, German South West Africa fell to the armed forces of the British colony of South Africa. South Africa was subsequently granted a trusteeship over South West Africa by the League of Nations, on condition that it "promote to the utmost the material and moral well-being and social progress of the inhabitants" and prepare the country for independence. Intending nothing of the sort, South Africa extended the apartheid system to South West Africa and used it as a safety valve for the emigration of poorer whites from its own territory. The League of Nations censured its "trustee", but did nothing to enforce the rights of black Africans in South West Africa.

The League's successor, the United Nations, has fared no better in protecting the people of its trusteeship. South Africa has violated its mandate by annexing South West Africa and has ignored all U.N. resolutions and actions through the International Court of Justice ordering it to withdraw. In 1966 the United Nations terminated South Africa's mandate over Namibia through a vote of the General Assembly, and the Security Council called on member states to discourage investment by their nationals in the territory. The International Court of Justice upheld these resolutions in 1971, and ruled:

> that States Members of the United Nations are under obligation to recognize the illegality of South Africa's presence in Namibia and the invalidity of its acts on behalf of or concerning Namibia, and to refrain from any acts and in particular any dealings with the Government of South Africa implying recognition of the legality

27. Peter Fraenkel, *The Namibians of South West Africa*, Minority Rights Group, London, 1974, p. 8.

of, or lending support or assistance to, such presence and administration.[28]

The Falconbridge Group defied both the United Nations and the International Court when, toward the end of 1971, it opened a copper mine, Oamites Mining Co. (Pty.) Ltd., 40 miles south of Windhoek, Namibia's administrative capital. It owns 75 per cent of the $7 million project in partnership with the government of South Africa, in flagrant violation of the International Court ruling. What has deflected Falconbridge from the path of international law and justice is profit. The after-tax rate of return on assets for Oamites in 1973 was a fabulous 57 per cent, with $3.2 million clear profit *after* deduction of interest payments and $2.1 million in taxes set aside for the illegal government, South Africa. By way of comparison, the 360 black labourers employed by Oamites at the equivalent of about $2 per day drew a total payroll under $400,000 for the year. The mine uses diesel scoop-trams and other capital-intensive technology typical of North American production arrangements, but the workers earn 20 times less than their North American counterparts, making possible the elevated rate of profit.

Falconbridge is availing itself of the advantages of near-perfect apartheid, for in Namibia the South African objective of separation of black male labourers from their families has been achieved. As in South Africa the black African peoples have been segregated in low-productivity land areas in the northern part of the territory, and are allowed only by special permit into the white area, which contains both the most productive agricultural lands and the bulk of Namibia's mineral wealth. For most of the last forty years Namibian workers have been controlled by the South West Africa Native Labour Association (SWANLA), a joint venture of employers and government. The SWANLA contract labour system, which the International Commission of Jurists condemns as "akin to slavery" was until very recently run just like a cattle auction.[29] Black workers were marshalled on the reserve, labelled A, B, or C according to size and age, sorted into truckloads and shipped to their employers. Under this system, which the Africans called "odalate" or "shackle", any person leaving the reserve was obliged to work for 12 to 18 months before returning. Families were not allowed to accompany their breadwinner into the "police zone" or white area.

Under these contracts wages ran at about $40 per month, although they could dip as low as $6 for child labour. The blacks faced the choice of seeing their families starve on the reserves or placing themselves at

28. *A Trust Betrayed: Namibia*, United Nations, New York (E.74.I.19), 1974, p. 37.
29. "Cracks in apartheid economics", *Sunday Times* (London), January 16, 1972.

SWANLA's mercy on the terms it decreed. This was made explicit by a South African functionary in 1973, in reference to the Ovambo people who constitute 50 per cent of the black population and 90 per cent of the wage labour force:

> You are mistaken if you think the Ovambos are coming here because they like it . . . They have had a very poor rainy season so far and I hear that large scale crop failures are expected. This means that we are going to have a heavy supply of labour this year again.[30]

When the weather does not produce the necessary labour, there are other means. In 1969 the South African government imposed a cash head tax designed to force workers out of Ovamboland and into the contract labour system.

Judge William Booth of the International Commission of Jurists in 1972 described the working conditions awaiting the Ovambos once they are in the clutches of their white masters:

> The men are housed in barracks type buildings with only a concrete locker type of bed for each man. The kitchen is quite unsanitary, with flies all over the place and cats chasing each other through the place. The food is served through openings in a wire fence separating the cooking area from the dining area. Porridge is lapped in a bowl with a shovel, a conglomeration of liquified vegetables is poured over the porridge and a piece of bread is also given each man. For meat, a hunk of bone is given on which there is some slight bit of meat.[31]

The conditions Booth observed are not unique, because both SWANLA and the system which replaced it in the early 1970s are designed to prevent competition on wage rates, living and working conditions. Another observer, Adam Raphael, recounted his Namibian experience in Britain's *Guardian Weekly* in 1973:

> In the Katutura compound near Windhoek, 5,000 Ovambos are housed in circumstances that would disgrace a nineteenth century prison. The cost to British and other employers is only (53 cents) per worker a day but that is no bargain. A visitor can only be appalled by the compound's unrelieved bleakness — the barbed wire fences; the concrete bunks in dank, overcrowded rooms in which up to 20 men sleep; the food being prepared with spades and pitchforks; above all, the overwhelming stench of urine

30. "Labour: the Achilles heel", *Financial Mail* (South Africa), March 2, 1973.
31. Counter Information Service, *Consolidated Gold Fields Ltd. Anti-Report*, London, 1973, p. 25.

which hangs over the compound. Its squalor is such that the local authority accepts that it must be demolished as a matter of urgency, but in Pretoria the Bantu Affairs Administration decrees that no funds are available.[32]

Once enmeshed in a contract a black Namibian has little choice but to suffer through it, because quitting exposes him to prosecution for breach of contract and desertion. Many employers don't even bother with the legal technicalities. Beatings are common punishment, and shootings by no means unknown.[33]

Falconbridge has taken full advantage of this rigid contract labour system. In 1973 its Oamites mine was carefully observing the apartheid colour code, with 360 blacks housed in the prescribed barracks sleeping on concrete bunks 14 to a room, and the overflow sheltered in tin shacks. The Canadian company's chief modification of apartheid seemed to have been the provision of foam rubber mattresses in the dormitories. Oamites' 82 coloured employees fared better with small two-bedroom houses, while 46 whites ruled the roost in much the same way as at the Blanket Mine in Rhodesia.[34]

With wages for its black workers at 1.44 Rand or about $2 per day, Falconbridge Oamites was paying only half the recognized minimum of the South African poverty datum line (PDL), a benchmark the Cape Town professor who performed the original research termed "not a 'human' standard of living".[35] The PDL is based on the cost of food, fuel and clothing required to sustain a family on a short term basis, but makes no allowance for any form of saving or for such elementary items as cooking utensils, bedding, medical bills, education costs, entertainment and other elementary expenditures. In the debate over how low a starvation wage can possibly be, Falconbridge claimed the South African PDL was inapplicable in Namibia because living costs were lower, but some British observers said they were higher.[36] In any case, Falconbridge came in well below the 15 Rand weekly minimum recommended by the Non-European Affairs department in Windhoek.

In reply to a Canadian YWCA inquiry asking if any blacks occupied positions of authority over whites, Falconbridge vice-president G.T.N. Woodrooffe informed the group "no—none have yet

---

32. Adam Raphael, "Namibian workers kept in squalor", *Guardian Weekly* (London), May 12, 1973.

33. *Sunday Times* (London), January 16, 1972.

34. Nangle, *op. cit.*

35. "Canadians are putting down black Africans", *Ottawa Citizen,* June 22, 1973.

36. Raphael, *op. cit.*

proven themselves capable to do so.''[37] He gave no indication of when a capable black might be discovered. In Hugh Nangle's assessment, "of all the Canadian companies I investigated in southern Africa, Falconbridge has the most depressing record.''[38] The company, however, seems intent on pursuing its established policies. Undaunted by charges in the press and by Canadian church groups that its operations in Namibia are both cruelly exploitive and illegal, Falconbridge Explorations Ltd. is searching for new prospects. In 1974 the *Cape Times* of South Africa reported that feasibility and technical studies on a copper-zinc-silver property at Okahandja north of Windhoek were well advanced and Falconbridge was preparing to invest a minimum of $13.5 million.[39]

REPRESSION AND THE NAMIBIAN RESISTANCE
The blacks of Namibia have not been passive in face of the oppression imposed by the government of South Africa, white South African employers and transnational mining corporations like Falconbridge. In 1972 a spontaneous strike spread from the ports to the main industrial and mine sites until 15,000 Ovambos had withdrawn their labour and returned to the northern homeland. Namibian industry was crippled, and the government headed off the crisis by promising to abolish SWANLA. According to Adam Raphael, the reform was a change in name only:

> Some minor improvements have since been made to the hated contract system . . . but (the) major grievances remain. The Ovambo are, however, helpless in the face of pass laws, employment permits, and influx control enforced by an efficient police state. Migrant workers in South West Africa are not even protected by minimum wage legislation as they are in the Republic. Instead, employers associations have been formed to fix wage rates to prevent competition for labour. The worker is thus (still) totally dependent on the goodwill or mercy of the employer. In many instances that last quality seems strained.[40]

The South African government has retaliated since the strike with a brutal crackdown on the largest political movement, the South West

---

37. Correspondence, Falconbridge vice-president G.T.N. Woodrooffe to Study and Action Committee, YWCA of Canada, December 4, 1972.

38. Nangle, *op. cit.*

39. "Copper Mine Project in S.W.A.", *Cape Times,* July 25th, 1974; see also *Northern Miner,* August 15, 1974. It appears that the project has been postponed due to depressed copper prices.

40. Raphael, *op. cit.*

Africa Peoples' Organization (SWAPO) which is recognized by the United Nations as the legitimate political representative of the Namibian people. In 1973 the South African government authorized public floggings as the penalty for membership in SWAPO and such minor defiances as singing SWAPO songs, using the name ''Namibia'' or wearing a shirt with SWAPO colours. The floggings, supervised by government-salaried tribal chiefs, intensified in the spring of 1974. *The Observer* of London reported a number of cases:

> Rachel was compelled to lie over a chair . . . in full view of a gathering of men, women and children. Four policemen each held a limb and she was flogged by a tribal policeman . . . with extreme violence. The tribal policeman wielded the Makalani cane, using two hands which he raised high in the air before striking.
> ''I was flogged in the same way,'' Elisa states. ''After my flogging I was barely able to walk. I walked as if I was crippled . . . When I removed my panties I found I was bleeding. I was unable to sit for a week thereafter.''[41]

The two women stated that they had never been charged or informed of the precise nature of their offense, nor were they allowed to call witnesses or defend themselves. Another victim, an Ovambo male, gave an account of his flogging, naked and in public, in a sworn affadavit:

> I am a family man and a member of my church congregation. I am 47 years of age and felt deeply humiliated. I lay down over a chair and the blows descended. They were agonizing . . . I was terrified that he would not only strike my buttocks but possibly injure my spine. The pain was terrible and produced open wounds. By the eighth stroke I lost consciousness . . .[42]

This government terrorism is designed to intimidate not only those punished, but all Namibians who dream of a day when their oppression will be ended. The full extent of white South African savagery was recently exposed before the U.N. Commission on Human Rights, which received evidence that the entire population of a Namibian village had been massacred in 1973 by South African air and ground forces. The assault, comparable to the widely publicized My Lai massacre in Vietnam, followed a SWAPO attack on a military base in which two SWAPO raiders and two South Africans were killed. A

41. ''Brutality backed by law'', *The Observer*, (London), April 7, 1974.
42. *Ibid*.

single survivor from the obliterated settlement was spirited out of
Namibia to Zambia. He was interviewed by Swedish reporters, and the
Swedes subsequently located the village to obtain pictures of the char-
red huts and bones of the dead. The massacre claimed over 100 lives.[43]

This outrage in Namibia is the most telling indicator of the status
of blacks under apartheid since the last reported mass killing, the
infamous Sharpeville massacre of 1960, in which South African troops
opened fire on a crowd peacefully demonstrating against the Pass Law,
killing 69 and wounding 178.

REFORM IN NAMIBIA: AN IMPOSSIBLE ILLUSION

The extremes of economic inequality in Namibia are even greater than
in South Africa. The last available information from 1967 showed that
whites enjoyed an income of about $200 a month for every man, woman
and child. Non-whites in the police zone received an average $39, while
blacks from the reserves subsisted on less than $8 per person per
month.[44]

United Nations reports indicate that as an exploited hinterland
Namibia is a crucial contributor to the economy of South Africa.
Between 30 and 50 per cent of the total value of production in the
territory is siphoned off by the South African government and private
business corporations, with mining the key method. Mining taxes from
Namibia between 1969 and 1971 yielded an average of $60 million per
year to the South African government,[45] while in 1971 foreign corporate profits, primarily from mining, reached $126 million[46], a com-
bined total more than twice the total income of all black Namibians.

This alliance between the South African government and the large
corporations including Falconbridge doing business in Namibia is sys-
tematically pillaging the territory at an increasing rate. While wages are
held at rock bottom, and social services for blacks are for practical
purposes non-existent, government expenditure is devoted to either
military security or roads and electric power installations which facili-
tate the extraction of raw materials. The Deputy Administrator of the
Territory, Dirk Mudge, is on record acknowledging that the South
African government in Namibia intends ''to give preference to the
necessary infrastructure instead of to other less than essential luxur-

43. Liberation News Service, No. 635, New York, August 14, 1974.
44. U.N. Department of Political Affairs, Trusteeship and Decolonization, *Decoloniza-
    tion*, Vol. 1, No. 3, December 1974.
45. *Algemeine Zeitung* (Namibia), November 23, 1971
46. *Report of the United Nations Council for Namibia*, United Nations (Twenty-eighth
    session, Agenda item 70, No.A/9024), New York, October 12, 1973, P.14

ies.''[47] In other words the product of Namibian labour and resources is not to be devoted to raising the living standards of black Namibians.

The South Africans and their corporate allies in this exercise are running a race against time. To the north of Namibia the Portuguese have given up the war against liberation forces in Angola, leaving South Africa with a new and difficult frontier to defend. The independent nations of Africa will not be able to deny encouragement to SWAPO in armed struggle from bases in Angola and Zambia against South Africa's occupation of Namibia. Most Africans recognize this as the only means by which the Namibian majority will ever regain its basic rights.

South Africa is, however, by far the strongest military power in Africa, and SWAPO alone can only wear away at its powerful enemy hoping that international political and economic pressures will finally force a South African withdrawal. The SWAPO leaders worry that before this happens, the natural resources of their country will have been seriously depleted leaving them little with which to build a new society. As long ago as 1970 SWAPO observed:

> Namibia is becoming one of the major copper producers in the world; this is the conclusion which can be drawn from the annual reports of the Association of Mining Companies, but the benefits do not accrue to the Namibian people. Our country's resources are being exhaused in an intense, short period and the profits are taken by the South African government, as well as transferred to foreign countries and South African companies, but nothing goes to the people . . . By keeping the population down . . . the South African government secures its foreign friends cheap and easy profit at the expense of the rightful owners of the country. We predict that the increasing investments in Namibia will lead to even harsher life conditions for our people, as this in itself is one of the necessary preconditions for this pernicious industrial expansion.[48]

Events of the last five years have proved this prediction accurate, except that five years has not been long enough to complete the looting. The Oamites mine is expected to produce until at least 1980.

APARTHEID'S SECRET SUPPORTERS
International pressure has not been brought to bear on the apartheid block in southern Africa except in relatively superficial ways. At the United Nations, the majority of the General Assembly supports

47. *Algemeine Zeitung* (Namibia), November 23, 1971.
48. Cited in W. Courtney and J. Davis, *Namibia: U.S. Corporate Involvement*, New York, 1972, p.24.

SWAPO and the right of the Namibian people to self-determination, but this majority represents other former colonial territories and has little military or economic power with which to enforce its convictions. The governments of the powerful industrial countries, including Britain, the United States and Canada, have offered rhetorical and U.N. voting support to the Namibian cause. In the case of Rhodesia they have applied half-hearted economic sanctions. But their words and statements of high political principle have not, in the final analysis, been matched by effective deeds.

In the case of Canada, the federal government has not lifted a finger against Falconbridge despite its sanction-breaking activities in Rhodesia and its flagrant violation of the U.N. position on Namibia for which Canada voted. In fact Canada may be violating the resolutions by allowing Falconbridge credit for taxes paid by Oamites to the South African government. Nor is Ottawa's studied indifference to the unethical behavior of the subsidiaries of one of its corporate citizens unique. Canada is dutifully following the great-power lead of the United States and Britain, which also have done very little to penalize their transnational corporations participating in the rape of Namibia or engaging in illegal commerce with Rhodesia.[49]

At the heart of this great default is the wish of all these governments to sustain the existence of apartheid South Africa, a policy which requires soft-pedalling on the buffer zones of Namibia and Rhodesia as well. This unspoken and shameful policy is based on several considerations. Southern Africa is a major present and future source of gold, diamonds and uranium as well as other raw materials to which the capitalist industrial countries wish to retain free access. The apartheid

49. Canada has publicly stated that it agrees with the judgment of the International Court of Justice which declared South Africa's presence in Namibia illegal. Canada has also affirmed that it "has sought to avoid all dealings with the Government of South Africa when it purported to act on behalf of Namibia or from which recognition of South African sovereignty over Namibia might have been implied." (See Canada's Communication with the UN Council for Namibia No. 285/73/Add.11, 21 August 1973). Canada has a double taxation agreement with South Africa whereby corporations can claim a Canadian tax credit on taxes paid to South Africa. If Falconbridge is able to claim such credits on taxes paid on its Namibian operations then Canada would be effectively recognizing South African sovereignty there. Also, if Falconbridge were receiving tax credits in Canada as a result of its operations in Namibia (and the subsequent taxes paid to South Africa), Canada would be in effect granting financial support to the company and facilitating commerce with Namibia. Canada's implied recognition and granting of tax credits would violate resolutions passed by the Security Council of the United Nations on July 29, 1970. According to international law, resolutions of the Security Council are binding on all UN member states. Thus far we have not been able to determine what tax arrangements are in force.

system provides that access at low prices with the accompanying benefit of high profits for the transnational corporations involved.

These commercial objectives are expressed politically as a desire to prevent the spread of communist influence in southern Africa, and the Republic of South Africa is regarded as a reliable buffer against communism. Communism has become a shorthand expression designating any social or political change which interferes with private capital investment, profit, trade, or the prices and availability of raw materials.

In military terms the policy objective of the great powers, as expressed through the North Atlantic Treaty Organization (NATO), is to maintain control of the high seas, the corollary of the free movement of goods, raw materials and capital on acceptable terms. The dilemma facing the NATO powers, including Canada, in Africa is that their objectives now require the support of apartheid. The defeat of their NATO ally Portugal in its colonial wars in Angola and Mozambique threatens to deny NATO powers any safe naval bases between the North Atlantic and the Philippines, a situation one analyst describes as "a strategic nightmare".[50] The NATO concern is that the Indian Ocean may soon no longer be an exclusive American preserve. It is this desire to maintain existing global power relations which makes the NATO allies cosy up to apartheid South Africa, a nation which will no doubt be more than willing to provide the desired naval bases and thus take out an effective insurance policy for its own survival in a hostile Africa.

In NATO countries like Canada this sacrifice of principle to expediency on the question of apartheid goes under the rubric of pragmatic politics. In African countries the proclivity of the democratic capitalist powers for alliances with fascist regimes, first Portugal and now, apparently, South Africa, cannot go unnoticed or unforgiven. People struggling for liberation from the cruel and oppressive colonialism in southern Africa inevitably find themselves lined up against the great capitalist powers and their transnational corporations.

50. Tad Szulc, "Why are we in Johannesburg?", *Esquire,* October 1974. NATO, in its Ottawa Declaration of June 19, 1974, articulated the new policy to which all member states have become committed: "The allies . . . are finally resolved to keep each other fully informed and to strengthen the practice of frank and timely consultations by all means which may be appropriate on matters relating to their common interests. . . . bearing in mind that these interests can be affected by events in other areas of the world." (Cited in Szulc, *op. cit.*) This strategy towards accommodation with South Africa is further evidenced by the contents of a secret White House document written by Henry Kissinger's staff which outlines how the U.S. will publicly press for liberalization of apartheid but privately act through military assistance to ensure the viability of the South African regime in the face of radically shifting political forces in Southern Africa. (*Ibid.*)

The real policy of Canada and other NATO countries toward southern African liberation will soon be put to the test. The U.N. High Commissioner for Namibia, Sean MacBride, announced in February 1975 that he was organizing the legal machinery to confiscate Oamites copper and all other materials shipped from Namibia in violation of the United Nations resolutions.[51] The degree of success or failure of this initiative will provide a further measure of the true intentions of the NATO powers toward the black peoples of southern Africa.

51. In September of 1974 the U.N. Council for Namibia passed a decree (U.N. No.A/AC.131/33) which in effect declared that without having permission from the Council any companies operating in Namibia were doing so illegally and that whatever resources were being taken from the territory were to be considered stolen goods. In order to protect the interests of the Namibian people and preserve their resources, the decree also allows for the seizure of such natural resources by the Council. Therefore any ships heading for European or other ports and carrying Namibian resources could be stopped and their cargoes impounded and held in trust for the Namibian People.

CHAPTER NINE

Transnational Empire

THE POLITICS OF MONOPOLY

Canada's economic future, the nation has been advised on more than one occasion by Trade and Commerce minister Alastair Gillespie, lies in the creation of more Canadian-based transnational corporations. The growing operations of the Falconbridge Group fit nicely into this Liberal game plan, giving the country a mining corporation which has escaped narrow national boundaries and sells in world markets from world-wide sources of supply.

A cursory reading of the Falconbridge annual report might even convey the impression that the organization is Canadian-controlled.

> At December 31, 1973 there were 11,104 shareholders, of whom 8,341 were of Canadian registry holding 4,499,416 shares. This represents 90 percent of the 4,955,412 shares outstanding after deduction of 45,483 shares held by subsidiaries.[1]

This information serves only to underline how deceiving appearances can be in corporate reporting. Canadian share registry is never a guarantee of Canadian ownership. More important in this case, one of those "Canadian" shareholders, McIntyre Mines, holds a controlling interest of 37 percent of Falconbridge common stock. McIntyre is in turn controlled from the United States by Superior Oil and Howard B. Keck.

Regardless of where they are controlled transnational corporations, in the view of their defenders, are a more efficient form of business organization than mere national companies and for this reason

---

1. Falconbridge Nickel Mines Ltd., *Annual Report 1973*, Toronto, 1974.

should be nurtured. Their superiority is demonstrated by higher profits, which in turn are attributed to higher productivity resulting from greater internal specialization, more and better research, and greater ability to apply the new technology generated by that research. All this contributes to both higher wages and a more rapid rate of economic growth. Therefore the only sensible policy for a forward-looking country is to encourage these large corporations for they are the key to progress and the way of the future.

The official government viewpoint is far from persuasive. There is every reason to suspect that the success of these huge corporations has less to do with efficiency in production than with other factors related to monopoly power: political manipulation of tax regulations and other legislation; market control and the suppression of competition; and preferred status in their relations with financial institutions. The Falconbridge record provides some useful clues on this score.

Since Howard Keck entered the picture in 1967, the performance of Falconbridge and related companies in terms of production and planning efficiency is not particularly impressive. The biggest success is the Falconbridge Dominicana project, through which the group consolidated its position as the world's number two nickel supplier. Offsetting that achievement are two costly fiascos: McIntyre's Smoky River Coal mine, and the abortive $65 million iron-nickel pellet refinery in Sudbury. On major capital programs, especially in Canada, the Superior Oil-McIntyre-Falconbridge complex would not win awards for "efficiency". It has, however, successfully palmed off a very large portion of the cost of its errors to the Alberta and Canadian taxpayers.

The growth of Keck's companies in spite of these failings highlights some of the more important aspects of their strength. One is privileged access to capital. A smaller organization might have been finished off by catastrophes like the two mentioned, but the Keck companies have reached a size which makes failure unimagineable. The potential for cross-subsidization among the various corporations and their intimate interdependence with banks guarantee that even such large reverses of fortune do not upset the basic stability of the group. During the Smoky River debacle Keck's key Canadian holding company, McIntyre, received a $3 million transfusion from Superior Oil. In addition its bank loans rose from $31 million in 1969 to $64 million in 1972. This is the sort of understanding many hard-pressed borrowers would like to have with their bank, but preferred treatment is the privilege of the large corporations which exchange directors with banking institutions.

Falconbridge and McIntyre are interlocked with investment bankers Dillon Read, the First National City Bank of New York, the First City National Bank of Houston, and the Canadian Imperial Bank of

Commerce, altogether a powerful array of financial connections. Nor must Howard Keck's chief Canadian lieutenant Marsh Cooper await the formality of board meetings to discuss financial arrangements with the CIBC's Neil McKinnon, although each is a director of the other's company. A short ride in the elevator of Toronto's Commerce Court tower, where Falconbridge is an $800,000 a year tenant of the CIBC and a major depositor, will bring them together in a jiffy.[2]

This mutual backscratching expresses what is essentially a political alliance between blocks of capital so large as to be substantially immune from traditional market discipline. Corporations, once they have attained this large size, resemble private governments. They are able within broad limits to levy taxes on the rest of the population at their own discretion for their own purposes without having to submit to the inconvenience of popular elections. Falconbridge and INCO provided a striking example of this power with their 54 percent nickel price increase in less than two years between 1972 and 1974. This type of corporate behavior in the areas of both financing and pricing is no proof of efficiency, but a convincing demonstration of monopoly power.

Another element of the Falconbridge Group's staying and growing power is its marketing connections. The Falconbridge Nickel sales organization, as supplier of a vital and sometimes informally rationed industrial commodity, has built strong ties with consumers of industrial metals. Now known as Falconbridge International, this sales organization has been a valuable asset in the diversification of the Falconbridge Group into the mining, refining and marketing of other products. The company's strong position in nickel is undoubtedly helpful in moving its output of commodities like copper for which sources of supply are more numerous and competition among suppliers keener. This dimension of Falconbridge's ability to generate profit, like its financial connections, has little to do with efficiency.[3]

2.   Other tenants of the CIBC'S Commerce Court Tower on King Street at Bay, a list that somewhat reflects the interest group that gathers around that particular bank, are: Brascan; Canadian Brazilian Services; Barclays Canada Ltd.; Blake, Cassels and Graydon; a representative office of the Department of Industry, Trade and Commerce; Mattagami Lake Mines Ltd.; McIntyre Mines Ltd.; Newmont Mining Corporation; Noranda Mines Ltd.; Sherritt Gordon; the South Africa Trade Commission; Texasgulf Inc.; Trans Canada Pipelines; and George Weston. In addition, many of Falconbridge's subsidiary companies, and those of McIntyre as well, are located in the building. This tenants list serves as a symbol of the degree of concentration and possiblities of communication among the members of the Canadian corporate elite.

3.   Falconbridge advertising lately has been stressing the diversified nature of the Group, its resources and its products: "Falconbridge has a wealth of seasoned management, research, metallurgical, mining, marketing and financing expertise to contribute to any venture in which it participates. Anywhere. Falconbridge, a mining and industrial group producing over 20 products in countries around the world." Advertisement, *Business Week*, February 10, 1975, p. 18.

For maximum effectiveness the market and financial power of a corporation and its financial group must be combined with strong influence in political decision-making. All governments impinge on corporate operations through taxation, pollution, anti-trust, labour and other legislation, and the effectiveness of its enforcement. Governments are often purchasers of a corporation's products as well. On another level, the foreign policies—diplomatic, economic and military — of a powerful government like the United States also have an important bearing on the affairs of the transnational corporation. All this makes close relations with important politicians and senior government functionaries essential, and there is ample evidence that the Falconbridge complex understands this part of the profit equation as well as anyone.

Historically government demand for nickel has been a prime feature of Falconbridge's growth. Its rise in the early years was intimately linked with state spending on armaments production. The second great surge in its expansion during the late 1940s and throughout the 1950s was based heavily on U.S. strategic stockpile contracts, part of a deliberate United States government policy to create alternate sources of nickel. With the non-communist world's military budgets running at about $200 billion annually, military procurement remains an important indirect source of demand for the company's products even though the direct sales pattern has been deemphasized.

If government policies have been central to Falconbridge's sales, they have also been important to its access to the raw material. The historic pattern of low royalties, low taxes and minimal refining requirements in Canada have been a large factor in the rapid growth of the company and the nickel industry. More recently the interventionist foreign policies of the United States have paved the way for industry expansion in the Philippines, Indonesia and Guatemala. For its part Falconbridge has been the beneficiary of one of the most blatant applications of American military force, the 1965 invasion of the Dominican Republic.

During the decisive 1950s decade of its development, the McIntyre-Falconbridge complex maintained high-level personal connections with both Ottawa and Washington. Jack Barrington and J.S.D. Tory provided links with the influential C.D. Howe in the Liberal cabinet, while Robert Anderson moved back and forth between top cabinet posts in Washington and the presidency of Falconbridge.

With the Superior Oil takeover in 1967, the Falconbridge group was drawn even more closely into the orbit of influence-peddling in Washington around the world's most powerful government. Howard Keck's exposure in 1956 in connection with the bribery of U.S. Congressmen provided a strong indicator of how government decisions were moulded to fit corporate needs during that period. The appointment as a Falconbridge director in the early 1970s of John Connally, veteran of Washington chicanery and potential presidential candidate, suggests that the influence game has remained an integral part of the successful business strategy of Howard Keck's corporations. Nor have Canadian political allies been slighted, judging by the appointment of E.C. "Smoky River" Manning to the board of McIntyre. This high-level diplomacy and exchange of personnel with government is a special brand of "efficiency" which is vital to the profit picture of the transnational corporation.

CORPORATE SOCIAL RESPONSIBILITY
In the political realm the large corporation does not rely exclusively on inducements to politicians to achieve its objectives. The moulding of opinion through public advertising and private lobbying is also of great importance, as Falconbridge's strong participation in the Mining Association of Canada attests. This informational activity is essentially manipulative in intent, since behind the high-minded description of public benefits from corporate activity for which we are asked to be thankful there usually lurks a threat. "Things will be done our way or they won't be done at all" is the message the large corporations bring, sometimes quite explicitly, to both citizens and governments.

In a world where private control of capital is tremendously concentrated in large corporations, and they in turn are allied through a handful of banks into highly centralized financial groups, this is not an idle bluff but a real and powerful weapon. The owners and managers of monopoly capital, operating on a world scale, are in a position to impose on governments many of the terms on which new investment and job creation will take place.

Canadians are most aware of this phenomenon in the field of resource exploitation, as provincial governments over the years have accepted humiliatingly low returns on the sale of their natural wealth. Even those governments honestly trying to drive a hard bargain have constantly faced the problem that some other province offers lower tax and royalty rates, less stringent pollution regulations, and so on. Those governments which attempt to raise the return to the public purse find that exploration and development within their jurisdiction slows down or halts until they restore the corporate profit margin to its expected level. A transnational corporation like Falconbridge plays this game even more effectively than a large national corporation. Its world-wide exploration activity gives it a smorgasbord of choice in investment decisions, great mobility for its capital, and correspondingly great bargaining power in its negotiations with any given political jurisdiction.

The mining corporations use this advantage extensively, often misleading those governments which are willing to be fooled. The *Canadian Mining Journal* in a recent editorial advised the Mining Association of Canada to stop "crying wolf" in its protests over proposed Canadian tax increases, and printed a long interview with "the old lion of finance" Eric Kierans in which he debunked some of the MAC's more tenuous claims:

> Actually, if you were to poll most of the other countries in the world you would find that they get a different version from these mining giants than is given to the Canadian government. They're told that if they want to tax, increase royalties or impose excess profits taxes and so on, then they (the mining giants) will do all of their investment in Canada. We are held up to them as being the country with the ideal tax system. And I guess we were. . . . One Australian economist told me a couple of years ago "If you fellows would only change your laws, you would enable us to get a decent return on our resources."[4]

The large corporation as "paper tiger" is an idea, however, that should not be carried too far. A study of the Falconbridge Group's 1973 consolidated balance sheet shows its overseas subsidiaries generating an increasing proportion of its profit with higher rates of return on capital than are provided by its integrated nickel facilities in Canada and Norway. Between them Falconbridge Dominicana and Oamites contributed fully one-quarter of the after-tax operating profit. Falcondo enjoyed a rate of return on assets of nearly 16 percent and Oamites a juicy 57 percent.

The integrated nickel section which includes the Manitoba and Sudbury mines and smelters and the Norwegian refinery yielded more return, about 40 percent of all profits, but the rate of return on producing assets was only 10 percent, apparently a much lower return to capital in the core of the company's operations. This is the reality underlying Marsh Cooper's rumblings about moving out of Canada for future nickel development.[5]

Falconbridge's attitude toward its social responsibility fluctuates to accomodate the imperatives of the balance sheet. When profits are

4. "CMJ Interview: Eric Kierans", *Canadian Mining Journal*, September 1974, p.21.
5. Not all of the company's Canadian mines show this low return. Falconbridge Copper, primarily Quebec-based, in 1973 yielded one-quarter of the Group profits with a return on assets of 59 percent, reflecting a great rush to take advantage of expiring tax privileges.

menaced by higher taxes or pollution regulations as in Canada, it threatens to shift investment elsewhere. The negative consequences of such behavior for its employees, however regrettable, cannot be avoided. Company officials are the first to point out that they run a business, not a charity.

The same attitude guides the company's behavior in Africa. Although Kilembe Copper was both profitable and socially important in the Ugandan economy, this did not prevent the Falconbridge Group from withdrawing capital as rapidly as possible just before president Obote forced it to sell Uganda a controlling interest in 1970. The implication was that its management team would be withdrawn entirely if the government did not restore Falconbridge's majority ownership. Dislocation in the lives of Ugandan people was a price the company seemed willing to pay in this tug of war over the profits from Uganda's resources.

In contrast with its ruthlessness in Uganda, Falconbridge has rejected any suggestion that it should get out of either Rhodesia or Namibia and cease its tacit support of the oppressive governments in those countries. One of the reasons given by company spokesmen is their concern about the suffering this might entail for their employees at the Blanket and Oamites mines, a posture contrary to the one struck in Uganda. The notable common factor in these situations is not concern for the welfare of employees, but an overriding concern for preserving capital and the opportunity to continue turning a profit, whatever that requires. The language of social responsibility, on those rare occasions when it crosses the lips of Falconbridge representatives, has a hollow ring.

MYTHICAL POLITICAL NEUTRALITY

Equally as dubious as its concept of social responsibility is the Falconbridge Group's professed political neutrality and its seemingly passive policy of obeying the laws of the land wherever it is doing business. Whether in Canada or the Dominican Republic Falconbridge plays an active role in creating laws favourable to itself, and then lives with them to the extent to which they are consistent with the higher law of the maximization of profit.

Falconbridge and subsidiaries have co-existed with a wide range of political philosophy in government, from Canada's liberal democracy to the Dominican Republic's militarized pseudo-democracy, Amin's military dictatorship in Uganda, and the apartheid regimes of Rhodesia, South Africa and Namibia. Their contribution of tax revenue and foreign exchange earnings to this motley collection demonstrates a

178 Falconbridge

rather weak attachment to the ideals of democracy and human rights, but cannot be mistaken for political neutrality.

What all these societies including Canada have in common is considerable freedom for private capital, and this is a political principle about which the corporate managers and owners care a great deal. In politics the company can tolerate Johannes Vorster, Joaquin Balaguer, Ian Smith and all they represent, but finds itself uncomfortable with an Obote or Juan Bosch or for that matter a David Lewis or Dave Barrett in Canada. Politicians and governments who obliterate human rights can be condoned, but those who threaten to encroach on property rights and advocate the use of wealth for the public good are quite unacceptable.

In a recent corroboration of this familiar political pattern, *Business Week* reported Falconbridge had opened negotiations with the military dictatorship of General Pinochet for the development of large copper deposits in Chile shortly after the bloody destruction of Salvador Allende's constitutionally elected government in that country.[6] Falconbridge has a $300 million investment plan for the 1500 million ton El Abra copper field, which has the potential to increase Chile's already large copper production by 50 percent.

Parallels between this situation in Chile and past events in the Dominican Republic are evident. In both countries the electorate chose a government promising extensive social and economic reforms. The United States intervened, bringing about the destruction of the elected government in favour of military dictatorship. Then like an enormous vulture Falconbridge moved in almost before the corpse of democracy was cold to negotiate a huge natural resources export project.

It can be argued that this sequence is mere coincidence, and that a corporate group like Falconbridge bears no responsibility for the behavior of either the United States government or its client military forces in the less developed countries. Such a view, however, seems unduly innocent and ignores the full scope of corporate interests and power. Falconbridge itself is to a large degree the creation of United States government economic policy, while the government elite is well populated with individuals attuned to corporate plans and needs. Both before and during the Keck era at Falconbridge the company has been

6. "Chile: A wobbly economy needs foreign help", *Business Week*, August 3, 1974, p. 30. Falconbridge has been publicly criticized by Canadian Church groups for this proposed investment on the grounds that it would aid the Chilean Junta, prop up the repressive machinery of the Chilean state, and extend the present reign of terror in Chile. On another Latin American front, Falconbridge is actively engaged in explorations in the Brazilian interior along with other "Canadian" companies—Noranda, INCO, Alcan, Cominco and Brascan. See: Swift and Draimin, "What's Canada Doing in Brazil?", *This Magazine*, Vol. 8, #5&6, January-February, 1975.

represented in the highest councils of American government and policy determination. This fusion of business and government is too pervasive to be ignored in explaining the uncannily frequent convergence of United States foreign policy with the interests of large corporations like Falconbridge.

A CORPORATE WORLD ORDER

As corporations like Falconbridge extend their control of trade, investment and technology on a worldwide scale, their overall political power is increasing relative to the power of the separate national governments and political parties with which they deal. This has led business philosophers to see in the mission of the transnational corporation a higher calling, the creation of a world order which transcends the particular and "irrational" social and political concerns of any municipality, province or nation state. The very nature of the large company allows it to ignore the most unwelcome pressures and demands of any particular social process, because there is always somewhere else to go. "Working through great corporations that straddle the earth," says George Ball, former U.S. undersecretary of State and chairman of the investment bank Lehman Brothers International, "men are able for the first time to utilize world resources with an efficiency dictated by the objective logic of profit." [7]

The Falconbridge Group illustrates Ball's thesis well. Copper from Uganda and iron and coal from British Columbia flow to customers in Japan. Ferro-nickel from the Dominican Republic and nickel-copper matte from Sudbury supply the industrial requirements of Europe, the United States and Japan while profits flow through Toronto to New York, Los Angeles and Houston. For such corporations the world has become a global factory and shopping centre. They deal not only in nickel, copper, automobiles, aspirins and coca-cola but in ideology and a "way of life", planning the future for millions of people.

This growth of transnational empire, with corporations breaking the bounds of national markets and national governments, is the dominant feature of recent decades and a dangerous stage in world history. These vast business organizations exercise tremendous power, but to whom are they responsible for the human consequences of their decisions? Both the ability and willingness of national governments to regulate them is limited. Internally they are highly centralized au-

7. R.J. Barnet and R.E. Muller, *Global Reach: The Power of the Multinational Corporations*, Simon and Schuster, New York, 1974, p. 13.

thoritarian institutions, so their thousands of employees are unlikely to provide effective checks and restraints on decision-making.

Management in transnational corporations answers to its share-holders, specifically its dominant shareholders. In Marsh Cooper's immortal words, "Howard Keck and I, in that order, run Falcon-bridge." The dominant shareholders like Keck generally acquire their right to guide the world's affairs through the inheritance of wealth and position. The power of decision-making is concentrated increasingly in the hands of a small economic elite accountable only to itself. This phenomenon is the very antithesis of democracy or any concept of decentralized and responsible authority.

If the prospects of democracy are dimmed by the overbearing power of the transnational corporations, this is not the only important human value which suffers. In guiding their affairs according to "the objective logic of profit" the leaders of this system are attempting in effect to throw the goals of equality of opportunity and equality of condition into the ashcan of history. With their ability to shift capital investment around the world in pursuit of low wages and low taxes, these corporations are vast engines for the accumulation of wealth under private control. The consequence is ever-mounting inequality between the owners of wealth and those whose living comes from work alone. This tragedy is most pronounced in the less developed countries plagued by crushing poverty and massive unemployment, but its effects are beginning to afflict working people in the industrial countries more severely as well.[8]

Growing inequality and the perpetuation of misery over great areas of the world is the cardinal failure in the new world order the transnational corporations are attempting to create. The dilemma is stated clearly in a comprehensive new work by Barnet and Muller, *Global Reach: The Power of the Multinational Corporations*:

> To promote a global vision which bypasses those parts of the planet in which most of its population lives, where the problems of survival are the starkest, and where political explosions are everyday occurences is beyond the capacity of even the most

8. Leo Johnson's work, *Poverty in Wealth,* (New Hogtown Press, Toronto, 1974) serves as a valuable insight into the growing gap between rich and poor in Canada:

    " . . . as a result of the rapid and disproportionate changes in income earned in each income level between 1946 and 1971, disparity between rich and poor earners has increased enormously. For example, in 1946 the richest ten per cent of earners received about 20 times as much income as the poorest ten per cent, whereas in 1971, they received 45 times as much. Similarly, in 1946 the income received by the richest decile equalled that received by the poorest 55 per cent of earners, whereas in 1971 their income equalled that of the poorest 64 per cent of earners." (p. 4).

accomplished masters of oversell. A Global Shopping Center in which 40 to 50 percent of the potential customers are living at the edge of starvation without electricity, plumbing, drinkable water, medical care, schools or jobs is not a marketable vision.[9]

Because the social order it offers is so bleak for so many, the resistance to private corporate organization of the world economy is multiplying and taking many forms. National liberation movements have sprung up in most less developed countries; and China, North Vietnam, North Korea and Cuba have isolated themselves almost completely from capitalist markets and investment in favour of more independent development strategies. Raw material-producing countries are moving toward the formation of cartels to increase their returns from trade, with OPEC showing the way. The trade union movement is working toward greater coordination of collective bargaining and secondary boycott activity across national boundaries, although this trend is far behind the international division of labour. Church groups in the industrial countries are taking increased interest in the social responsibility of business and the moral implications of their own investment portfolios. In many countries the socialist political parties are increasing their popular support. All these developments are in one way or another responses to the excessive power of the transnational corporations and its negative human consequences.

For their part the Howard Kecks, Marsh Coopers and other members of the world's economic elite are generally satisfied with their stewardship over the enormous undemocratic power and privilege they exercise, and are unlikely to surrender it gladly. But while they continue to employ the rhetoric of liberty in defense of the *status quo*, it is becoming more obvious that freedom of private wealth is not the same as human freedom. The confusion between the two is becoming more difficult to sell with each passing year.

It is too soon to guess with any assurance how the dilemmas created by the transnational corporations will be resolved. Their very size, power and unresponsiveness to anything but the profit motive makes the notion of reform seem distant and difficult. Nevertheless, if the human ideals of liberty, equality, solidarity and justice are to retain any meaning in the modern world, these concentrations of irresponsible power must be dismantled and replaced by institutions tied more firmly to real human needs. By their performance the transnational corporations will continue to provide support for this proposition; history will be determined by how all of us respond to the challenge.

9.   R. Barnet and R. Muller, *op. cit.*, p. 124.

Index